The Dessert Book

First published in 2002 by Mercer University Press

The University Press of Kentucky

Scholarly publisher for the Commonwealth,
serving Bellarmine University, Berea College, Centre
College of Kentucky, Eastern Kentucky University,
The Filson Historical Society, Georgetown College,
Kentucky Historical Society, Kentucky State University,
Morehead State University, Murray State University,
Northern Kentucky University, Transylvania University,
University of Kentucky, University of Louisville,
and Western Kentucky University.
All rights reserved.

Editorial and Sales Offices: The University Press of Kentucky
663 South Limestone Street, Lexington, Kentucky 40508-4008
www.kentuckypress.com

The Library of Congress has cataloged the Mercer University Press
edition of this book as follows:

The Dessert Book
edited by Louis B. Hatchett, Jr. 1st ed.
p. cm.
ISBN 0-86554-810-2 (hardcover: alk paper)
1. Desserts
I. Hatchett, Louis
TX773 .D818 2002
641.8'6-dc21
2002151070

ISBN 978-0-8131-4465-8 (pbk.: alk. paper)
ISBN 978-0-8131-4467-2 (pdf)
ISBN 978-0-8131-4466-5 (epub)

The Dessert Book

Duncan Hines

Edited by
Louis Hatchett

Foreword by
Michael and Jane Stern

UNIVERSITY PRESS OF KENTUCKY

For Linda Priscilla

Contents

Foreword

I<small>N THE</small> 1940s and 1950s, Duncan Hines was the most respected restaurant reviewer in America, known for reliable recommendations of eating places in cities and on back roads from coast to coast. While Hines's pioneering road trips are now history, his name lives on to many shoppers as a dependable brand of cake mix.

That legacy is fitting, for while Hines was an omnivore, he had a special fondness for cake and just about all desserts—as he put it, "from the old standby, apple pie, to such exotic creations as zabaglione." How fortunate that his passion has been captured in *The Dessert Book*. First published in 1955, it is a treasury of recipes gathered over two decades of travel, from restaurants Hines liked as well as from friends and family. Here are such renowned classics as mile-high Lemon Chiffon Pie from Stone's in Marshalltown, Iowa, and Date Nut Torte from the L. S. Ayers Tea Room in Indianapolis (now part of a museum). Here, too, are creative ways to use Duncan Hines's own cake mixes, such as Banana Nut Cake using Devil's Food Cake Mix and Cherry Coconut Angel Food Cake.

The scope of this cookbook is astonishing: more than five hundred recipes in every conceivable category—pies, cakes, and cookies, of course, but also ice cream and toppings, waffles and fritters, pinwheels, slumps, shortcakes, Fromage à la Crème and Peaches Flambée Royale. As Hines's followers learned to expect from his restaurant reviews, the recipes are clear and precise, easy to follow, and sure to yield happy results. "By following one of my recipes," he wrote, "you will surprise yourself with perfect results—and how easy!" These words precede a recipe for one of New York's most cherished dishes—Lindy's Cheese Cake.

Beyond the recipes, the pages come alive with handy marginalia, such as "Cooked fruits usually have a better flavor and retain more of their natural sweetness if served hot." And, "Cheese cake is best the second day because it mellows in flavor." Hines includes valuable advice about reducing and increasing recipes, about what freezes well and what doesn't, and what utensils are most useful for dessert making. Best of all, each category is introduced with the words of wisdom, wit, and history that make Duncan Hines a joy to read. Did you know, for instance, that waffles are said to have originated when a thirteenth-century Crusader, dressed in armor, accidentally sat on some freshly baked oat cakes his wife had just made? He flattened the cakes, leaving an imprint of his chain mail in them. He was hungry enough to eat them anyway, and his wife was so delighted by the way the corrugated oat cakes held melting butter that she used her hubby's armor thenceforth to shape her cakes.

Anyone with a ravening sweet tooth has got to love this book, for in Duncan Hines's world, dessert is no afterthought. It is, he writes, "like the final act in a good play . . . long remembered with pleasure."

Michael and Jane Stern

Preface

FOR THOSE who are unaware, in the 1940s and 1950s surveys showed that the most respected name in the food industry was Duncan Hines. Beginning in 1936, he published *Adventures in Good Eating*, an annual restaurant guide that eventually forced the restaurant industry—particularly those eating establishments in out-of-the-way places—into the modern era; with that single book he helped pave the way for the quality restaurant meals that we expect today. In 1938 he began publishing an annual guide for travelers seeking quality overnight lodgings, which he called *Lodging for a Night*. In 1948 he published *Duncan Hines Vacation Guide*, which was a guidebook for people seeking that era's quality vacation spots throughout America. And in 1939 he began publishing an annually updated cookbook, *Adventures in Good Cooking*, which consisted of recipes taken from many of the nation's finest restaurants as well as from individuals who were as discriminating about quality food as he was.

When Procter and Gamble bought the rights to Duncan Hines's name in August 1956 and began putting his name on its cake mix packages, a lot of this history was forgotten by the American public. When Hines died in 1959, he was soon forgotten as a celebrity, but his name lives on today via America's supermarket shelves.

In my book *Duncan Hines: The Man behind the Cake Mix* (Macon, Ga.: Mercer University Press, 2001), I describe two books that Duncan Hines published in 1955. In July 1953 Duncan Hines, then seventy-three, wanted to semi-retire; so he sold his publishing operation, Adventures in Good Eating, Inc., to Roy Park, his business partner in Hines-Park Foods. At the time of the sale and transfer, Hines was publishing his three annual guidebooks and cookbook, which were all still popular.

Later that year Park moved the operations of Adventures in Good Eating, Inc., from Bowling Green, Kentucky, to Ithaca, New York, and changed its name to the Duncan Hines Institute. From this location, he was not only responsible for sales of the books but he was also the CEO for Hines-Park Foods, which produced about 250 products for the Duncan Hines label.

While Park continued to update and expand the annual editions of Hines's popular guidebooks and kept the cookbook fresh with new contributions, he also put together a couple of other publishing ventures featuring Duncan Hines. With his business partner's cooperation, Park arranged to have published Hines's autobiography, *Duncan Hines' Food Odyssey* (New York: Thomas Y. Crowell, 1955), but even more popular was their other effort, *Duncan Hines' Dessert Book* (New York: Pocket Books, 1955), which sold hundreds of thousands of copies over the next decade.

Duncan Hines' Dessert Book was originally a standard paperback book that sold for 35 cents. Depending on the edition, the cover carried a picture of chocolate cake (or some other tantalizing edible) along with the familiar "Duncan Hines" logo emblazoned across the top. The *Dessert Book*'s organization was a simple one. The recipes were arranged in the same manner and style as they had been in his popular cookbook *Adventures in Good Cooking*, with the ingredients on the left side of the page and the directions on the right. The book was distributed in early 1955 and had an initial print run of 250,000 copies.*

*In previous editions of *Duncan Hines' Dessert Book*, Park made every attempt to ensure that there was no confusion when a sugary concoction was being described; each recipe had dotted lines that connected its ingredients to the cooking directions. Some of these directions, incidentally, were more elaborate and detailed than they had been in *Adventures in Good Cooking*. Because it was estimated that it could reach a larger cross section of the population than *Adventures in Good Cooking* ever had, Park believed that easy-to-read instructions were essential to the book's success. No doubt many readers of *Adventures in Good Cooking* occasionally

Duncan Hines' Dessert Book, like its older sister publication, was compiled from recipes submitted from restaurants and assorted individuals. Contributions submitted by both individuals and restaurants were given credit. As was the case with *Adventures in Good Cooking,* any blank areas that made a page look awkward were filled with household hints, suggestions, admonitions, and an assortment of Duncan Hines's famous bon mots. In subsequent editions, picture sketches were provided when they were thought to be of value to the reader.

By early July 1954 the editorial outline had taken shape. The book began with one hundred recipes for cake. They included various recipes for conventional cakes, mix cakes, sponge cakes, chiffon and angel food cakes, fruit cakes, coffee and upside down cakes, tortes and cheese cakes. Next came dessert cakes not frequently produced in American homes: recipes for petit fours, cupcakes, meringues, cream puffs, and éclairs, among many others. Finally, there came forty selections of the many things that one could pour onto a cake: frostings, icings, fillings, and sauces.

Having exhausted the subject of cakes, the book next turned to other dessert forms: cobblers, dumplings, shortcakes, and turnovers. The number of recipes in these four dessert groups came to twenty-five. This was followed first by twenty-five variations of cornstarch pudding and then by forty recipes for custard-styled desserts. The latter came in two forms: baked puddings, as in bread pudding, and soft pudding, as in soft custard.

As the user turned the pages, he next found recipes for ten forms of fruit dessert, including frozen fruit dishes, ambrosia, baked fruit, and a recipe for Apple Brown Betty. Next came twenty recipes of various cheese desserts, such as cheese cracker specialties and cheese cakes; these were accompanied with serving suggestions. The book's next section was a compilation of forty gelatin desserts

---

wished that they had been blessed with dotted lines to keep track of the book's sometimes elaborate instructions. Indeed, it is clear that *Adventures in Good Cooking* was not for the kitchen novice; occasionally some of the recipes are quite difficult. For this edition of *The Dessert Book,* we have updated the format of the recipes by removing the dotted lines and listing the ingredients separately, in a manner intuitive to contemporary readers.

that covered charlottes, bavarians, whips, and sponges, among other delectable treats. This was followed by five recipes for whips and sponges not using gelatin.

Recipes for one hundred types of pie encompassed the next category. After a discussion on pie crusts came concoctions for nearly every pie known to mankind, including apple pie, crumb meringue pie, and coconut pie. There were also recipes for the many things that could be poured into a pie crust: fruit filling, cream filling, custard filling, chiffon, parfait, and sponge filling. Concluding this section were recipes for tarts, turnovers, and "refrigerator pies."

The next to the last section of the book consisted of ten recipes for soufflés and fondues, ten more for assorted steamed puddings, and another fifteen covering tapioca, cereal, and rice desserts. Finally came fifty recipes for cookies of all kinds, twenty recipes for cooked and uncooked sauces, and, rounding off the book's contents, ten miscellaneous recipes, including Swedish pancakes, crêpes Suzette, waffles, waffle brownies, shortcake, fruit fritters, and doughnuts. The book contained a total of 555 recipes.

Many of these recipes had been tested in the kitchen of the wife of Hines's brother's son, Geraldine Hines. Hines's third wife, Clara, later took her place and tested many more. Those recipes that came after the business transfer in 1953 were tested in the Duncan Hines Test Kitchen in Ithaca, New York.

In the companion book to this volume, *Adventures in Good Cooking*, I've included some information about the restaurants from which many of the recipes in that volume and this one came. Below I identify some of the individuals who contributed the recipes found in both volumes.

Mrs. Thomas A. Williams, Nashville, Tennessee, was the wife of a vice president of the Williams Printing Company, which published Duncan Hines's guidebooks and his cookbook. The Williams firm continued to publish his books from 1939 until July 1953, when Roy Park took over Hines's operation.

Francis E. Fowler Jr., Los Angeles, California, was an entrepreneur and lifelong art collector whose greatest commercial success was in developing and marketing a sweet whiskey he named Southern Comfort. Every Christmas the Fowlers sent Duncan Hines a case of Southern Comfort, which he generously distributed among members of his family. When Hines and his wife went to Los Angeles, they always saw the Fowlers and dined with them as frequently as they could. The Fowlers owned a set of gold dishes that had belonged to a czar of Russia, and on special occasions they served meals on them. Fowler is best remembered today as the namesake of the Fowler Museum of Cultural History on the UCLA campus, which holds a major portion of his silver collection.

Mrs. Louis (Idella) Weathers, Elkton, Kentucky, was a woman whose daughter, Elizabeth Ann, was married to Duncan Hines's nephew, Duncan Ludlow Hines. Mrs. Weathers was known to be a wonderful cook who presided over the kitchen with the help of a black cook named Donie (pronounced DOUGH-nee).

Charlie Grider, Bowling Green, Kentucky, was a distant Hines relative. Grider was considered by many to be an excellent cook.

Edmund H. Singmaster, Philadelphia, Pennsylvania, was perhaps Hines's most cherished "dinner detective." Edmund Singmaster was an elderly gentlemen whose exacting demands for good eating may have even exceeded Duncan Hines's own. He actually lived in Germantown, a suburb of Philadelphia. The two got to know each other so well that by 1941 Singmaster and his wife would accompany the Hineses on several gustatory prowls when the Kentucky couple came to town. Sometimes the Singmasters would go with them to far-flung eateries, even as far away as Maine or Wisconsin. Singmaster's opinions became in Hines's estimation something close to the word of God when it came to restaurant recommendations. If Singmaster recommended a restaurant, then the place went into Hines's book, and no questions were asked. Hines knew that Singmaster would recommend only those restaurants that were both heavenly to dine in and immaculately clean.

Mrs. W[ill]. B. (Louise) Taylor, Bowling Green, Kentucky, was the granddaughter of John J. Valentine, the president of the Wells Fargo Company who obtained for Duncan Hines a job with his firm in December 1898. Hines's father and Mr. Valentine were close friends, and as these recipes attest, the friendship between the two families continued long after the two elder men had passed away.

Mrs. Taylor had a wonderful cook named Antha, who made

delicious corncakes. The problem with duplicating recipes from Antha is that she prepared her meals with no measures; a pinch of salt here, another pinch of sugar there, a handful of cornmeal, and perhaps a half dozen other ingredients were the only measurements she knew. Antha's cooking was all done by feel, and Duncan Hines marveled at her skill and wondered how she made it taste so good. Hines's own maid, Myrtle Potter, was another such cook, and at one time or another over the many years she was employed by the Hineses she prepared practically all the recipes found in this book and its companion, *Adventures in Good Cooking*. It could very well be that some of the recipes listed here under Duncan Hines's name originated with Mrs. Potter herself.

Elsie Smythe, Bowling Green, Kentucky, was also a granddaughter of John J. Valentine and the sister of Mrs. W. B. Taylor and Mrs. R. T. Cooksey. She had lived in California and moved back to her hometown of Bowling Green in her later years. On her return, she brought back several recipes from out West, and Duncan Hines thought enough of many of them for inclusion here.

Mrs. R[ichard]. T. Cooksey, Madison, Wisconsin, was the third granddaughter of John J. Valentine. She married a doctor who moved to Wisconsin. She was also an excellent cook, and a few of her contributions are included here along with those of her sisters.

Mrs. C[larence]. H. Welch, Tucson, Arizona, is the daughter of Duncan Hines's only sister. Her maiden name was Annie Fore Hines. She married Clarence H. Welch, a young man in the United States Army Air Corps, who retired to become the personnel manager of a Howard Hughes firm in Tucson and then later became a stockbroker before he retired. Mrs. Welch had a reputation as a wonderful cook, and because she was with her husband in so many places over the years, her recipes come from as many locations as there are recipes in this book.

Mrs. Roy (Jane) Morningstar, Bowling Green, Kentucky, was Duncan Hines's niece. She was his brother Porter's daughter. When Mrs. Morningstar first saw her name listed as the originator of the recipe for Scalloped Oysters in *Adventures in Good Cooking* (# 196), she told him, "This isn't my recipe for scalloped oysters." Duncan

Hines replied, "No, it's not. The recipe came from a can of oysters. But I couldn't say that, so I put your name on it." What brand he got it from no one knows, but it's mighty good just the same.

C[harlotte]. C[ombs]. Moore, Henderson, Kentucky, was the sister-in-law of Duncan Hines's brother Porter, as well as a distant cousin.

Marion Flexner, Louisville, Kentucky, wrote a popular regional cookbook called *Out of Kentucky Kitchens* (University Press of Kentucky, 1949), for which Duncan Hines wrote the preface. She and Duncan Hines had some correspondence and greatly admired each other.

Fred Waring, New York, New York, was a famous musical entertainer from the early 1920s until his death on July 29, 1984. Not only was he the inventor of the popular Waring Food Blender, but he was also one of Duncan Hines's dinner detectives. Always on the lookout for a good recipe, he created by his own hand several dishes included here.

Mrs. H[enry]. H. (Nell) Baird, Bowling Green, Kentucky, whose husband headed that town's Scott Tobacco Company, was a popular hostess in the middle half of the twentieth century. She and Nellie, her servant of many years who originally hailed from Tennessee, created scores of heavenly dishes for her many luncheons and dinners.

Mrs. Rhea G. Price, Bowling Green, Kentucky, was a friend of Duncan and Clara Hines. With help from her cook Annie Covington, Mrs. Price created and served many delicious recipes to her guests throughout the 1930s and 1940s at her home south of Bowling Green.

Mrs. McKenzie (Louise) Moss, Bowling Green, Kentucky, was the daughter of Duncan Hines's brother Porter.

Mrs. Bland (Bena) Farnsworth, Bowling Green, Kentucky, was another cousin of Duncan Hines. Noted for her culinary skills, she was also in the same Bowling Green literary and women's clubs as was Clara Hines.

Gertrude Chaffin Wellman, Cleveland, Ohio, was a relative of Duncan Hines's first wife, Florence Chaffin Hines.

Due to neglect, this book has mainly been forgotten. But when its contents are tried, they are guaranteed to pack a wallop on the tongue. As always, Duncan Hines never recommended anything unless it was extraordinarily good. If he recommended it, he really meant it. So when he approved his name to be associated with the delectable desserts found in these pages, he promised his readers that a rich treat, one not quickly forgotten, would delightfully entertain their taste buds and make them pine for more.

Louis Hatchett

Introduction

ONE OF the most important courses in any meal is the dessert. It is the finale in any full-course Adventure in Good Eating—and, like the final act in a good play, is long remembered with pleasure.

I am in the fortunate position of being a professional taster. I work and eat at the same time. In my work I have sampled thousands of desserts, ranging from the old standby, apple pie, to such exotic creations as zabaglione. When I enjoy a particularly good dessert at one of the places listed in my books, *Adventures in Good Eating, Lodging for a Night,* and *Vacation Guide,* I often ask for the recipe. It is a matter of extreme gratification to me that so many places I recommend have consented to release their prized recipes for publication in my book, *Adventures in Good Cooking and the Art of Carving in the Home.*

This *Duncan Hines' Dessert Book* contains a selection of the dessert recipes that I have taken from my private collection, which has been built up over the years through the generosity of friends who have been willing to share with me their prized recipes.

You will note that my recipes are easy to follow. I list the ingredients in the order they are used. Opposite the list of ingredients I tell in specific language the steps to be taken. Although some of the creations are exotic and sound mysterious, actually any person who follows the directions carefully can come forth with a delectable dessert.

For the most satisfying results from any recipe you should take precautions from beginning to end. Before you begin, make certain you have on hand the exact ingredients the recipe calls for. Follow directions carefully, use exact level measurements, and know your temperatures. You should have your oven tested occasionally to see that the temperature is the same throughout all corners, front and back. Never proceed by guess.

I should like to acknowledge the assistance that has been given to me in the preparation of this book by:

My wife, Clara, who is an artist with foods as well as a delightful traveling companion, and who often goes into the kitchen to observe a famous chef while he puts together some of his creations.

E. L. Ackley, Director of Quality Control, and Marie W. Layer, Home Economist, Hines-Park Foods, Inc., Ithaca, New York, who have assisted with the testing of the recipes.

Nebraska Consolidated Mills Company, Omaha, Nebraska, manufacturers of the Cake Mixes that bear my name, who put the findings of their Test Kitchen at our disposal in the preparation of this book.

My associate, Roy H. Park, of the Duncan Hines Institute, Ithaca, New York, who has worked with the publishers on the manifold details of bringing out this publication.

And so, ladies—and gentlemen—let's go into the kitchen now and set forth on a new adventure in the preparation of good desserts. May you have fun in the doing as well as in the eating. Good luck!

Duncan Hines

2 pints	=	1 quart
4 quarts	=	1 gallon
8 quarts	=	1 peck
4 pecks	=	1 bushel
1 pony	=	$1/3$ oz.
1 jigger	=	1 $1/2$ oz.
1 shell	=	1 $1/2$ oz.
16 oz.	=	1 lb.
2 cups	=	1 pint
1 pint	=	1 lb. liquid or fat
4 cups	=	1 quart or 32 oz.

1 wine glass = 4 oz. = 8 tablespoons = $1/2$ cup
(*This is a claret glass and is most commonly used in the average home*)
1 sherry glass = 3 oz. = 6 tablespoons = $1/3$ cup
1 port glass = 2 oz. = 4 tablespoons = $1/4$ cup

Table silverware spoons do not correspond accurately with the capacity of measuring spoons.

ᔓ Food Weights and Measures

This table is for approximate weights and measures of various foods and is intended as a handy guide in estimating quantities. Courtesy of *Restaurant Management Magazine*, 222 East 42nd Street, New York City, N.Y.

Ingredient	Weights	Approximate Measures
Allspice (ground)	1 oz.	5 tablespoons
Allspice (whole)	1 oz.	6 tablespoons
Almonds (shelled, chopped)	1 oz.	$1/4$ cup
Apple (juice)	8 oz.	1 cup
Apples (dried)	1 lb.	5 cups
Apricots (dry)	1 lb.	3 cups

Ingredient	Weights	Approximate Measures
Apricots (soaked and cooked)	1 lb.	4 cups and juice
Baking powder	1 oz.	3 tablespoons
Bananas (mashed)	1 lb.	2 cups
Bread	1 lb.	12 slices, ½ inch thick
Bread crumbs (dried, sifted)	4 oz.	1 cup
Butter	1 lb.	2 cups
Butter	1 oz.	2 tablespoons
Butter	Size of an egg	¼ cup
Cashew nuts	1 lb.	4 cups
Cheese (cream)	1 lb.	2 cups
Cheese (cream, Philadelphia)	6 oz.	1 package
Cheese (cubed)	1 lb.	2⅔ cups
Cherries (candied)	1 lb.	3 cups
Chestnuts (in shell)	1 lb.	2 cups—meats
Chocolate (grated)	1 oz.	4 tablespoons
Chocolate (melted)	1 lb.	2 cups
Cider	8 oz.	1 cup
Cinnamon (ground)	1 oz.	4 tablespoons
Cinnamon (stick)	¾ oz.	4 (5-inch size)
Cloves (ground)	1 oz.	4 tablespoons
Cloves (whole)	1 oz.	6 tablespoons
Cocoa (ground)	1 oz.	4 tablespoons
Coconut (shredded)	1 lb.	6 cups
Coffee (ground fine)	1 lb.	5 cups
Cornmeal	1 lb.	3 cups
Cornstarch	1 oz.	3 tablespoons
Cracker crumbs	2½ oz.	1 cup
Crackers (graham, crushed)	1 cup	12 crackers
Cranberries	1 lb.	4 cups
Cranberry sauce (strained)	1 lb.	2 cups
Cream of tartar	1 oz.	3 tablespoons
Currants (dried)	1 lb.	3 cups
Currants (dried)	10 oz.	1 package
Dates (pitted)	1 lb.	3 cups
Eggs (1 unbeaten)	1½ oz.	3 tablespoons
Eggs (whites)—1 cup	8 oz.	8 to 10
Eggs (whole)	1 cup	4 to 6 medium
Eggs (yolks)—1 cup	8 oz.	12 to 16

Ingredient	Weights	Approximate Measures
Figs (dried, cut-up)	1 lb.	2 ¾ cups
Filberts (shelled)	1 lb.	3 ½ cups
Flour (bread)	1 oz.	3 to 4 tablespoons
Flour (bread, sifted)	1 lb.	4 cups
Flour (cake, sifted)	1 lb.	4 ½ cups
Flour (graham, sifted)	1 lb.	3 ½ to 3 ¾ cups
Flour (pastry, sifted)	4 oz.	1 cup
Flour (rice)	1 lb.	2 cups
Flour (rye, sifted)	1 lb.	5 ½ cups
Flour (whole wheat)	1 lb.	3 ¾ cups
Gelatin (granulated)	1 lb.	4 cups
Gelatin (prepared)	1 oz.	2 ½ cups
Ginger (ground)	1 lb.	6 tablespoons
Grapefruit juice	11 oz.	1 cup
Grapes (cut and seeded)	8 oz.	2 to 3 cups
Honey	1 lb.	1 cup
Lard	8 oz.	1 cup
Lemon juice	1 cup	4 to 5 lemons
Lemon rind	1 lemon	2 teaspoons
Lemons	1 lb.	3 to 5 lemons
Milk (condensed, sweetened)	11 oz.	1 cup
Milk (evaporated)	1 lb.	2 cups
Mixed spices	1 lb.	4 ⅔ cups
Molasses	12 oz.	1 cup
Nutmeg (ground)	1 oz.	4 ⅔ tablespoons
Oatmeal (quick-cook)	1 lb.	3 cups
Oats (rolled, quick-cook)	2 ¾ oz.	1 cup
Oils	1 lb.	2 cups
Orange (rind, grated)	½ oz.	2 tablespoons
Peaches (dried)	1 lb.	3 cups
Peaches (fresh, sliced)	1 lb.	2 to 2 ½ cups
Peanut butter	1 lb.	1 ⅔ cups
Peanuts (shelled, jumbo)	1 lb.	3 cups
Pecans (shelled)	1 lb.	4 cups
Pineapple (candied)	1 lb.	7 rings
Pineapple (canned, sliced and diced)	3 slices	1 cup
Pineapple (canned, tidbits)	1 lb.	2 cups
Pineapple (juice)	8 oz.	1 cup

Ingredient	Weights	Approximate Measures
Prunes (cooked, pitted)	1 lb.	3 cups
Raisins (seeded)	1 lb.	2 cups
Raisins (seedless)	1 lb.	3 cups
Raisins (seedless)	5 ⅓ oz.	1 cup
Rhubarb (edible part, cooked)	1 lb.	2 ¼ cups
Rye meal	2 ⅓ oz.	1 cup
Salt	1 oz.	1 ¾ tablespoons
Soda	1 oz.	2 ½ tablespoons
Strawberries (whole)	1 quart	3 ½ cups
Sugar (brown, firmly packed)	1 lb.	2 ¼ cups
Sugar (brown, loosely packed)	1 lb.	3 cups
Sugar (confectioners')	4 ½ oz.	1 cup
Sugar (confectioners' sifted)	1 lb.	3 ½ cups
Sugar (granulated)	1 lb.	2 cups
Sugar (powdered)	6 ½ oz.	1 cup
Tapioca (minute)	1 lb.	2 ½ cups
Tapioca (pearl)	5 oz.	1 cup
Tea (dry)	2 oz.	1 cup
Vanilla	1 oz.	2 tablespoons
Vinegar	8 oz.	1 cup
Walnuts (English, shelled)	4 oz.	1 cup
Water	8 oz.	1 cup
Yeast	½ oz.	1 cake

∾ Sweetening Value of Sugar Substitutes

Equivalents of 1 cup sugar:

¾ to 1 cup honey
1 cup brown sugar
1 cup maple sugar
1 cup maple syrup
1 ½ cups sorghum or molasses
1 ½ cups cane syrup
2 cups corn syrup

ᴖ Recommended Temperatures

Stovetop and Oven

Simmering water	180° F.	Slow oven	300–325° F.
Boiling water	212° F.	Moderate oven	350–375° F.
Boiled icings	238–240° F.	Hot oven	400–425° F.
Jellying stage	218–222° F.	Very hot oven	450–475° F.
Very slow oven	250–275° F.	Extremely hot oven	500–525° F.

Deep-Fat Frying

Doughnuts	370–380° F.
Fritters	370–380° F.

Breads

Baking powder biscuits	450–475° F.	12–15 minutes

Cakes and Pies

Angel food cake	325° F.	60–75 minutes
Cupcakes	350–375º F.	20–30 minutes
Layer cake	375° F.	25–35 minutes
Loaf cake	350° F.	45–60 minutes
Sponge cake	325° F.	40–60 minutes
Pie shells	450° F.	12–15 minutes
Prebaked shell with filling	350° F.	25–30 minutes
One-crust pie (custard type)	400° F.	25–30 minutes
Or, begin at	450° F.,	10 minutes
and then reset to	325° F.	25–30 minutes
Two-crust pie (fruit pies)	425° F.	45–50 minutes
Or, begin at	450° F.,	15 minutes
and then reset to	350° F.	35–45 minutes

∾ Substitutes

It is always best to use the ingredients stated in the recipe; however, if they are not on hand, here is a list of satisfactory substitutes.

FOR	USE
1 cup sifted all-purpose flour	1 cup plus 2 tablespoons sifted cake flour
1 cup sifted cake flour	1 cup minus 2 tablespoons sifted all-purpose flour
1 cup sifted pastry flour	1 cup minus 2 tablespoons sifted all-purpose flour
1 tablespoon cornstarch (for thickening)	2 tablespoons flour (approximately)
1 teaspoon baking powder	¼ teaspoon soda plus ½ teaspoon cream of tartar
1 cup fresh sweet milk	½ cup evaporated milk plus ½ cup water
1 cup fresh sweet milk	1 cup sour milk or buttermilk plus ½ teaspoon soda (decrease baking powder by 2 teaspoons)
1 cup sour milk or buttermilk	1 cup fresh sweet milk with 1 tablespoon lemon juice or vinegar added
1 square (1 oz.) unsweetened chocolate	3 to 4 tablespoons cocoa plus ½ teaspoon shortening

∾ Baking and Cooking Terms

Bake: To cook by dry heat, usually in the oven.

Batter: A mixture of flour and liquid, usually in combination with other ingredients thin enough to pour.

Beat: To mix vigorously with an over-over motion.

Blanch: To remove the skins from fruits or nuts by dipping in boiling water.

Blend: To mix thoroughly together two or more ingredients.

Boil: To cook in water, or in a liquid consisting mostly of water, in which bubbles rise continually and break on the surface.

Broil: To cook directly under a hot heated unit or flame, or over live coals.

Brush: To spread thinly, usually with a brush, but sometimes done with a piece of cloth or paper.

Caramelize: To melt sugar to a golden brown color over low heat.

Chill: To allow a mixture to become thoroughly cold but not frozen.

Chop: To cut into coarse or fine pieces with a chopper or knife.

Combine: *See* Blend.

Core: To remove the core from certain fruits.

Cream: To soften fat, butter, cheese, etc., until it is light and creamy.

Cream together: To work one or more foods together until soft. Usually this applies to sugar and shortening.

Crumble: To break into smaller particles, usually using the fingers.

Cube: To cut into small squares.

Cut in: To mix fat with dry ingredients using two knifes, a fork, or pastry blender.

Defrost: To bring a food to room temperature.

Dice: To cut into cubes.

Dip: To coat a food with a dry or moist substance like flour or beaten egg.

Dissolve: To make a solution from a dry and liquid ingredient.

Dot: To scatter bits of fat or cheese over the surface of food.

Drain: To remove the liquid from foods, usually using a sieve or strainer.

Dust: To sprinkle lightly with flour or sugar.

Envelope: Usually refers to gelatin—1 envelope equals 1 tablespoon.

Flake: To break lightly apart into small pieces with a fork.

Flour: To sprinkle or cover with a thin film of flour.

Fold in: To mix by cutting down through the batter, lifting up, and then folding over before cutting down again. It is usually done with a large spoon, flat wire whip, rubber scraper, etc.

Fry: To cook in hot fat.

Grate: To rub against a grater to tear food into small pieces or shreds.

Grind: To change a food into small particles by the cutting and crushing motion of a food grinder.

Halve: To cut into two equal parts.

Heat: To cause a mixture or liquid to become hot by the use of a flame.

Knead: To work into a smooth, satiny mass with the hands, using a rolling, pressing, and folding-over motion.

Macerate: To soften or separate parts of a substance by steeping in liquid.

Marinate: To let food stand in a marinade, usually an oil and acid mixture like French dressing.

Mash: To reduce a food to a soft, smooth state by crushing or beating.

Melt: To change a solid to a liquid by heating.

Mix: To combine two or more ingredients until evenly blended.

Pare: To cut off the outside covering with a knife.

Peel: To strip off the outside covering.

Pinch: Amount of substance that can be contained between thumb and forefinger.

Preheat: To heat the oven to the desired temperature before putting in the food.

Press: To pack down a mixture, with the fingers or the bottom of a cup, into a pan.

Puree: To press through a fine sieve.

Quarter: To cut into four equal parts.

Roll: To place on a board and spread thin with a rolling pin.

Rub: To smear two substances together.

Saute: To brown or cook in a small amount of fat.

Scald: To heat a liquid to just below the boiling point.

Scrape: To remove the outside skin by rubbing the surface with a sharp knife.

Sift: To put dry ingredients through a sieve.

Simmer: To cook in liquid just below the boiling point. It is done on the top of the stove.

Skin: To remove the outer covering.

Slightly beat: To mix together lightly (a few strokes).

Sliver: To cut or shred into long pieces.

Soak: To suck up and absorb liquid.

Sprinkle: To scatter a dry ingredient over the surface of a food.

Steam: To cook in the steam that arises from a pan of boiling water or other liquid.

Stir: To mix, usually with a spoon, using a circular motion.

Stuff: To fill a cavity or hole with a mixture.

Sugaring: To sprinkle with sugar.

Toast: To brown by means of dry heat.

Top: To crown or cap.

Warm: To heat to moderate degree.

Whip: To beat rapidly, using a flat wire whisk, rotary egg beater, or electric mixer at high speed, to incorporate air and to increase the volume.

❧ Useful Kitchen Utensils for Dessert Preparation

Measuring

1. Set of standard measuring spoons
2. Nest of measuring cups with lips for liquids and plain rims for dry ingredients
3. Pint and quart measuring cups
4. Utility tray
5. Metal spatula

Mixing

6. Kitchen fork and knife
7. Flat wire whip
8. Pastry blender
9. Wooden spoon
10. Rotary egg beater
11. Electric mixer
12. Flour sifter
13. Mixing bowls
14. Rubber spatula

Food Preparation

15. Paring knife
16. Bread knife
17. Straight-edged knives
18. Flexible spatula
19. Grapefruit knife
20. Apple corer
21. Strawberry huller
22. Kitchen scissors
23. Food chopper
24. Wire strainers: very fine, medium, and coarse
25. Pastry brush
26. Set of graters
27. Lemon squeezer
28. Can opener, jar opener, bottle opener, and corkscrew
29. Timer
30. Cookie cutters
31. Cookie press
32. Rolling pin
33. Pastry canvas
34. Breadboard

Top of the Stove Cooking

35. Saucepans and covers, several sizes
36. Double boiler, large and small
37. Large kettle with steamer
38. Deep-fat frying basket
39. Heavy skillets, large and small
40. Pancake griddle
41. Pancake turner
42. Coffee maker
43. Teakettle
44. Waffle iron

Baking

45. Square pans, 8-inch and 9-inch
46. Round layer pans, 8-inch and 9-inch
47. Oblong pan, 13 × 9 × 2-inch
48. Loaf pan, 10 × 5 × 3-inch
49. Tube pans, 9-inch and 10-inch
50. Pie pans, 7-inch, 8-inch, and 9-inch
51. Baking sheets
52. Jelly roll pan, 15 ½ × 10 ½ × ½-inch
53. Ring molds, several sizes
54. Wire cooling racks
55. Oven thermometer
56. Muffin pans
57. Casserole with covers, several sizes
58. Individual custard cups
59. Pudding molds

How to Freeze Desserts

THERE ARE many advantages to the home freezer. Food can be prepared ahead when time is available and when it is convenient. For example, fruit pies and other fruit desserts can be made up in season when fresh fruit is easy to find and cheaper to buy. Then, too, with a freezer there is no need to worry about what to serve unexpected guests.

Cakes, cookies, fruits, ice cream, ice cream desserts, and most pies can be frozen satisfactorily. Proper choice of material and correct wrapping is very important to successful freezing. The wrapping material should be moisture-vapor proof, strong and tough, free of odor, and pliable and easy to work with. Aluminum foil, polyethylene, and pliofilm are excellent and readily available. The foods should be very tightly wrapped and sealed.

To protect them against rough handling, it is a good idea to place baked goods in paper plates or on cardboard and then wrap. They may also be wrapped and placed in a sturdy box.

Label and date all packages. Be careful not to overload your freezer as it causes the temperature to rise. Specific directions for cakes, cookies, fruits, ice cream, ice cream desserts, pies, and pastries follow below:

Cakes—All kinds of baked cakes may be frozen. They may be frosted or unfrosted; however, they keep better and longer if unfrosted. If frosted, use a butter or penuche-type frosting. Cool cakes first before wrapping, and if frosted freeze before wrapping so as not to upset the frosting. Unwrap frosted cakes before thawing while unfrosted cakes should be left wrapped during the thawing period. Two hours at room temperature are sufficient for thawing. Frozen cakes may be stored 3 to 4 months.

Cookies—Baked cookies or cookie dough may be frozen. Baked cookies should be packed very carefully before freezing to prevent breakage. Freeze baked cookies in covered containers, and thaw the frozen cookies in the original container at room temperature. It takes from 15 to 30 minutes. Cookie doughs, other than refrigerator cookie dough, should be packed into freezer containers. Refrigerator dough should first be molded, then wrapped in sheet wrapping and sealed with tape; when used, the dough should be thawed in the refrigerator until it is soft enough to slice easily. Other doughs should be thawed until they can be handled easily.

Fruits (general directions)—Freeze only sound, fully ripe fruit. Make a sugar-water syrup and chill before packaging. To prevent darkening, add ½ teaspoon ascorbic acid for each quart of syrup. Add syrup to fruit in liquid-tight containers and fill to within ¾ an inch from the top. Freeze according to directions furnished with your freezer or obtained from some other reliable source.

Ice Cream and Ice Cream Desserts—Freeze ice creams in tight containers to prevent loss of flavor and accumulation of ice crystals. The richer the ice cream mixture, the lower the freezing and storing temperature required. Ice cream may be stored for a month. Ice cream desserts should be carefully wrapped to protect the flavor. They should not be kept *too long*.

Pies—Fruit pies, vegetable pies (pumpkin and squash), mince, and chiffon pies all freeze well. Custard pies do not freeze satisfactorily, and meringue toppings shrink and become tough. Some juicy fruits and berries may require more thickening when put in a pie to be frozen. Fruit and mince pie may be frozen baked or unbaked. (Pies frozen unbaked have a slightly fresher flavor.) All fruit pies should be thawed in the oven. Chiffon pies should be set before freezing. Baked pumpkin pie may be frozen for a short period of time; however, for longer storage, it is better to freeze the unbaked filling. Be sure to thaw pies before baking. Pie shells may be frozen baked or unbaked. Pies may be made and frozen in regular pie plates or special paper baking plates, but if baked, be sure to cool first. Do not slit the top crust of unbaked pies. On the whole it is easier to freeze pie before wrapping. To protect the top of pies, cover with paper pie plate before placing in the freezer bags or other wrapping material. Be sure pies are setting level while freezing. To thaw chiffon pies, unwrap them and set them in the refrigerator for 1 to 1 ½ hours. Frozen fruit and mince pies should also be unwrapped when thawed. When you use a frozen unbaked pie, slit the top crust and bake in hot oven (425° F.) 40 to 60 minutes or until done. Frozen baked pies should be heated in a moderate oven (375° F.) 30 to 50 minutes or until the center is bubbling. Unbaked pie shells should be unwrapped and thawed at room temperature or in a moderate oven. Baked pastry and pastry circles should be thawed completely before using. Pies may be stored up to two months.

Reducing and Increasing Recipes

To MAKE half a recipe use exactly one-half the amount of each ingredient. To double a recipe, use exactly twice the amount of each ingredient. Refer to the tables "Food Weights and Measures" and "Equivalent Measures and Weights" for help in dividing or multiplying the ingredient.

If the modified recipe calls for uneven amounts of flour, liquid, eggs, etc., remember the following proportions:

$$\frac{3}{8} \text{ cup} = \frac{1}{4} \text{ cup} + 2 \text{ tablespoons}$$
$$\frac{5}{8} \text{ cup} = \frac{1}{2} \text{ cup} + 2 \text{ tablespoons}$$
$$\frac{7}{8} \text{ cup} = \frac{3}{4} \text{ cup} + 2 \text{ tablespoons}$$

If the modified recipe figures out to be part of an egg, beat up one whole egg, measure with a tablespoon, and divide.

Baking pans for half recipes of cakes, pies, etc. should measure half the area but have the same depth of those for the whole recipe.

Approximate the baking time and oven temperature. When doubling the recipe, use two pans of the same size indicated for the original recipe or a pan double in area. Thus the same baking time and temperature may be maintained so that the batter will be the same depth in the pan.

RECIPES

Cakes

My mother keeps in two big books
The secrets of the things she cooks.
If I could ever learn to bake,
I'd send my brother Bill a cake.
But mother says it's hard to learn
To bake cakes that never burn.

THIS OLD nursery rhyme applies no more. Today any woman can be queen of the "castle" by making a perfect cake. A perfect cake does not depend upon luck or knack. Our recipes, unlike our grandmother's, are carefully balanced in ingredients and precisely written to give the clearest directions. If you use top-quality ingredients, measure accurately, follow the recipe exactly, have proper sized pans, use a good oven, and follow the baking time and temperature—perfect results will be your reward every time. Those are the secrets of cake baking.

In the eighteenth century "Animated Specialties" were the pride and joy of French chefs. Huge cakes and pies were made that, when cut, released birds, frogs, or butterflies. The larger, more fantastic cakes concealed dwarfs who jumped out. Strange as it may seem, cakes were part of the entertainment program in the castle.

In early times, particularly in England, every religious occasion was celebrated with a cake.

Many of the original English recipes and traditions continue unchanged. To this day, cakes are thrown from the tower of Biddenden Church in Kent on the Eve of Epiphany. Back in the twelfth century, two sisters gave money to build this church, and the thrown cakes are symbolic of the donors.

There is an interesting tale about Mother's Day and cakes. The origin of our Mother's Day is Mothering Sunday, which is known in the Church of England as Refreshment Sunday or the Fourth Sunday in Lent. Like the evergreen tree at Christmastime, cake was traditional for this event.

Usually sons and daughters (especially those living away) went "a-mothering" with a gift of a cake. The cake was eaten while the family reunited in worship. Eventually, the day became an occasion to honor all mothers.

Two of our familiar cakes, the plum or fruit cake and the bride's cake, also have their origins in a religious event. The fruit cake, made of fruits and spices, represented the gifts of the Wise Men to the Christ Child. The present-day bride's cake is a descendant of the honey cake, which was an important part of the marriage ceremony and from which we get the word *honeymoon*.

We can trace many more of our present-day practices, expressions, and recipes to cakes of one kind or another from the four corners of the earth. I am sure that many a bride in many a land was chosen, by men of good appetite, for her cake-making abilities as much as for her handsome features and ample dowry. And you know, even though it is out of style to say so, I believe that many of today's young prospective husbands keep their eyes peeled for a good cake baker. The joke on them is the fact that it is so easy to make excellent cakes.

In fact, the old saying "You can't eat your cake and have it too" no longer applies. Today you can eat your cake and tomorrow make another identical one. And when you know that friends are coming, whether it is the teenage crowd, the afternoon bridge club, your husband's poker club, or dinner guests—bake a cake!

❧ 1-2-3-4 Cake

Ingredients

3 cups sifted flour	4 egg yolks
4 teaspoons baking powder	1 cup milk
¼ teaspoon salt	1 teaspoon vanilla
1 cup butter	4 egg whites
2 cups sugar	

Directions (Makes two 9-inch layers)

Sift together first three ingredients three times. Set aside.

Cream butter; add sugar gradually, and cream together until light and fluffy.

Add yolks, one at a time, beating well after each addition. Add milk.

Fold in vanilla. Beat egg whites until stiff but not dry. Fold in carefully. Pour batter into two round 9-inch layer pans that have been lined on bottoms with paper. Bake in moderate oven at 375° about 25 minutes. This cake may also be baked in three 8-inch layer pans. Cool and frost with Orange Butter Cream Frosting and sprinkle with coconut.

➥ *Cake pans cost so little that you should have a set of each size in your kitchen if you wish to be a successful cake maker.*

❧ One Egg Cake

Ingredients

2 cups sifted cake flour	1 cup sugar
2 teaspoons baking powder	1 egg
¾ teaspoon salt	⅞ cup milk
⅓ cup butter	1 teaspoon vanilla

Directions (Makes two 8-inch layers)

Sift together first three ingredients three times. Set aside.

Cream butter; add sugar gradually, and cream together until light and fluffy.

Add egg to the creamed mixture and beat well.

Add flour, alternately with milk, beating well after each addition.

Stir in vanilla. Pour batter into two round 8-inch layer pans that have been lined on bottoms with paper. Bake in moderate oven at 375° about 25 minutes. This cake may also be baked in the 9 × 9 × 2-inch pan.

❧ Economical Gold Cake

Ingredients

2 cups sifted cake flour	1 cup plus 2 tablespoons sugar
2 teaspoons baking powder	3 egg yolks
½ teaspoon salt	¾ cup milk
½ cup butter	1 teaspoon vanilla

Directions (Makes two 8-inch layers)

Sift together first three ingredients three times. Set aside.

Cream butter; add sugar gradually, and cream together until light and fluffy.

Beat yolks until very thick and lemon-colored; add to the above butter mixture and beat well.

Add flour, alternately with milk, beating after each addition until smooth.

Add vanilla and blend. Pour batter into two round 8-inch layer pans that have been lined on bottoms with paper. Bake in moderate oven at 375° for 20 to 30 minutes. This cake may also be baked in the 9 × 9 × 2-inch pan at 375° for 35 to 40 minutes.

❧ Rich Butter Cake

Ingredients

2 ¼ cups sifted cake flour	1 ½ cups sugar
2 ¼ teaspoons baking powder	3 eggs
½ teaspoon salt	⅔ cup milk
¾ cup butter	1 teaspoon vanilla

Directions (Makes two 9-inch layers)

Sift together first three ingredients three times. Set aside.

Cream butter; add sugar gradually, and cream together until light and fluffy.

Add eggs one at a time, beating well after each addition.

Add flour, alternately with milk, beating after each addition until smooth.

Add vanilla and blend. Pour batter into two round 9-inch layer pans that have been lined on bottoms with paper. Bake in moderate oven at 375° about 25 minutes. This cake may also be baked in two 8 × 8 × 2-inch square pans about 30 minutes.

ᕦ White Cake

Ingredients

½ cup butter
1 ¾ cups sugar, sifted
4 egg yolks
3 cups flour
1 cup milk

½ teaspoon salt
3 teaspoons baking powder
2 egg whites, beaten
2 teaspoons lemon extract

Directions (Makes two 9-inch layers)

Cream butter and sugar together.

Add yolks to above.

Sift flour three times. Add just a little to mixture.

Add milk alternately with remaining flour. Hold out 1 cup of flour.

Add salt and baking powder to final cup of flour and stir into mixture.

Fold in beaten egg whites.

Add lemon extract to mixture. Pour batter into two 9-inch cake pans that have been greased and floured. Bake in 350° oven for 35 minutes. Fill and frost when cold.

ᕦ White Cake

Ingredients

2 ⅔ cups sifted cake flour
3 teaspoons baking powder
1 teaspoon salt
5 egg whites

½ cup sugar
⅔ cup vegetable shortening
1 ¼ cups sugar
1 cup milk

Directions (Makes two 9-inch layers)

Sift together first three ingredients three times. Set aside.

Beat egg whites until frothy throughout. Add ½ cup sugar, 2 tablespoons at a time, beating after each addition until blended. Beat only to soft peaks. Set meringue aside.

Cream shortening; add 1 ¼ cup sugar gradually, and cream together until light and fluffy.

Add flour, alternately with milk, beating after each addition until smooth.

Add vanilla and blend. Stir in meringue until well blended. Pour batter into two round 9-inch layer pans that have been lined on bottoms with paper. Bake in moderate oven at 375° for 25 to 30 minutes or until done.

⁓ White Cake Supreme

Ingredients

1 cup butter	½ teaspoon salt
2 cups sugar	1 cup milk
3 ½ cups cake flour	1 teaspoon vanilla
4 teaspoons baking powder	8 egg whites

Directions (Makes two 9-inch layers)

Beat butter until creamy. Add sugar gradually and blend until very light and creamy.

Sift flour and measure. Add baking powder and salt, and sift all together two or three times. Stir into butter mixture alternately with milk. Beat batter until smooth. Add vanilla. Remove from beater.

Beat egg whites until stiff and fairly dry. Fold into batter. Place in two greased, paper-lined 9-inch cake pans. Bake in 350° oven for 40 minutes. Can also be baked in three 8-inch pans at 375° for about 25 minutes.

⁓ Orange Cake

Francis Fowler Jr., Los Angeles, California

Ingredients

1 tablespoon grated orange rind	2 ¼ cups cake flour
¼ cup orange juice, strained	3 ½ teaspoons baking powder
¾ cup butter	½ teaspoon salt
1 ½ cups sugar	¾ cup water
3 egg yolks, beaten	3 egg whites, beaten

Directions (Makes two 9-inch layers)

Put rind in juice and let stand while making the cake. Save the pulp for filling.

Cream butter; add sugar gradually and cream thoroughly.

Add yolks to mixture.

Sift together dry ingredients. Add water to the orange juice and add alternately with the sifted dry ingredients to the above mixture.

Fold egg whites into mixture. Pour into two 9-inch layer pans that have been well greased. Bake in 350° oven for 30 to 35 minutes. Cool and spread with Clear Orange Filling.

∾ Hot Milk Cake

Ingredients

2 cups sifted flour	2 tablespoons butter
2 teaspoons baking powder	4 eggs
¼ teaspoon salt	2 cups sugar
1 cup milk, scalded	2 teaspoons vanilla

Directions (Makes two 9-inch layers)

Sift together first three ingredients three times. Set aside.

Add butter to scalded milk. Set aside.

Beat eggs until thick and lemon colored. Add sugar gradually and
continue beating until very thick. Quickly add flour mixture and
stir until just mixed. Stir in hot milk.

Add vanilla. Pour batter into two 9-inch layer pans that have been
lined on bottoms with paper. Bake in moderate oven at 350° about
35 minutes. Frost with your favorite frosting.

∾ Orange Juice Cake

Ingredients

2 ⅓ cups sifted cake flour	1 ¾ teaspoon grated orange rind
2 ¾ teaspoons baking powder	½ cup milk
¼ teaspoon soda	¼ cup orange juice
1 teaspoon salt	¼ teaspoon almond extract
1 ½ cups sugar	3 eggs
⅔ cup butter	

Directions (Makes two 9-inch layers)

Sift together dry ingredients. Set aside.

Stir butter just to soften. Add grated orange rind. Sift in dry
ingredients.

Combine milk, orange juice, and almond extract. Add to the above
mixture and mix until all flour is dampened. Beat 2 minutes at
a low mixer speed or 300 vigorous strokes by hand. Add eggs to
above mixture and beat 1 minute longer in mixer or 150 strokes by
hand. Pour batter into two round 9-inch layer pans that have been
lined on bottoms with paper. Bake in moderate oven at 375° for
25 to 30 minutes. Cool and frost with Seven Minute Frosting and
sprinkle with coconut.

❦ Orange Layer Cake

Damon's, Cleveland, Ohio

Use your favorite yellow cake recipe, but when mixing dough, substitute ¼ of the amount of liquid stipulated with orange juice. Cool and frost with Orange Butter Cream Icing.

❦ Aunt Susan's Clabber Cake

The Anna Maude, Oklahoma City, Oklahoma

Ingredients

½ lb. butter
2 cups sugar
2 eggs, beaten
2 cups clabber

3 ½ cups cake flour
2 teaspoons soda
3 ⅓ tablespoons cocoa

Directions (Serves 16)

Cream butter and sugar together.
Add eggs and clabber to mixture.
Add remaining ingredients to mixture. Stir well. Pour batter into greased and floured pan. Bake in a 350° oven for 45 minutes.

❦ Buttermilk Cake

Ingredients

2 ½ cups sifted cake flour
1 ½ teaspoons baking powder
½ teaspoon soda
1 teaspoon salt
1 ⅔ cups sugar

¾ cup butter
¾ cup buttermilk or sour milk
1 teaspoon vanilla
3 eggs

Directions (Makes two 9-inch layers)

Sift together dry ingredients. Set aside.
Stir butter just to soften. Sift in dry ingredients.
Add buttermilk and vanilla to the above and mix until all flour is dampened. Beat 2 minutes at a low speed of electric mixer or 300 vigorous strokes by hand. Add eggs and beat 1 minute longer in mixer or 150 strokes by hand. Pour batter into two round 9-inch layer pans that have been lined on bottoms with paper. Bake in moderate oven at 350° about 35 minutes. This cake may also be baked in two 9 × 9 × 2-inch baking pans at 350° for 25 to 30 minutes or in the 13 × 9 × 2-inch baking pan for 35 to 40 minutes.

⌒ Minnehaha Cake

Ingredients

3 egg whites	2 teaspoons baking powder
½ cup sugar	½ teaspoon salt
½ cup butter	½ cup milk
½ cup sugar	1 teaspoon vanilla
1 ½ cups flour	

Directions (Makes two 8-inch layers)

Beat egg whites until stiff and add ½ cup sugar, beating until blended. Set aside.

Cream butter and remaining sugar.

Sift dry ingredients; add to creamed mixture alternately with milk. Beat smooth.

Add vanilla. Fold in beaten egg whites. Pour batter into two buttered, 8-inch layer cake pans. Bake at 350° for 30 to 35 minutes. Cool and spread with Festive Frosting.

⌒ Burnt Sugar Cake

The Anna Maude, Oklahoma City, Oklahoma

Ingredients

1 cup butter	3 cups cake flour, sifted
2 cups sugar	4 eggs
4 tablespoons caramelized sugar syrup	1 tablespoon baking powder
¾ cup milk	1 teaspoon vanilla

Directions (Makes two 9-inch layers)

Cream butter and sugar together.

Make a syrup by melting granulated sugar in an iron skillet. (May be made up in quantity and kept on hand.) Combine syrup and milk.

Add flour to creamed mixture alternately with milk and syrup. Add eggs, one at a time, beating well after each addition.

Add baking powder and vanilla last. Pour batter into two 9-inch layer pans that have been greased and floured. Bake in a 350° oven for 40 minutes.

ᕐᗢ *Banana Cake*

Ingredients

½ cup butter	2 cups cake flour
1 ½ cups sugar	1 teaspoon baking powder
2 egg yolks	½ cup chopped nuts
1 scant cup crushed bananas	1 teaspoon vanilla
5 tablespoons buttermilk	2 egg whites
1 teaspoon soda	

Directions (Makes one 10-inch square layer)

Cream butter and sugar together in electric mixer until light and fluffy.

Add yolks to above and beat well.

Add crushed bananas. Dissolve soda in buttermilk and stir into mixture.

Sift flour twice, adding baking powder to second sifting. Add nuts to flour and beat into mixture. Add vanilla and fold in stiffly beaten egg whites. Pour into greased and lined 10-inch square cake pan and bake in 350° oven for 40 to 50 minutes or until cake tester comes out clean. Let cool, and ice with Maple Frosting.

ᕐᗢ *Grandma Shield's Montgomery Cake-Pie*

Water Gate Inn, Washington, D.C.

Ingredients

1 cup sugar	2 teaspoons double-acting
¼ cup shortening	baking powder
1 egg, beaten	½ cup milk
1 ½ cups sifted cake flour	1 teaspoon lemon extract

Directions (Makes two 8-inch layers)

Cream together sugar and shortening until well blended. Add egg and mix well.

Sift baking powder with flour. Add to above mixture, alternately with milk, in small amounts. Beat well. Add lemon extract and mix well. Pour batter into two greased 8-inch round cake pans and bake in 350° oven for 25 to 30 minutes or until done. Cool and spread filling between layers and on top of cake.

Filling

Ingredients

1 cup sugar
4 ½ tablespoons cornstarch
¼ teaspoon salt
2 lemons

1 cup dark corn syrup
2 cups water
1 teaspoon lemon extract
3 eggs

Directions

Mix together first three ingredients.

Grate lemon rinds; then squeeze lemons to extract juice. Add grated rind and juice to water, corn syrup, and lemon extract. Add to the above mixture. Beat eggs and add to above. Cook in top of double boiler over hot water, stirring constantly until thickened. Cool.

➤ Here's a simple way to find out if your cake is done. Stick in a toothpick, and if it comes out clean, it is done. Or you can lightly touch the top of the cake with your little finger, and if it leaves no imprint, then it is done.

➤ Poppy Seed Cake

Lake Breeze Resort, Three Lakes, Wisconsin

Ingredients

1 cup poppy seeds
¾ cup scalded milk
1 ½ cups sugar
¾ cup butter

¾ cup cold milk
3 teaspoons baking powder
3 cups flour
4 egg whites, beaten

Directions (Makes three 9-inch layers)

Soak together first three ingredients overnight.

Cream sugar and butter together. Stir in milk.

Sift together baking powder and flour three times and blend all ingredients together.

Fold beaten egg whites into mixture. Bake in three layers in 9-inch cake pans in 350° oven for 25 to 30 minutes. Cool and fill with Lemon Filling. Frost with White Icing.

Allenwood Fudge Cake

Ingredients

2 squares unsweetened chocolate
½ cup milk
1 tablespoon butter
1 egg yolk
1 cup sugar

½ cup milk
1 teaspoon vanilla
1 ¾ cups flour
1 teaspoon soda

Directions (Makes two 8-inch layers)

Melt chocolate in ½ cup milk, stirring constantly, until like custard.
Add butter and egg yolk to the above mixture. Let cool.
Add sugar, remaining milk, and vanilla to the mixture.
Blend together flour and soda, and add to mixture. Pour into greased and floured 8-inch cake pans and bake in 375° oven for about 10 minutes; then lower the temperature to about 350° and bake for another 25 to 30 minutes.

➤ *Cooked fruits usually have a better flavor and retain more of their natural sweetness if served hot.*

Fudge Cake

Ingredients

4 squares unsweetened chocolate
½ cup hot water
½ cup sugar
2 cups sifted cake flour
1 teaspoon soda
1 teaspoon salt

½ cup butter
1 ¼ cups sugar
3 eggs
⅔ cup milk
1 teaspoon vanilla

Directions (Makes two 9-inch layers)

Heat chocolate with hot water in top of double boiler. Cook and stir over boiling water until chocolate is melted and mixture thickens.
Add ½ cup sugar to the above mixture and cook and stir 2 minutes longer. Cool to lukewarm while mixing cake.
Sift together cake flour, soda, and salt three times. Set aside.
Cream butter; add sugar gradually, and cream together until light and fluffy.
Add eggs one at a time, beating well after each addition.

Add flour mixture, alternately with milk, in small amounts, beating after each addition until smooth.

Add vanilla with chocolate mixture to the batter. Stir until blended. Pour batter into two round 9-inch layer pans that have been lined on bottoms with paper. Bake in moderate oven at 350° for 25 to 30 minutes. This cake may also be baked in the 13 × 9 × 2-inch pan about 40 minutes. Cool and frost with Sea Foam Frosting or Mocha Butter Cream Frosting.

➥ *You cannot expect perfect results in making cake unless you are certain that the ingredients are of top quality and always fresh.*

ᔐ Eight-Yolk Fudge Cake

Violet Bray Berry, Berkeley, California

Ingredients

2 cups sugar, sifted	¾ teaspoon soda
¾ cup butter	2 teaspoons baking powder
8 egg yolks	¼ teaspoon salt
2 squares unsweetened chocolate	1 ¼ cups buttermilk
2 ½ cups flour	1 teaspoon vanilla

Directions (Makes three 9-inch layers)

Cream sugar and butter until light and fine grained.

Beat egg yolks until thick and lemon colored and add to above. Melt chocolate and add to mixture.

Sift dry ingredients four times. Alternately add to above mixture with buttermilk.

Add vanilla to mixture. Pour into three 9-inch layer pans that have been greased and floured. Bake in 350° oven for 30 minutes.

ᔐ Fudge Cake à la Anchorage-by-the-Sea

Anchorage-by-the-Sea, Mattapoisett, Massachusetts

Ingredients

3 eggs, separated	1 ½ teaspoons baking powder
1 ½ cups sugar	½ cup butter
¾ cup milk	2 squares unsweetened chocolate
1 ½ cups cake flour	1 teaspoon vanilla

Directions (Serves 8)

Beat egg yolks with sugar. Add milk and flour, which has been sifted
with the baking powder.

Melt chocolate with butter and add to above. Then add stiffly beaten
egg whites and vanilla. Pour batter into two 8-inch layer pans that
have been greased and floured. Bake in moderate oven at 350°
about 35 minutes. Cool and frost with Fudge Frosting.

ᰡ *Fudge Pecan Cake Ball*

Take a day-old chocolate cake without frosting and crumble until
very fine. Take a scoop or slice of brick ice cream and roll in crumbs,
pressing rather hard so the ice cream will collect as much of the
crumbs as possible. Place in a serving dish and cover with chocolate
syrup. Top with chopped pecans.

ᰡ *Cocoa Devil's Food Cake*

Ingredients

1 ½ cups sifted cake flour
1 teaspoon soda
1 teaspoon salt
⅓ cup sugar
½ cup cocoa

½ cup butter
⅞ cup milk
1 teaspoon vanilla
2 eggs

Directions (Makes two 8-inch layers)

Sift together first five ingredients. Set aside.

Stir butter just to soften. Sift in dry ingredients.

Add ¾ cup of the milk and vanilla to the above mixture. Mix until all
flour is dampened. Beat 2 minutes at a low speed of electric mixer
or 300 vigorous strokes by hand.

Add eggs and remaining milk. Beat 1 minute longer in the mixer or
150 strokes by hand. Pour batter into two round 8-inch layer pans
that have been lined on bottoms with paper. Bake in moderate
oven at 350° for about 35 minutes. This cake may also be baked in
the 9 × 9 × 2-inch pan for 35 to 40 minutes.

◆ *Part of the success in your cake making lies in using the proper size pan. Never try to crowd a 9-inch cake into an 8-inch pan, or you will have cake batter all over the bottom of your oven. If you try to put an 8-inch cake into a 9-inch pan, then the result will be a product that is thin and tough. Cake tins cost so little that you should have a set of each in your kitchen if you wish to be a successful cake maker.*

ᔓ Devil's Food Cake

Ingredients

2 cups sifted cake flour	3 egg yolks
1 teaspoon baking powder	3 squares unsweetened
½ cup butter	chocolate, melted
1 ¼ cups firmly packed brown	1 cup milk
sugar	1 teaspoon vanilla

Directions (Makes two 9-inch layers)

Sift together first two ingredients three times. Set aside.

Cream butter; add brown sugar gradually and cream together until light and fluffy.

Add egg yolks, one at a time, beating well after each addition. Add melted chocolate to the above and blend thoroughly.

Add flour, alternately with milk, in small amounts, beating after each addition until smooth.

Stir in vanilla. Pour batter into two round 9-inch layer pans, which have been lined on bottoms with paper. Bake in moderate oven at 350° about 30 minutes.

ᔓ Devil's Food Cake

Ingredients

2 cups sugar	2 ½ cups cake flour
2 tablespoons butter	2 teaspoons soda
4 egg yolks	4 egg whites
1 cup sour cream	
3 squares unsweetened chocolate	
¾ cup water	

Directions *(Makes two 9-inch layers)*

Cream together sugar and butter.

Beat yolks, add sour cream, and add to above, mixing well.

Melt chocolate in water in top of double boiler, and add to above.

Sift cake flour, and measure. Dissolve soda in a little water. Add flour to above mixture, and then stir in soda.

Beat egg whites until stiff and fold into batter. Bake in two 9-inch layers at 350° until straw comes out dry. Ice with a boiled white icing.

∼ Devil's Food Cake

Ingredients

2 cups sugar	1 cup buttermilk
2 tablespoons butter	3 cups cake flour
3 eggs	2 teaspoons soda
¼ teaspoon salt	4 squares unsweetened chocolate
2 teaspoons vanilla	1 cup sweet milk

Directions *(Makes two 9-inch layers)*

Cream together butter and sugar until fluffy. Beat eggs and stir into creamed mixture with salt and vanilla.

Add buttermilk to the above.

Sift together cake flour and soda, and add to mixture.

Heat milk and chocolate in double boiler until chocolate is dissolved. Stir into cake batter; place in two 9-inch pans that have been greased and lined with paper, and bake in 325° oven for 1 hour.

∼ Sour Cream Devil's Food Cake

Ingredients

2 cups sifted cake flour	3 squares unsweetened
1 ¼ teaspoons soda	chocolate, melted
½ teaspoon salt	1 teaspoon vanilla
⅓ cup butter	½ cup sour cream
1 ¼ cups sugar	1 cup sweet milk
1 egg	

Directions (Makes two 9-inch layers)

Sift together first three ingredients three times. Set aside.

Cream butter; add sugar gradually, and cream together until light and fluffy.

Add egg to creamed mixture and beat well.

Stir chocolate and vanilla into the above and blend thoroughly. Add ¼ of the flour mixture and blend.

Add sour cream to above, and beat well.

Add remaining flour, alternately with milk, beating after each addition until smooth. Pour batter into two round 9-inch layer pans that have been lined on bottoms with paper. Bake in moderate oven at 350° for 30 to 35 minutes.

ᕼ *Party Devil's Food Cake*

Ingredients

2 ¼ cups sifted cake flour	3 eggs
2 teaspoons soda	3 squares unsweetened
½ teaspoon salt	chocolate, melted
½ cup butter	½ cup buttermilk or sour milk
2 ½ cups firmly packed brown	1 teaspoon vanilla
sugar	1 cup boiling water

Directions (Makes three 8-inch layers)

Sift together first three ingredients three times. Set aside.

Cream butter; add sugar gradually, and cream together until light and fluffy.

Add eggs, one at a time, beating well after each addition.

Add chocolate to the above mixture and blend thoroughly.

Add flour, alternately with milk, beating after each addition until smooth.

Stir in vanilla and water and blend. (Batter will be thin.) Pour batter into three 8-inch layer pans, which have been lined on bottoms with paper. Bake in moderate oven at 375° for 25 to 30 minutes. Cool and frost tops and sides with double the Cocoa Whipped Cream recipe.

❧ Chocolate Cake Supreme

Ingredients

½ cup butter
2 cups sugar
4 squares unsweetened chocolate
2 egg yolks
1 teaspoon vanilla

2 ½ cups cake flour
2 teaspoons baking powder
½ teaspoon salt
1 ½ cups sweet milk
2 egg whites

Directions (Makes two 9-inch layers)

Cream butter and sugar together until fluffy.
Melt chocolate in double boiler and add to above.
Beat yolks, add vanilla to beaten yolks, and add to above.
Sift together dry ingredients three times.
Add milk alternately with flour mixture to the above.
Beat egg whites stiff and fold into mixture. Place in two 9-inch cake pans that have been greased, paper lined, and lightly greased again. Bake in 350° oven for about 30 minutes or until done. Cool and spread with Chocolate Frosting.

➤ *In order to ensure perfect cakes, be sure that your oven temperature is correct. Every good cook should have an oven thermometer and test the stove front and back, top and bottom to see that the oven heats evenly. Always have the oven preheated to the temperature called for in the recipe before putting in the cake or pie. After a cake has cooled, keep it fresh and moist by storing it in a container that has a tight cover.*

❧ Buttermilk Chocolate Cake

Ingredients

2 cups sifted cake flour
¼ teaspoon salt
½ cup butter
1 ¼ cups sugar
2 eggs
1 cup buttermilk

2 squares unsweetened
chocolate, melted
1 tablespoon vinegar
½ teaspoon vanilla
1 teaspoon soda

Directions (Makes two 8-inch layers)

Sift cake flour and salt together three times.

Cream butter; add sugar gradually, and cream together until light and fluffy.

Add eggs, one at a time, beating well after each addition.

Add flour, alternately with milk, adding four parts flour and three parts milk, beating well after each addition until smooth.

Add remaining ingredients and blend thoroughly. Pour batter into two 8-inch layer pans that have been lined on the bottoms with paper. Bake in moderate oven at 350° about 35 minutes or until done. Cool and frost with Seven Minute Frosting.

❧ Buttermilk Chocolate Cake

Ingredients

3 cups sifted cake flour
½ teaspoon salt
¾ cup butter
2 ¼ cups sugar
3 eggs
1 ½ cups buttermilk

3 squares unsweetened chocolate, melted
1 ½ tablespoons vinegar
1 teaspoon vanilla
1 ½ teaspoons soda

Directions (Makes three 8-inch layers)

Use directions for Buttermilk Chocolate Cake (two 8-inch layers), substituting the listed ingredients.

❧ Mild Chocolate Cake

Ingredients

1 ¾ cups sifted cake flour
2 teaspoons baking powder
¼ teaspoon soda
1 teaspoon salt
1 ½ cups sugar
½ cup butter

1 cup plus 2 tablespoons undiluted evaporated milk
1 ¼ teaspoons vanilla
2 eggs
2 squares unsweetened chocolate, melted

Directions (Makes two 9-inch layers)

Sift together first five ingredients. Set aside.

Stir butter just to soften. Sift in dry ingredients.

Add evaporated milk and vanilla, and mix until all flour is dampened. Beat 2 minutes at a low speed of electric mixer or 300 vigorous strokes by hand.

Add eggs and chocolate to above mixture and beat 1 minute longer in mixer or 150 strokes by hand.

Pour batter into two round 9-inch layer pans that have been lined on bottoms with paper. Bake in moderate oven at 350° for 30 to 35 minutes. Cool and frost with Butter Cream Frosting.

⌒ "My Eureka Cake"

Ingredients

½ cup water	1 cup sifted cake flour
2 squares unsweetened chocolate	¾ teaspoon soda
¼ cup butter	¼ cup sour milk
1 cup sugar	1 egg

Directions (Makes one 8-inch square cake)

Pour water in a saucepan with chocolate and butter. Bring to a boil to melt. Let cool.

Measure sugar into a bowl.

Combine flour, soda, and milk, and add to above mixture. Add cooled chocolate.

Stir egg quickly into the mixture. (Batter must be thin.) Pour into an 8-inch square pan that has been greased and floured. Bake in 350° oven for 30 minutes or until cake tester comes out clean. Cool and spread with Mocha Frosting or Cocoa Whipped Cream.

⌒ Chocolate Chip Cake

The Derings, Green Lake, Wisconsin

Ingredients

½ cup shortening	1 cup water
1 ½ cups sugar	3 egg whites, stiffly beaten
1 ½ teaspoons vanilla	1 square unsweetened chocolate, grated
1 teaspoon salt	
2 ¼ cups sifted flour	
2 ½ teaspoons baking powder	

Directions (Makes two 8-inch layers)

Blend together the first four ingredients.

Sift together the flour and baking powder.

Add sifted dry ingredients alternately with water to the creamed
  mixture.

Fold egg whites into the batter. Then add grated chocolate. Bake in
  8-inch layer pans in a 350° oven for 30 to 35 minutes. Cool and
  frost with Creamy Soft Chocolate Frosting.

ᴄᴡ *Sugar Plum Cake*

Ingredients

1 tablespoon butter	2 cups flour
1 cup sugar	1 teaspoon baking powder
1 cup sour cream	¼ teaspoon salt
½ cup cocoa	1 teaspoon soda
½ cup hot water	8 teaspoons cold water
2 eggs, beaten	

Directions (Makes two 8-inch layers)

Cream butter, sugar, and sour cream together.

Add cocoa, hot water, and eggs to above.

Sift flour, baking powder, and salt. Add to mixture.

Dissolve soda in cold water. Add to the mixture. Stir well. Bake in
  two 8-inch pans or one 12 × 9-inch loaf pan, lightly greased and
  floured. Bake in 350° oven for 30 minutes. While cake is warm,
  spread with Date Nut Frosting.

ᴄᴡ *Spice Cake*

Ingredients

2 ½ cups sifted cake flour	½ cup butter
1 teaspoon baking powder	⅔ cup soft, firmly packed brown
1 teaspoon soda	sugar
¾ teaspoon salt	1 cup milk
¾ teaspoon cinnamon	2 tablespoons milk
¾ teaspoon cloves	2 eggs
1 cup sugar	

Directions (Makes two 9-inch layers)

Sift together first seven ingredients. Set aside.

Stir butter just to soften. Sift in dry ingredients.

Add brown sugar to the above and mix until all flour is dampened.
Beat 2 minutes at a low speed of electric mixer or 300 vigorous
strokes by hand.

Add remaining ingredients and beat 1 minute longer in mixer or 150
strokes by hand. Pour batter into two round 9-inch layer pans or
two 9 × 9 × 2-inch square pans that have been lined on bottoms
with paper. Bake in moderate oven at 375° for 25 to 30 minutes.

➽ *Fruits for cake may be cut easily by using a pair of scissors and
dipping frequently in water. Fruit that has been soaked in warm water
a few minutes blends well with other ingredients.*

ᕫ Spiced Layer Cake with Seafoam Frosting

Williamsburg Inn, Williamsburg, Virginia

Ingredients

⅓ cup butter	¼ teaspoon ginger
1 cup sugar	¼ teaspoon mace
1 egg	¼ teaspoon allspice
1 egg yolk	¼ teaspoon nutmeg
2 tablespoons molasses	¾ teaspoon cloves
2 cups sifted flour	¾ teaspoon cinnamon
2 teaspoons baking powder	¾ cup milk
¼ teaspoon salt	

Directions (Makes two 8-inch layers)

Cream butter thoroughly. Add sugar gradually and cream until light
and fluffy.

Add egg and egg yolk to butter mixture and beat well.

Add molasses and mix thoroughly.

Sift dry ingredients together three times. Add to creamed mixture
alternately with milk, beating after each addition until smooth.
Pour batter into two greased 8-inch layer pans and bake in 375°
oven for about 25 minutes or until done. Cool and frost with
Seafoam Frosting.

ᴄᴡ Hart's Old-Fashioned Spice Cake

Hart's Old Tyme Coffee House, Moose Lake, Minnesota

Ingredients

2 cups brown sugar
½ cup shortening (butter
  preferred)
3 whole eggs or 5 egg yolks
1 teaspoon allspice
1 teaspoon cinnamon

1 teaspoon ground cloves
2 cup pastry flour
1 teaspoon soda
½ teaspoon salt
1 cup heavy sour cream

Directions (Makes one 12 × 7 ½ × 2-inch cake)

Cream shortening and sugar together until thoroughly blended.
Beat egg yolks well. Add yolks and spices to above and beat well.
Sift together flour, soda, and salt. Add to mixture alternately with
  sour cream. If whole eggs are used, fold in beaten egg whites. Pour
  batter into a 12 × 7 ½ × 2-inch cake pan. Bake in 350° oven for
  50 minutes or until cake starts to shrink from sides of pan. Cool
  and frost with Sour Cream Frosting.

ᴄᴡ Spiced Molasses Cake

Ingredients

1 ¾ cups sifted cake flour
2 teaspoons baking powder
¾ teaspoon salt
¼ teaspoon cloves
½ teaspoon nutmeg
½ teaspoon allspice
1 teaspoon cinnamon

½ cup butter
2 teaspoons grated orange rind
1 cup sugar
2 eggs
⅔ cup milk
1 teaspoon vanilla
2 tablespoons molasses

Directions (Makes two 8-inch layers)

Sift together first seven ingredients three times. Set aside.
Cream butter and orange rind. Add sugar gradually, and cream
  together until light and fluffy.
Add eggs one at a time, beating well after each addition.
Combine remaining ingredients. Add flour, alternately with milk
  mixture, beating after each addition. Pour batter into two round
  8-inch layer pans that have been lined on bottoms with paper.
  Bake in moderate oven at 375° about 35 minutes.

ᕙ Hickory Nut Cake

Ingredients

2 ½ cups sifted cake flour
3 teaspoons baking powder
1 teaspoon salt
1 ½ cups sugar
½ cup butter

⅞ cup milk
1 teaspoon vanilla
2 eggs
1 cup chopped hickory nuts

Directions (Makes two 9-inch layers)

Sift together first four ingredients. Set aside.

Stir butter just to soften. Sift in dry ingredients.

Add ¾ cup of the milk and vanilla to the above mixture. Mix until all the flour is dampened. Then beat 2 minutes at a low speed of electric mixer or 300 vigorous strokes by hand.

Add eggs with remaining milk. Beat 1 minute longer in mixer or 150 strokes by hand. Stir in nuts. Pour batter into two round 9-inch layer pans that have been lined on bottoms with paper. Bake in moderate oven at 375° for 20 to 25 minutes. This cake may also be baked in three round 8-inch layers at 375° for about 20 minutes.

ᕙ Hazel Nut (Filberts) Cake

Mrs. Carl F. G. Neuhaus, Chicago, Illinois

Ingredients

1 cup butter
2 cups sugar
3 cups flour
Pinch of salt
2 teaspoons baking powder
1 cup milk

6 egg whites, stiffly beaten
1 ½ cups chopped hazel nuts
(put through No. 2 size meat chopper)
1 teaspoon cinnamon
½ teaspoon cloves

Directions (Makes two 9-inch layers)

Cream butter and gradually add sugar.

Sift flour three times, last time with salt and baking powder. Add to the above mixture alternately with milk.

Fold in stiffly beaten egg whites. Then add remaining ingredients. Pour batter into two 9-inch cake pans that have been greased and floured well. Bake in 375° oven until top springs back when lightly pressed with fingers. Cool and frost with Butter Cream Frosting.

> ❧ One of the most important kitchen tools is a set of accurate measuring spoons. If you would get the best out of every recipe, you must follow it to the letter.

∾ Pecan Cake

Ingredients

3 cups sifted cake flour
2 teaspoons baking powder
¾ teaspoon salt
1 cup butter
1 ¾ cups sugar
3 eggs

1 egg yolk
¾ cup milk
1 teaspoon orange extract
1 teaspoon almond extract
1 cup finely chopped pecans

Directions (Makes one 10-inch tube cake)

Sift together first three ingredients three times. Set aside.

Cream butter; add sugar gradually, and cream together until light and fluffy.

Add eggs and yolk to the above mixture and beat well.

Add flour, alternately with milk, beating after each addition until smooth.

Add remaining ingredients to the above and mix well. Pour batter into a 9- to 10-inch tube pan that has been greased and lightly floured. Bake in moderate oven at 375° for 60 minutes, or until wire cake tester comes out clean and dry. (Cool slightly before removing from pan.) Serve unfrosted to accompany fruit desserts or ice cream. May be frosted if desired.

∾ Prune and Nut Spice Cake

The Maine Maid, Jericho, Long Island, New York

Ingredients

½ cup butter
1 cup sugar
2 eggs, beaten
1 cup sour milk
2 teaspoons soda
2 cups flour

1 ½ teaspoons cinnamon
½ teaspoon cloves
½ teaspoon salt
½ teaspoon allspice
¾ cup chopped stewed prunes
¾ cup chopped nuts

Directions (Makes two 9-inch layers)

Cream butter and sugar. Add beaten eggs, then sour milk in which
soda has been dissolved.

Sift together flour, salt, and spices and add to above mixture.

Add nuts to prunes; dust lightly with flour, add to above, and mix.
Pour batter into two 9-inch layer cake pans that have been greased
and floured. Bake in 375° oven for 20 to 30 minutes or until done.
Put together with any desired filling.

ᠸ *Fairy Loaf Cake*

Dorothy Dean, *The Spokesman-Review*,
Spokane, Washington

Ingredients

8 egg yolks	½ teaspoon salt
1 ¼ cups sugar	1 cup water
½ cup salad oil	1 ½ teaspoons vanilla or
2 ¾ cups sifted cake flour	1 teaspoon vanilla and
3 teaspoons double-acting	½ teaspoon lemon or whatever
baking powder	flavoring you prefer

Directions (Makes one 10-inch tube cake)

Beat egg yolks until fluffy. Add sugar gradually and beat in thoroughly. Add oil and beat until fluffy.

Sift flour with baking powder and salt. Add to first mixture alternately with water and flavoring, beating carefully. The batter will
be thin. Bake in a 10-inch tube pan or in a 13 × 9 × 2-inch pan, or a
10 × 16-inch pan at 350° to 375° for 35 to 50 minutes. This is a good
cake to cut into small pieces and frost for petit fours. If desired,
slice the tube cake crosswise, in three equal layers, and frost with
Butter Rum Frosting.

～ Prune Layer Cake

Mrs. Alonzo Newton Benn, Chicago, Illinois

Ingredients

⅓ cup butter	1 ½ cups flour
1 ⅛ cups sugar	½ teaspoon baking soda
2 egg yolks, beaten	1 ½ teaspoons baking powder
1 egg, beaten	¼ teaspoon salt
5 tablespoons milk	1 teaspoon cinnamon
1 ⅛ cups stewed prunes,	1 teaspoon cloves
chopped	1 teaspoon nutmeg
1 teaspoon lemon juice	

Directions (Serves 10 to 12)

Cream butter and sugar together.

Add egg yolks, egg, and milk to above mixture and stir well.

Add chopped prunes and lemon juice to mixture and stir.

Sift together remaining ingredients and add to mixture; stir lightly.
Pour batter into two 9-inch round cake pans that have been greased and floured. Bake in 375° oven for 25 to 30 minutes. Cool and cover with a boiled white icing. This delicious cake remains fresh for some time.

～ Luncheon Cake

Mrs. H. V. Cameron, Chatham, Ontario, Canada

Ingredients

1 lb. butter	1 ¼ lbs. all-purpose flour
1 lb. sugar	1 ½ lbs. raisins
10 eggs	½ lb. mixed candied fruit peel

Directions (Makes two loaf cakes)

Cream butter until fluffy; add sugar and beat 5 minutes.

Add eggs, 2 at a time, to the above mixture, until 6 have been added; beat 5 minutes after each addition. Add the remaining 4 eggs one at a time, beating 5 minutes after each one.

Combine fruit and flour lightly. Add to the above, mixing well. Pour into two 9 × 5-inch loaf pans. Bake in a 300° F. oven for 1 hour.

∾ Orange Gold Loaf

Ingredients

2 ¼ cups sifted cake flour	½ cup butter
2 teaspoons baking powder	2 teaspoons grated orange rind
¾ teaspoon salt	5 egg yolks
1 cup sugar	⅔ cup milk

Directions (Makes one 10 × 3-inch loaf cake)

Sift together first four ingredients. Set aside.

Stir butter just to soften.

Add rind, yolks, and ⅓ cup milk to dry ingredients, and mix until all flour is dampened. Beat 2 minutes at a low speed of electric mixer or 300 vigorous strokes by hand.

Add remaining milk to the above mixture and beat 1 minute in electric mixer or 150 strokes by hand. Pour batter into a 10 × 3-inch loaf pan that has been lined on bottom with paper. Bake in moderate oven at 350° for 60 to 70 minutes. (Cake will have a crack on top.)

∾ Angel Peppermint Loaf Cake

Ingredients

½ cup sifted cake flour	½ teaspoon vanilla
¼ cup sifted sugar	¼ teaspoon almond extract
⅔ cup egg whites	½ cup sugar
⅛ teaspoon salt	2 tablespoons finely crushed
½ teaspoon cream of tartar	peppermint stick candy

Directions (Serves 8)

Sift together cake flour and ¼ cup sugar three times. Set aside.

Combine egg whites, salt, cream of tartar, vanilla, and almond extract in a large bowl. Beat with flat wire whip, egg beater, or at a high speed of electric mixer until soft peaks are formed.

Add ½ cup sugar to the egg whites, 2 tablespoons at a time, beating after each addition.

Fold in flour mixture, ½ at a time.

Fold crushed candy into batter. Pour batter into ungreased 10 × 5 × 3-inch loaf pan. Bake in moderate oven at 375° about 25 minutes. Cool upside down 1 hour. Serve plain or with ice cream and Chocolate Sauce.

❧ Hoagy Cake

Dunton's Cafeteria, Dallas, Texas

Ingredients

1 ¼ cups sugar
½ cup butter
2 eggs, well beaten
1 ¼ cups buttermilk
1 teaspoon soda

½ teaspoon salt
1 teaspoon baking powder
2 cups sifted cake flour
Grated rind of 2 oranges
½ cup chopped nuts

Directions (Makes one 13 × 9 × 2-inch cake)

Cream butter and sugar; add well-beaten eggs.

Combine soda, baking powder, and salt with flour and add alternately with buttermilk to above.

Add orange rind and chopped nuts to above; pour batter into a 13 × 9 × 2-inch pan that has been greased and floured. Bake in 350° oven for 30 minutes or until done.

Sauce

Ingredients

1 cup sugar
Juice of 2 oranges

Juice of 1 lemon

Directions

Combine sugar with juice of oranges and lemon and cook for 5 minutes. While cake is still in pan, pour sauce over cake. Cut and serve immediately.

❧ Sultana Cake

Mrs. David Donald, Pittsfield, Massachusetts

Ingredients

1 lb. butter
1 lb. sugar
8 eggs
1 ½ cups milk
8 cups cake flour

3 teaspoons baking powder
1 lb. sultana raisins
½ lb. orange peel
Orange and lemon to flavor

Directions (Makes 3 loaves)

Cream together butter and sugar.
Mix eggs into the above.
Slowly add milk to the mixture.
Sift cake flour and baking powder and add to mixture.

Add remaining ingredients to mixture. Pour batter into three loaf
pans that have been greased and lightly floured. Bake in 350° oven
for 1 hour or more.

◠ Pound Cake

Ingredients

½ lb. butter	2 cups flour, measured after two
1 ¾ cups sugar	siftings
5 whole eggs	Vanilla
	Mace

Directions (Makes one loaf cake)

Cream butter until fluffy. Beat like the devil.

Add sugar to creamed butter. Cream until fluffy and light.

Drop in 1 whole egg at a time, while beating, until you have dropped
in 5.

Stop the beater and fold in flour. Do not beat, as that makes it tough.
Flavor with a little vanilla and mace. Bake in loaf pan about 45
minutes at 300°. Turn oven up to 325° for 15 minutes or until
brown.

The old-fashioned recipe called for brandy, nutmeg, and mace instead
of vanilla. Do you have the brandy?

◠ Applesauce Cake

Ingredients

1 ½ cups brown sugar	½ teaspoon cinnamon
¾ cup butter	½ teaspoon cloves
3 teaspoons soda	½ teaspoon allspice
1 ½ cups applesauce	1 cup raisins
3 cups flour	1 cup nuts

Directions (Makes one 10-inch square layer)

Cream together brown sugar and butter until smooth.

Dissolve soda in applesauce, and add to butter and sugar mixture.

Sift flour; measure and sift again with spices. Add raisins and nuts to
flour and stir all into batter. Bake in a 10-inch square cake pan or
in a 13 × 9 × 2-inch pan that has been greased and lined with waxed
paper. Bake in 350° oven for 25 to 30 minutes or until done. Ice
with boiled white icing.

> ☞ *Here is a simple way to find out if your cake is done. Stick in a toothpick, and if it comes out clean, then it is done. Or lightly touch the top of the cake with your little finger, and if it leaves no imprint, then it is done.*

∾ Applesauce Cake

Ingredients

3 cups sifted flour	¾ cup brown sugar
2 teaspoons soda	2 eggs
¼ teaspoon salt	2 cups thick applesauce
2 teaspoons cinnamon	2 cups chopped walnuts
1 ½ teaspoons cloves	2 cups chopped raisins
½ cup butter	1 cup chopped dates

Directions (Makes two loaf cakes)

Sift together first five ingredients three times. Set aside.

Cream butter; add brown sugar gradually, and cream together until light and fluffy.

Add eggs, one at a time, beating well after each addition.

Add flour mixture, alternately with applesauce, beating well after each addition until smooth.

Beat in remaining ingredients. Pour batter into two 6 x 3-inch loaf pans, which have been lined on bottoms with paper. Bake in slow oven at 325° about 60 minutes. (This cake will keep moist for several days if stored in a tightly covered cake box.)

∾ Gingerbread

Ingredients

1 cup boiling water	1 teaspoon baking powder
1 cup shortening	1 teaspoon soda
1 cup brown sugar	1 teaspoon salt
1 cup molasses	1 ½ teaspoons ginger
3 eggs, beaten	1 ½ teaspoons cinnamon
3 cups flour	

Directions (Makes one 13 × 9 × 3-inch cake)

Pour water over shortening.

Add sugar, molasses, and eggs to the above.

Sift together remaining ingredients and add to the mixture. Beat with an egg beater until smooth. Pour batter into a greased and floured 13 × 9 × 3-inch pan. Bake in 350° oven for 30 to 40 minutes.

◦๛ *Sour Cream Gingerbread*

Ingredients

1 cup flour	½ teaspoon cloves
¼ teaspoon salt	⅔ cup thick sour cream
¼ cup sugar	3 tablespoons butter
½ teaspoon soda	⅓ cup dark molasses
1 ½ teaspoons ginger	1 egg
1 teaspoon cinnamon	

Directions (Serves 6)

Mix and sift all dry ingredients in mixing bowl. Heat cream; remove from fire and add butter and stir until melted. Add molasses. Beat egg and pour into it the other ingredients gradually, beating constantly. Add this to dry ingredients, mixing only enough to make a smooth batter. Pour into a buttered 8-inch square cake pan, and bake in 350° oven for 25 to 30 minutes or until done. Serve hot with whipped cream or hot buttered rum sauce.

◦๛ *Sponge Cake*

Ingredients

12 egg yolks, beaten	12 egg whites, beaten
½ cup sugar	Pinch of salt
Juice of 1 lemon	½ cup sugar
1 cup flour, sifted 4 times	1 teaspoon vanilla

Directions (Makes one 10-inch tube cake)

Beat in ½ cup sugar with egg yolks, a teaspoon at a time.

Add lemon juice and flour alternately to above until it becomes a smooth dough.

Slowly beat ½ cup sugar and pinch of salt into the egg whites. Cut into the batter.

Add vanilla to mixture. Pour batter into an ungreased 10-inch tube pan. Bake in a 325° oven for 1 hour and 15 minutes. (We use this delicious sponge cake to make our famous "Ice Cream Sandwiches." One slice of cake, with coffee ice cream and butterscotch sauce. It's "yummy.")

∼ Sponge Cake

Ingredients

6 egg yolks	1 teaspoon vanilla extract
1 cup sugar	6 egg whites
1 cup sifted cake flour	½ teaspoon cream of tartar
¼ cup cold water	½ teaspoon salt
1 teaspoon lemon extract	

Directions (Makes one 10-inch tube cake)

Beat egg yolks until very thick and lemon colored.

Beat sugar into yolks very gradually.

Add flour gradually to the above mixture alternately with water. Beat until blended. Add flavorings.

Combine egg white, cream of tartar, and salt in large bowl and beat with wire whip or rotary egg beater until just stiff enough to hold a peak. Gradually and carefully fold the egg yolk mixture into the beaten egg whites. Pour batter into an ungreased 10-inch tube pan. Bake in slow oven at 325° for 60 to 65 minutes. Invert and cool in pan, 1 to 2 hours. Loosen from sides and center tube with knife and gently pull out. Serve plain or frost with Butter Cream Frosting. Or serve a wedge of cake covered with ice cream topped with fresh berries, Fudge Sauce, or Butterscotch Sauce.

∼ Egg Yolk Sponge Cake

Ingredients

2 cups sifted cake flour	1 ¾ cups sugar
2 teaspoons baking powder	½ cup cold water
½ teaspoon salt	1 tablespoon grated orange rind
11 egg yolks (¾ cup)	1 tablespoon orange juice
1 whole egg	

Directions (Makes one 10-inch tube cake)

Sift together first three ingredients. Set aside.

Beat egg yolks and egg together until thick and lemon colored.

Beat sugar into above very gradually.

Combine remaining ingredients. Add flour gradually to the above mixture alternately with water. Beat until well blended. Pour batter into an ungreased 10-inch tube pan. Bake in slow oven at 325° for 60 to 65 minutes. Invert and cool 1 to 2 hours.

∾ Chocolate Sponge Cake

Ingredients

¼ lb. or 4 squares unsweetened chocolate	1 ¼ cups flour
1 cup milk	1 teaspoon baking powder
5 eggs	Pinch of salt
2 cups sugar	1 teaspoon vanilla

Directions (Makes three 8-inch or two 10-inch layers)

Shave chocolate and add to milk. Cook over slow fire, stirring constantly until thick. Let stand until cool.

Separate eggs and put whites aside.

Cream egg yolks and sugar well. Add chocolate and milk mixture.

Sift together dry ingredients and add to above.

Add vanilla to above. Beat the egg whites and fold into cake mixture. Pour batter into three 8-inch layer pans or two 10-inch layer pans that have been greased and floured. Bake in 350° oven until a straw or cake tester pulls out clean. Do not overbake or cake will be dry. Ice with caramel or chocolate icing.

∾ Daffodil Cake

Ingredients

1 ¼ cups sifted cake flour	1 ½ teaspoons cream of tartar
½ cup sifted sugar	¾ teaspoon vanilla
1 ¼ cups egg whites	1 cup sugar
¼ teaspoon salt	

Directions (Makes one 10-inch tube cake)

Sift together cake flour and sugar three times. Set aside.

Combine egg whites, salt, and cream of tartar, and vanilla in large bowl. Beat with flat wire whip, egg beater, or at a high speed of electric mixer until whites are stiff enough to hold up in soft peaks, but still moist and glossy.

Add sugar to the egg whites, 4 tablespoons at a time, beating after each addition until blended. Sift about ¼ of the flour mixture over beaten egg whites. Fold in with 15 fold-over strokes, turning bowl often. Fold in remaining flour in same manner. Pour batter into ungreased 10-inch tube pan. Bake in slow oven at 325° for 60 minutes.

ᝰ *Sunshine Cake*

Ingredients

5 egg yolks (⅓ cup)	8 egg whites (1 cup)
½ cup sugar	½ teaspoon cream of tartar
1 cup sifted cake flour	½ teaspoon salt
2 tablespoons cold water	1 cup sugar
1 teaspoon vanilla	

Directions (Makes one 10-inch tube cake)

Beat egg yolks until very thick and lemon colored.

Beat sugar into yolks very gradually.

Add flour gradually to the above mixture alternately with water. Beat until blended. Add vanilla.

Combine egg whites, cream of tartar, and salt in large bowl and beat with wire whip or rotary egg beater until just stiff enough to hold a peak.

Gradually beat sugar into stiffly beaten egg whites. Slowly and carefully fold the egg yolk mixture into the beaten egg whites. Pour batter into an ungreased 10-inch tube pan. Bake in slow oven at 325° for 60 to 65 minutes. Invert and cool in pan 1 to 2 hours. Loosen from sides and center tube with knife and gently pull out. Serve plain or frosted.

～ Sunshine Cake

Ingredients

1 cup flour	2 tablespoons flour
1 teaspoon baking powder	3 tablespoons cold water
1 ½ teaspoons cornstarch	1 teaspoon vanilla
½ teaspoon salt	4 egg whites, beaten
4 egg yolks, beaten	½ cup sugar
½ cup sugar	

Directions (Makes one 10-inch tube cake)

Sift together first three ingredients three times.

Beat yolks and sugar together.

Add flour, cold water, and vanilla to egg mixture and stir into dry
ingredients.

Fold egg whites and sugar into mixture and pour into 10-inch tube
pan. Bake in 300° oven for 45 minutes, then in 350° oven for
15 minutes. Invert pan until the cake is cold.

～ Angel Food Cake with Eggnog Filling

Mrs. Gordon Pilkington, St. Louis, Missouri

Ingredients

1 ½ cups egg whites	½ teaspoon almond extract
1 teaspoon cream of tartar	1 teaspoon vanilla
Pinch of salt	1 tablespoon strained lemon
1 cup sifted cake flour	juice
1 ½ cups less 2 tablespoons sifted sugar	

Directions (Serves 16)

Whip egg whites with wire whisk until frothy; add cream of tartar
and salt. Beat until stiff but not dry. Remove wire whisk.

Sift flour and sugar together several times and fold a small amount at
a time into the egg whites.

Add almond extract, vanilla, and lemon juice, and pour batter into
a 9- to 10-inch tube pan. Bake at 325° for about an hour. Remove
from oven and invert the pan. Let stand until cold.

Remove from pan and slice crosswise into four layers.

Eggnog Filling

Ingredients

½ lb. butter	1 pint whipping cream
1 lb. powdered sugar, sifted	2 tablespoons sugar
5 egg yolks	2 tablespoons whiskey
½ cup bourbon whiskey or rum	¼ lb. chopped toasted almonds
¼ lb. chopped toasted almonds	¼ lb. macaroon crumbs
¼ lb. crushed macaroon crumbs	Cherries and green leaves

Directions

Cream butter. Add powdered sugar to butter and whip until creamy. Add yolks to the above and mix well.

Fold in ½ cup bourbon whiskey, ¼ lb. chopped almonds, and ¼ lb. crushed macaroon crumbs. Fill layers of cake.

Whip cream and add sugar and 2 tablespoons whiskey. Coat outside of cake with whipped cream.

Cover whipped cream with ¼ lb. almonds and ¼ lb. macaroon crumbs, mixed together.

Decorate with cherries and green leaves.

ᐭ *Ribbon Cake*

Lemon and Chocolate Layers

Ingredients

½ cup shortening	1 cup plus 2 tablespoons milk
1 ½ cups sugar	½ teaspoon lemon extract
2 eggs	1 ½ squares unsweetened
2 ¼ cups cake flour	chocolate
2 ½ teaspoons baking powder	1 tablespoon milk
1 teaspoon salt	

Directions (Makes a 9-inch four-layer cake)

Cream together shortening and sugar thoroughly. Add eggs, one at a time, and beat until fluffy.

Sift flour, measure, add other dry ingredients, and sift together. Add to butter and sugar mixture, alternately with milk, and blend well. Divide batter into two equal portions.

Mix lemon flavor into one portion of batter.

Melt chocolate in milk and let cool slightly. Then stir into other portion of cake batter. Pour each batter into a greased, paper-lined 9-inch cake pan. Bake in moderate oven at 375° for 25 minutes or until done.

Silver and Pink Layers

Ingredients

5 egg whites	3 teaspoons baking powder
½ cup sugar	1 teaspoon salt
⅔ cup shortening	1 cup milk
1 ¼ cups sugar	1 teaspoon peppermint extract
1 teaspoon vanilla	A drop or two of red food
2 ⅔ cups cake flour	coloring

Directions

Beat egg whites until fairly stiff; gradually add ½ cup sugar and beat until meringue stands up in peaks.

Cream shortening until fluffy; add 1 ¼ cup sugar gradually and vanilla. Beat until smooth and creamy.

Sift flour, measure, add other dry ingredients, and sift again. Add to creamed mixture alternately with milk. Mix well until smooth. Fold in beaten egg whites and blend well. Divide into two equal portions.

Flavor one portion of batter with peppermint extract and add red coloring to make a delicate pink. Pour each batter into a greased, paper-lined 9-inch cake pan and bake in 375° oven for 30 minutes or until done. Let all layers cool.

Frosting

Ingredients

4 cups sugar	4 egg whites
1 teaspoon cream of tartar	2 teaspoons vanilla
1 ½ cups water	Few drops red food coloring

Directions

Combine sugar, cream of tartar, and water and let come to boil. Cook to 240°.

Beat egg whites until stiff. Pour syrup into whites, little by little, beating constantly. Add vanilla and just enough coloring to give a delicate pink color.

Beat until of spreading consistency. Place chocolate layer first on plate, frost; then the lemon-flavored layer, frost; then add the pink layer, frost; and last the silver layer. Frost top and sides of cake.

Lane Cake

Dr. T. J. Leblanc, Cincinnati, Ohio

Ingredients

1 cup butter
2 cups sugar
3 ¼ cups flour
3 teaspoons baking powder

1 cup milk
8 egg whites, beaten
1 tablespoon vanilla

Directions (Makes two 10-inch layers or one tube cake)

Cream butter and sugar together until very light.

Sift dry ingredients together four times. Add milk to creamed mixture, alternately with the flour.

Add vanilla to egg whites and fold into mixture. Bake in two 10-inch layer pans or one tube pan in 350° oven for 40 to 50 minutes, or until cake springs to touch. Test with straw.

Lane Cake Filling

Ingredients

½ cup butter
1 cup sugar
7 egg yolks, beaten
1 cup raisins, chopped

1 cup nut meats, chopped
1 teaspoon vanilla
1 wineglass brandy

Directions

Cream butter and sugar together.

Add egg yolks and cook in double boiler, stirring constantly until smooth and thick. Remove from fire.

Add raisins, nut meats, and vanilla to mixture while it is still hot.

Add brandy to mixture and spread over the cake.

Fresh Coconut Angel Cake

The White Turkey Town House, New York City

Ingredients

12 egg whites
1 teaspoon salt
1 teaspoon cream of tartar

1 cup pastry flour
1 cup sugar

Directions (Makes one 10-inch tube cake)

Beat together egg whites and salt until foamy.

Add cream of tartar to eggs and beat until stiff, but moist. Sift flour and sugar together three or four times and carefully fold into the beaten eggs. Pour into a 10-inch tube pan free of grease and bake in 300° oven for 50 minutes. Turn off oven and let cake remain for another 10 minutes. Cool and frost with Boiled Frosting. Sprinkle top with fresh grated coconut.

> ➤ *Cakes should always be cooled thoroughly before frosting.*

ᏑᎳ *Cherry Sponge*

Mrs. A. E. R. Peterka, Cleveland, Ohio

Ingredients

3 egg yolks, beaten
3 tablespoons sugar
3 egg whites, beaten

3 teaspoons flour
1 ½ cups sweet black cherries

Directions (Serves 4)

Beat sugar into yolks until smooth and lemon colored.
Put whites on top of yolks.
Sift flour over the egg whites. Fold in lightly. Put mixture in an 8-inch square or round cake pan, 1 ½ inches deep.
Wash and dry cherries. Drop into the egg batter so they are distributed evenly over the surface. Bake in 320° oven for 10 to 15 minutes or until lightly browned. Let cool, slice, and then dust with powdered sugar and serve.

ᏑᎳ *Patio Ice Cream Cake*

Terrace Patio, Ft. Lauderdale, Florida

Ingredients

2 eggs
1 cup sugar
½ cup milk
1 teaspoon butter

1 cup flour
1 ½ teaspoons baking powder
½ teaspoon salt
½ teaspoon vanilla

Directions

Beat eggs well and add sugar. (Use an electric mixer if possible.) Bring milk just to a boil; add butter and add to egg mixture.
Sift dry ingredients together. Add to egg mixture gradually. Add vanilla. Pour batter into 8-inch greased and floured square pan. Bake in a 350° oven for 20 minutes or until done.

Patio Caramel Sauce

Ingredients

1 cup brown sugar	Pinch of salt
1 cup dark corn syrup	1 teaspoon vanilla
¼ cup granulated sugar	Vanilla ice cream
¼ cup butter	Whipped cream
½ cup coffee cream	Slivered toasted almonds

Directions

Boil sugar and syrup together for 5 minutes.

Caramelize sugar; add to syrup. Add butter and boil a few minutes longer.

Remove from fire and stir in cream, salt, and vanilla. When ready to serve, cut cake in squares. Split each square and place vanilla ice cream between layers. Put whipped cream over top and drip Caramel Sauce over all. Sprinkle with toasted almonds.

➧ *It is best to wait until cakes cool before slicing.*

ᴄᴡ De Luxe Coffee Cake

Mrs. Gordon Pilkington, St. Louis, Missouri

Ingredients

¾ cup butter	1 cup sweet milk
1 ½ cups sugar	Grated rind of 1 lemon
3 eggs	2 tablespoons lemon juice
3 cups flour	Chopped pecans
Pinch of salt	Powdered sugar
3 teaspoons baking powder	

Directions (Makes one 10-inch tube cake)

Cream butter and sugar well.

Add eggs, one at a time, and beat well.

Sift flour and measure. Add salt and baking powder and sift again. Add to butter and sugar mixture, alternately with milk. Mix well.

Add lemon rind and juice. Grease deep 10-inch tube pan with butter. Sprinkle with flour and cover bottom thickly with pecans. Pour batter into pan and bake at 350° for 50 to 60 minutes, or until done. Turn out and cover nut-covered top thickly with powdered sugar. If desired, a cup each of raisins and pecans can be added to batter. If so, flour with a little extra flour before stirring into batter.

Banana Dutch Coffee Cake

Home Economics Department,
Fruit Dispatch Company, New York City

Ingredients

1 cup sifted flour
1 1/4 teaspoons baking powder
1/2 teaspoon salt
2 tablespoons sugar
1/4 cup shortening
1 egg, well beaten
3 tablespoons milk
3 bananas (firm)
2 tablespoons butter, melted
2 tablespoons sugar
1/4 teaspoon cinnamon
1 teaspoon grated orange rind

Directions (Serves 6 to 8)

Sift together dry ingredients.
Cut shortening into the above.
Mix together egg and milk and stir into flour mixture. The dough should be stiff. Turn into a well-greased baking pan.
Peel and slice bananas into 1/2-inch diagonal pieces. Cover dough with bananas.
Brush butter over the bananas.
Mix together remaining ingredients and sprinkle over the bananas. Bake in 350° oven about 35 minutes. Serve hot for breakfast or as dessert with whipped cream or Lemon Hard Sauce. (*See* Dessert Sauces Section.)

If you do not have the proper pan size, do not fill the pan more than 2/3 full of batter.

Chocolate Fudge Upside Down Cake

Cathryn's, Portland, Oregon

Ingredients

3/4 cup sugar
1 tablespoon butter
1/2 cup milk
1 cup flour
1/4 teaspoon salt
1 teaspoon baking powder
1 1/2 tablespoons cocoa
1/2 cup walnuts, chopped
1/2 cup sugar
1/2 cup brown sugar
1/4 cup cocoa
1 1/4 cups boiling water

Directions (Makes one 9-inch square cake)

Cream butter and ¾ cup sugar together.

Add milk to the above and stir.

Sift together flour, salt, and baking powder, and add to mixture. Stir well and put in 9-inch buttered, square pan.

Sprinkle with nuts.

Mix ½ cup sugar, brown sugar, and cocoa well together and spread over top.

Pour boiling water over the top of all. Bake in 350° oven for 30 minutes. Let cool in pan.

∽ Apricot Coconut Upside Down Cake

Ingredients

¼ lb. dried apricots	2 cups cake flour
¼ lb. butter	2 teaspoons baking powder
1 cup brown sugar	½ teaspoon salt
½ cup butter	1 cup milk
1 cup sugar	Freshly grated coconut
2 eggs	

Directions (Makes one large upside down cake)

Apricots should be simmered gently until tender but not mushy. In a heavy, large iron skillet, melt ¼ lb. butter; spread brown sugar evenly over butter and place a layer of apricot halves to cover the bottom.

Cream ½ cup butter and 1 cup sugar together.

Beat eggs into above mixture thoroughly.

Sift flour and measure. Add baking powder and salt and sift together twice. Add flour mixture, alternately with milk, to the creamed mixture. Pour batter over the apricots in the skillet and bake in a 350° oven for 35 minutes or until done. Turn out on large round platter and top with freshly grated coconut.

❧ *Torte*

Ingredients

6 egg whites
1 ½ cups sugar
1 ½ teaspoons vinegar
1 teaspoon vanilla

¼ teaspoon almond extract
1 quart strawberries
½ cup sugar, superfine
1 cup whipping cream, whipped

Directions (Serves 10 to 12)

Beat egg whites stiff, adding sugar gradually.

Add vinegar, vanilla, and almond extract to the above. Drop on
brown paper placed on cookie sheet, using a spoon that holds
about 2 tablespoons. After they are placed on the sheet, make an
indentation with the back of the spoon. Bake in 300° oven for
45 minutes; then raise the temperature to 325° for 15 minutes.
Remove from paper using a spatula. If they stick, reheat the sheet
and try again.

Do not crush the berries. Add superfine sugar and fill each indentation with berries.

Top each meringue with whipped cream. If berries are not used,
peaches may be upturned and filled with a soft custard.

Custard

Ingredients

3 cups milk
½ cup sugar
or
2 cups milk
1 cup peach juice

⅓ cup sugar
6 egg yolks, beaten
⅓ cup sugar
1 teaspoon salt
⅛ teaspoon almond flavoring

Directions

Scald choice of liquids with sugar.

Put remaining ingredients in double boiler and pour scalded liquid
over. Cook slowly until mixture coats a spoon. Stir while cooking.
Cool.

➥ There are four basic principles that should not be overlooked in cooking any dish—proper and accurate measurements, proper cooking temperature, proper length of cooking time, and proper time of serving.

➤ Baked Cherry Torte

Henry F. Boxman's Restaurant, Bloomington, Indiana

Ingredients

1 egg	½ teaspoon soda
1 ¼ cups sugar	1 teaspoon cinnamon
2 cups well-drained cherries	1 tablespoon melted butter
1 cup pastry flour	1 teaspoon almond extract
¼ teaspoon salt	½ cup cut pecans

Directions (Serves 12)

Beat egg. Gradually add sugar and continue beating until sugar is dissolved in egg. Fold in cherries.

Sift dry ingredients. Fold into above mixture.

Add melted butter and flavoring. Turn batter into a greased pan.

Scatter cut pecans over top of batter. Bake in 350° oven about 45 minutes. Cool. Prepare sauce.

Sauce

Ingredients

1 cup cold cherry juice (add water to make 1 cup)	1 tablespoon butter
¼ cup sugar	2 drops almond extract
1 tablespoon cornstarch	½ cup whipped cream, sweetened
⅛ teaspoon salt	

Directions

Combine dry ingredients with several tablespoons of the cold cherry juice. Heat remaining liquid. Add first mixture to the hot cherry juice and cook until thick and no starch taste remains. Taste for sweetness, and add more sugar if needed.

Add butter and almond extract, and cool.

Serve torte cold topped with whipped cream and then add cherry sauce on top of whipped cream.

⌒ Blitz Torte

Ingredients

1 ¾ cups sifted cake flour	½ cup butter
2 ¼ teaspoons baking powder	⅔ cup milk
¾ teaspoon salt	1 teaspoon vanilla
1 cup plus 2 tablespoons sugar	2 eggs
4 egg whites	⅓ cup slivered blanched
1 cup sugar	almonds

Directions (Makes two 9-inch layers)

Sift together first four ingredients. Set aside.

Beat egg whites until frothy throughout. Add 1 cup sugar, 2 tablespoons at a time, beating after each addition until blended. Continue beating until stiff peaks are formed. Set aside.

Stir butter just to soften. Sift in dry ingredients.

Add milk and vanilla to above mixture and mix until all flour is dampened. Beat 2 minutes at a low speed of electric mixer or 300 vigorous strokes by hand.

Add eggs and beat 1 minute longer in mixer or 150 strokes by hand. Pour batter into two round 9-inch layer pans that have been lined on bottoms with paper.

Spread egg-white meringue over batter.

Sprinkle almonds over top. Bake in moderate oven at 350° for 35 to 40 minutes, or until the meringue is lightly browned; cake is done when cake tester is inserted. Cool and spread Pineapple Filling between layers and whipped cream on sides.

⌒ Date Nut Torte

L. S. Ayers Tea Room, Indianapolis, Indiana

Ingredients

½ cup egg whites	¼ teaspoon baking powder
1 ½ teaspoons water	½ cup walnuts or pecans
⅝ cup sugar	1 cup chopped dates
1 cup cake crumbs	

Directions (Serves 9)

Whip egg whites until stiff; add water gradually.

Add sugar to egg whites, beating during the addition.

Combine cake crumbs with baking powder, nuts, and dates, and add to above mixture. Pour into an ungreased 9-inch square cake pan. Bake at 325° for 30 minutes.

～ Fruit Cake

Virginia McDonald's Tea Room, Gallatin, Missouri

Ingredients

4 lbs. seeded raisins	1 teaspoon allspice
2 cups peach brandy	1 teaspoon cloves
2 cups butter	1 teaspoon cinnamon
2 cups sugar	3 cups candied citron, cut
10 egg yolks, beaten until thick	1 cup figs, cut
10 egg whites, stiffly beaten	1 cup dates, cut
2 cups sifted flour	1 cup candied lemon peel, cut
1 teaspoon baking powder	1 cup candied orange peel, cut
½ teaspoon soda	2 cups almonds, finely chopped
1 cup molasses	2 cups pecans, finely chopped

Directions (Serves 12 to 15)

Soak raisins in brandy overnight.

Cream butter and sugar until light and fluffy. Add beaten egg yolks.

Fold beaten egg whites into the above. Sift flour and baking powder together. Add to the above mixture.

Combine soda and molasses and add to mixture.

Combine allspice, cloves, and cinnamon, and add to mixture.

Add remaining ingredients and the raisins to the batter. Mix together thoroughly. Pour batter into loaf pans, which have been greased and lined with waxed paper or heavy brown paper. Fill pans about ¾ full. Or bake fruit cake in an old-fashioned corset box if you have one. Line box with greased brown paper. After pouring in the batter, cover with greased brown paper, and then put on the box lid. Bake in slow oven at 300° for 3 to 4 hours or until done. Cover fruit cakes with brown paper about halfway through baking to prevent them from browning too much.

➥ Have you ever eaten a cold baked apple? Then try one with a little cinnamon, nutmeg, and warm milk. You may bake these while using the oven for something else, letting them cool and then storing them in the refrigerator for later use. Stale bread may be toasted at the same time and will add flavor as well as proteins along with your baked apple and warm milk.

~ Gumdrop Fruit Cake

Dolores Restaurant and Drive-In, Oklahoma City, Oklahoma

Ingredients

1 cup butter
2 cups sugar
2 eggs, beaten
4 cups flour
1 teaspoon cinnamon
¼ teaspoon nutmeg
¼ teaspoon cloves
¼ teaspoon salt

1 ½ cups sieved applesauce
1 teaspoon soda
1 tablespoon hot water
1 teaspoon vanilla
1 to 2 lbs. gumdrops
1 lb. white raisins
1 cup pecans

Directions (Makes 2 or 3 small loaf cakes)

Cream butter and sugar together.

Add eggs to the above.

Sift together dry ingredients. Put a little aside to mix with raisins, nuts, and gumdrops. Add the remainder to the above alternately with the applesauce.

Dissolve soda in hot water and stir into mixture.

Add vanilla to mixture.

Cut gumdrops in pieces with scissors. (Do not use any black gumdrops.)

Fry pecans in a little butter and add to gumdrops and raisins. Mix in the flour and add to the mixture. Line two or three small loaf pans with greased parchment or heavy paper and bake in 300° to 325° oven for 2 hours. If oven glass or casseroles are used, do not line with paper but bake at a lower temperature of 275° to 300°.

~ Dark Fruit Cake

Ingredients

¾ lb. butter
2 cups sugar
8 egg yolks
4 cups flour
1 tablespoon cinnamon
½ teaspoon cloves
1 teaspoon nutmeg
3 teaspoons soda
½ cup cold water
8 egg whites, beaten
2 lbs. moist raisins

2 lbs. currants
¼ lb. candied orange peel, cut
¼ lb. candied lemon peel, cut
½ lb. citron, cut
¼ lb. candied cherries, cut
¼ lb. candied pineapple, cut
¼ lb. candied fruit mix
¾ lb. walnuts, broken
½ lb. pecans, broken
1 cup sherry wine

Directions (Makes about 12 lbs.)

Cream butter and sugar together.

Add yolks to above.

Hold out a little flour to mix later with fruits. Sift flour and spices together and add to mixture.

Mix soda and water together and stir into mixture.

Fold beaten egg whites into mixture.

Mix fruits and nuts with the flour held out. Stir into mixture.

Stir in the wine. Bake in 350° oven for about 75 minutes; then turn oven down to 300° and bake another 75 minutes, or about 3 hours. Be careful not to bake too fast, or the cake will burn.

ᔆ *Christmas Nut Cake*

Ingredients

½ lb. butter	⅓ cup whiskey
½ lb. sugar	¾ lb. raisins
5 egg yolks	½ lb. hickory nuts or pecans
¼ cup sour cream	1 package candied red cherries
¼ teaspoon soda	⅛ lb. citron
½ lb. flour	5 egg whites
½ whole nutmeg, grated	

Directions (Makes one 10-inch tube cake)

Cream butter and sugar together in electric mixer.

Add yolks to above, one at a time. Remove from beater.

Dissolve soda in sour cream and add to above, stirring lightly.

Sift flour and nutmeg together. Add to above alternately with whiskey.

Chop fruit and nuts and cover well with extra flour. Fold gently into above mixture.

Beat egg whites stiff and fold into above. Pour in greased 10-inch tube pan with paper in bottom. Place in 300° oven. Put pan of water on lower level and bake for 2 hours or until done. This cake cannot be kept for any length of time but must be eaten within a week.

❧ Christmas Wine Cake

Dupuis Tavern, Port Angeles, Washington

Ingredients

2 cups sugar
1 cup butter
2 eggs
3 ½ cups flour
½ teaspoon salt
1 teaspoon soda
1 teaspoon cinnamon

1 teaspoon cloves
2 cups unsweetened applesauce
1 cup chopped mixed candied
    fruit
1 cup raisins
1 cup nuts

Directions (Makes about 30 cupcakes)

Cream butter and sugar until fluffy. Add eggs and beat well.

Sift flour and measure. Retain ½ cup to flour the fruits and nuts. To remaining flour add other dry ingredients and sift again. Stir into creamed mixture.

Heat applesauce to the boiling point and add to batter.

Combine fruit and nuts and flour well with the ½ cup reserved flour. Stir into batter and mix well. Spoon batter into paper-lined muffin pans, filling ⅔ full. Bake for 30 minutes in a 350° oven. Serve warm with wine sauce.

Wine Sauce

Ingredients

3 cups sugar
½ teaspoon salt
6 tablespoons cornstarch

6 cups currant or claret wine
Few drops red coloring

Directions

Mix together sugar, salt, and cornstarch. Stir in wine; mix well and cook over slow fire until thick and clear. Add a few drops of red coloring to make ruby red. Serve hot over cakes.

❧ Jam Cake

Ingredients

1 cup shortening
1 ¼ cups sugar
5 eggs
2 cups blackberry jam
2 ½ cups flour
1 tablespoon cocoa
1 teaspoon cinnamon

½ teaspoon allspice
½ teaspoon nutmeg
1 teaspoon cloves
½ teaspoon mace
Pinch of salt
1 teaspoon soda
1 cup buttermilk

Directions (Makes two 9-inch square layers)

Cream shortening and beat in sugar.

Add eggs one at a time and blend well. Stir in jam until well mixed.

Sift flour, measure, and add cocoa, spices, and salt. Sift again.

Dissolve soda in buttermilk and add to creamed mixture alternately with flour and spices. Blend well and pour batter into two 9-inch square cake pans that have been greased and lined on bottoms with paper. Bake in 350° oven for about 30 minutes or until done. Ice with Caramel Fudge Icing.

❧ Blackberry Jam Cake

Ingredients

3 cups sifted flour	2 cups sugar
1 teaspoon soda	4 egg yolks
2 teaspoons cinnamon	1 cup buttermilk or sour milk
1 teaspoon nutmeg	1 teaspoon vanilla
1 teaspoon cloves	1 cup blackberry jam
1 teaspoon allspice	4 egg whites, stiffly beaten
1 cup soft butter	

Directions (Serves 15 to 20)

Sift together first six ingredients three times.

Cream butter; add sugar gradually, and cream together until light and fluffy.

Add yolks, one at a time, beating well after each addition.

Add flour mixture, alternately with milk, in small amounts, beating after each addition until smooth.

Add vanilla and jam to mixture and mix well.

Fold in beaten egg whites. Pour batter into a 9- to 10-inch tube pan that has been greased and floured on the bottom. Bake in slow oven at 325° for 30 minutes. Increase heat to 350° and continue baking for about 55 minutes or until done. Cool. Frost top and sides with Boiled Frosting (using 3 egg whites) or Quick Brown Sugar Icing.

∾ Jelly Roll

Ingredients

¾ cup sifted cake flour
¾ teaspoon baking powder
¼ teaspoon salt

4 eggs
¾ cup sugar
1 teaspoon vanilla

Directions (Makes one jelly roll)

Sift together first three ingredients. Set aside.

Beat eggs in small bowl. Add sugar gradually, and beat until thick and lemon colored. Gradually fold in flour mixture.

Fold in vanilla. Spread batter in a 15 × 10-inch jelly roll pan that has been lined on bottom with paper. Bake in hot oven at 400° for 13 minutes. Immediately turn cake out onto cloth sprinkled lightly with confectioners' sugar. Quickly remove paper and cut off crisp edges of cake. Roll up cake. Place on rack to cool. When cool, unroll, spread with 1 cup tart jelly, and reroll. Sprinkle with more confectioners' sugar.

∾ Chocolate Roll

Old English Inn, Omaha, Nebraska

Ingredients

6 eggs
1 cup powdered sugar
3 tablespoons cocoa

1 tablespoon flour
1 pint whipping cream, whipped

Directions (Serves 9)

Separate eggs, and beat yolks and whites separately. Fold the yolks into the whites.

Sift dry ingredients and fold into egg mixture. Line a greased, flat cake pan, 12 × 18 inches, with heavy waxed paper. Grease the waxed paper and pour in the batter.

Bake in a 375° oven until done, approximately 25 to 30 minutes. Turn cake pan over onto a dampened tea towel. Remove the waxed paper and roll lengthwise in the towel. Let cool.

Unroll the cooled cake and spread with whipped cream. Reroll and frost with Mocha Icing.

ᕙ Chocolate Roll

Ruttgar's by the Sea, Fort Lauderdale, Florida

Ingredients

5 egg yolks
1 cup confectioners' sugar
¼ cup flour
½ teaspoon salt

5 tablespoons cocoa
1 teaspoon vanilla extract
5 egg whites, stiffly beaten

Directions (Serves 8)

Beat egg yolks until thick and lemon colored. Add sifted dry ingredients and beat until well blended. Add vanilla and fold in egg
whites. Spread in greased, paper-lined 10 ½ × 15-inch jelly roll pan.
Bake in moderate hot oven at 375° for 15 to 20 minutes. Turn out
onto towel sprinkled with confectioners' sugar. Remove paper; cut
off crisp edges; roll up. Cool. Unroll and spread with sweetened,
whipped cream. Roll like jelly roll and dust with confectioners'
sugar.

ᕙ Refrigerator Cake

Ingredients

3 tablespoons butter
¾ cup powdered sugar
3 egg yolks, beaten
½ cup strong cold coffee
2 tablespoons brandy

3 egg whites, beaten
24 ladyfingers
½ cup sherry wine
1 pint whipping cream, whipped

Directions (Serves 6 to 8)

Cream butter and sugar together.
Add yolks to above mixture.
Add coffee to mixture, drop by drop, constantly stirring.
Add brandy to mixture, drop by drop, constantly stirring.
Fold egg whites into mixture.
Dip ladyfingers in sherry. Line the bottom and sides of a mold. Cover
   with half the coffee mixture.
Cover the coffee mixture with whipped cream and on top of the
   cream put the rest of the mixture. Top that with nuts and fruit
   (candied orange peel, candied lemon peel, candied cherries, and
   pistachio nuts), if desired. Place in refrigerator and chill until firm.

Chocolate Sauce

Ingredients

1 ½ cups sugar　　　　　　½ teaspoon vanilla
½ cup water　　　　　　　¼ cup cream
4 squares unsweetened chocolate

Directions

Boil sugar and water together 5 minutes.

Melt chocolate over hot water, and when the syrup is partially cooled, add to above.

Add vanilla to mixture and put in double boiler to keep warm until ready to serve.

Add cream to sauce just before serving.

∾ *Mocha Refrigerator Cake*

Mrs. E. H. Salter, Vernon Manor, Cincinnati, Ohio

Ingredients

½ cup butter　　　　　　　1 cup whipping cream, whipped
1 cup powdered sugar　　　1 teaspoon vanilla
2 egg yolks, beaten　　　　Sponge cake or ladyfingers
⅓ cup very strong coffee, cooled

Directions

Cream butter and sugar; add beaten yolks. Then add the cooled coffee very slowly, a little at a time, beating constantly until smooth. Add whipped cream and vanilla.

Line a mold with waxed paper, then with sponge cake or ladyfingers. Pour into this the above mixture. Cover with sponge cake and place in refrigerator 12 to 24 hours. Or make the alternate layers of sponge cake and filling as preferred.

∾ *Pineapple Refrigerator Cake*

Colony House, Trevor, Wisconsin

Ingredients

½ lb. vanilla wafers or butter　　2 eggs
　cookies　　　　　　　　　　½ pint whipping cream
½ cup butter　　　　　　　　　1 can (9 oz.) crushed pineapple,
1 ½ cups powdered sugar　　　　　drained

Directions (Makes one 12 × 8 × 2-inch cake)

Grind the wafers or roll them into crumbs and put half of them in the
bottom of a buttered 12 × 8 × 2-inch pan. Cream butter and sugar.
Add eggs, one at a time, and beat until smooth and creamy. Pour
this mixture over the crumbs.

Whip cream; add the pineapple and pour over the first mixture.
Cover with the rest of the crumbs and put in the refrigerator
overnight.

ᕀ Chocolate Chip Cake

Duncan Hines Division, Nebraska Consolidated
Mills Company, Omaha, Nebraska

(Using White Cake Mix) Use recipe as directed on package of White
Cake Mix. Just before turning batter into cake pans, fold in ½ cup
semisweet chocolate pieces or coarsely grated unsweetened chocolate. Bake as directed on package.

ᕀ Banana Nut Cake

Duncan Hines Division, Nebraska Consolidated
Mills Company, Omaha, Nebraska

(Using Devil's Food Cake Mix) Use recipe on package of Devil's Food
Cake Mix, substituting 1 cup mashed bananas for cup of liquid. Add
2 tablespoons soft shortening and fold in ⅔ cup chopped nuts. Bake
5 minutes longer than directed on package.

ᕀ Orange Cake

Duncan Hines Division, Nebraska Consolidated
Mills Company, Omaha, Nebraska

(Using Yellow Cake Mix) Use recipe as directed on package of Yellow
Cake Mix, substituting fresh or frozen orange juice for liquid. Bake
as directed on package. Frost with orange frosting.

∾ Cherry Coconut Angel Food Cake

Duncan Hines Division, Nebraska Consolidated
Mills Company, Omaha, Nebraska

(Using Angel Food Cake Mix) Use recipe as directed on package of
Angel Food Cake Mix, adding ¾ teaspoon almond extract. Just
before pouring batter into pan, fold in ½ cup well-drained, chopped
maraschino cherries and ½ cup finely shredded coconut. Bake as
directed on package.

∾ Whipped Cream Cake

Ingredients

2 ¼ cups sifted cake flour
1 ½ cups sugar
2 teaspoons baking powder
½ teaspoon salt

1 ½ cups heavy cream, 30–35
    percent butterfat
3 eggs, very well beaten
1 ½ teaspoons vanilla

Directions (Makes two 9-inch layers)

Sift together dry ingredients. Set aside.

Whip cream until stiff.

Fold well-beaten eggs into whipped cream. Then fold in flour
   mixture. Blend in vanilla. Pour batter into two round 9-inch
   layer pans that have been lined on bottoms with paper. Bake in
   moderate oven at 350° for 30 to 35 minutes. Serve unfrosted.

∾ Mazarin Cake

Ingredients

½ cup soft butter
¼ cup confectioners' sugar

1 egg yolk
1 cup flour

Directions (Serves 10)

Work together butter and sugar with pastry blender or fingers until
   well blended.

Add yolk and flour to above mixture and stir until smooth. Chill
   about 1 hour.

Roll dough on lightly floured board to fit a 9-inch buttered pie pan.

Filling

Ingredients

½ cup sugar
⅓ cup soft butter
⅔ cup blanched almonds, finely ground
2 eggs
½ teaspoon almond extract

Directions

Work together butter and sugar until smooth.

Add remaining ingredients and mix together until well blended. Pour into prepared pie pan. Bake in slow oven at 300° about 45 minutes. Cool. Sprinkle top with confectioners' sugar.

Orange Tea Cakes

Chalet Suzanne, Lake Wales, Florida

Ingredients

1 ¼ cups almonds, chopped about the size of rice kernels
½ lb. orange peel, chopped
2 cups cake flour
2 ½ cups powdered sugar
1 pint heavy cream
A few drops orange coloring

Directions

Place first four ingredients in a mixing bowl. Blend.

Mix heavy cream and coloring into ingredients and put into pastry bag with a No. 5 or No. 6 tube. Lay out in little mounds on a heavily greased pan. Bake in 340° oven. Do not allow to brown, as cakes should retain their orange color. Ice the bottoms with temperate sweet chocolate.

Baba au Rhum

The Toll House, Whitman, Massachusetts

Ingredients

2 egg whites
2 egg yolks
1 cup sugar
1 cup flour
1 teaspoon baking powder
Pinch of salt
½ cup hot milk
1 tablespoon butter
½ teaspoon lemon extract
½ teaspoon vanilla

Directions (Serves 6)

Beat egg whites stiff. Beat egg yolks until light; add to whites and beat together.

Add sugar slowly and beat with spoon for 5 minutes.

Sift dry ingredients together and add to egg mixture. Melt butter in hot milk and beat into mixture. Add lemon extract and vanilla. Pour into Mary Ann pan and bake in 360° oven for 25 to 30 minutes. Makes 6 Mary Anns.

Buttered Rum Sauce

Ingredients

2 cups sugar	1 tablespoon butter
1 cup cold water	⅓ cup rum

Directions

Boil sugar and water for 2 minutes. Remove from heat and add butter. Cool and add rum. Soak the cake in rum sauce; then place in serving dish. Fill center with vanilla ice cream and garnish with whipped cream. Serve at once.

◟ Orange Cupcakes

Mission Inn, Riverside, California

Ingredients

2 tablespoons shortening	1 tablespoon baking powder
1 cup sugar	½ teaspoon salt
2 eggs, slightly beaten	½ cup milk
Juice of 2 oranges	Rind of 2 oranges, grated
3 cups flour	

Directions (Makes 12)

Cream together shortening and sugar.

Add eggs and orange juice to mixture.

Sift dry ingredients together and stir into the above mixture. Leave a little of the flour to stir in later.

Add milk to mixture.

Add orange rind to mixture with the balance of the flour. Pour batter into greased muffin pans and bake in 350° oven for 30 minutes.

ᴄᴡ Iced Brandied Cupcakes

Icing

Ingredients

8 tablespoons powdered sugar 1 tablespoon currant jelly
2 tablespoons brandy

Directions (Makes 18)

Mix ingredients together until smooth; place in refrigerator to set
   while making cakes.

Cupcakes

Ingredients

3 cups flour ½ lb. butter
½ cup sugar 1 tablespoon brandy
1 tablespoon baking powder

Directions

Sift flour once; mix with sugar and baking powder. Work in butter.
   Last, add brandy. Put in Mary Ann pans; prick with fork; bake
   in 350° oven for 5 to 10 minutes or until slightly brown. Remove
   from oven and allow to cool while filling is being prepared.

Filling

Ingredients

1 cup powdered sugar 1 teaspoon vanilla
¼ lb. butter 1 cup heavy cream

Directions

Cream butter, sugar, and vanilla together.
Whip cream lightly and add to above. Remove cakes from Mary Ann
   pans and fill with above mixture. Spread with prepared icing and
   top with half pecan. Set in refrigerator for a few hours.

ᕱ Little Apple Cakes

Mrs. Mathew Jackson, Chicago, Illinois

Ingredients

½ cup lard
1 cup sugar
1 egg, beaten
2 cups flour
½ teaspoon soda
1 teaspoon salt
2 teaspoons baking powder
½ teaspoon cinnamon

½ teaspoon cloves
½ teaspoon nutmeg
½ cup nuts, broken
1 cup chopped apples
½ cup chopped dates
1 teaspoon vanilla
½ cup cold coffee

Directions (Makes 12 large or 18 small cakes)

Cream lard and sugar together. Add beaten egg. Stir remaining ingredients into the mixture, in the order listed, and bake in Gem tins in a 350° oven for 30 to 40 minutes.

Frostings and Fillings

A GOOD CAKE deserves a luscious frosting. To some people the frosting is more important than the cake itself. It is this final touch that adds flavor, color, moistness, and glamour. Most frostings will suit any number of cakes. However, the cake specialist knows when and how to use them to best advantage. A rich butter-type frosting glamorizes the plain cake; a light fluffy frosting or a cooked fondant type best suits the rich cake; and a simple glaze or icing enhances the angel food or chiffon.

Choosing and preparing the frosting are only the first steps. They must be followed by careful workmanship to ensure the best success. If you want to add raisins, nut meats, or pineapple to the icing, wait until the last minute to do so. The natural acid or oil in fruits and nuts is apt to thin the icing if added too soon.

First, allow the cake to cool thoroughly before icing it. If the cake is too warm it will cause the frosting to run, which will spoil the effect you want.

After brushing all the crumbs from the sides of the cake, place the first layer top-side down on the cake plate. Then spread the frosting or filling almost to the edge of the cake. Allow the filling to set slightly before adding another layer. Place the top layer on the filling, bottom-side down. Frost the sides first, using a wide flexible spatula. Spread with an easy upward stroke and keep the sides of the cake straight. Finally spread the frosting on top, making deep graceful swirls with a spatula, back of a spoon, or knife handle.

Once the cake has been frosted you can further glamorize it by adding special decoration. A plain cake can be transformed into one for a festive occasion by garnishing with tinted or toasted coconut, chopped or sliced nuts, grated or melted chocolate, tiny fresh flowers, candied or fresh fruits, and small candies such as gumdrops, peppermints, cinnamon candies, small chocolate patties, or chocolate-covered nuts.

Many remarkable creations can be squeezed out of your pastry bag or cake decorator. If your cake is a seasonal one, then you may want to decorate it in a pattern, such as a Christmas tree, a peppermint candy cane, or a valentine heart shaped from cinnamon candies. Whatever you use to decorate your cake, here is your chance to express your individuality. Perhaps you'll come up with a brand new idea.

A special filling different from the frosting will enhance the flavor of your cake. It can give a plain cake a new taste appeal or make a rich cake more appetizing.

A custard filling, or perhaps a fruit, whipped cream, or raisin and nut filling will give variety. By a simple variation of your cream filling you can have caramel, mocha or chocolate, orange, lemon, coconut, or banana.

Sometimes you may want to tie in your filling and frosting to create the same mood: some grated orange rind in your icing to match an orange filling, or pineapple to go with a pineapple cream filling. The same idea can be carried through with coconut, banana, nuts, and many other ingredients.

Here is a nice idea for a dessert surprise: cut angel food or sponge cake horizontally through the middle and fill with whipped cream and fruit. Then frost with whipped cream. Strawberries, raspberries, and blackberries all lend themselves to this combination. Such a cake should be refrigerated or served immediately.

❧ Boiled Frosting

The White Turkey Town House, New York City

Ingredients

2 cups sugar
1 cup water

3 egg whites
1 coconut, grated

Directions (Frosts 10-inch tube cake)

Boil sugar and water until it forms a soft ball when dropped in cold water.

Whip egg whites until stiff. Slowly add the sugar syrup and whip until cold. Spread over cake.

Sprinkle top generously with fresh grated coconut.

❧ Caramel Frosting

Ingredients

¼ lb. butter
1 cup brown sugar, firmly packed

¼ cup cream
4 cups sifted confectioners' sugar

Directions (Frosts 9-inch layer cake)

Melt butter; add brown sugar; stir and let come to a boil. Cook for 1 minute or until slightly thick. Cool slightly.

When sugar and butter mixture has cooled, add cream and beat smooth. Stir in confectioners' sugar and beat until of spreading consistency. May have to add a little extra cream if too thick.

❧ Creamy Orange Frosting

Ingredients

½ cup butter
⅛ teaspoon salt
1 box (1 lb.) sifted confectioners' sugar

1 egg or 2 egg yolks
1 ½ teaspoons grated orange rind
2 tablespoons milk (about)

Directions (Frosts 9-inch layer cake)

Cream butter until soft. Add salt and part of sugar gradually, beating well after each addition.

Add egg and rind to above mixture and blend well.

Add remaining sugar, alternately with the milk until frosting is of right consistency to spread. Beat after each addition of sugar. Add a little orange food coloring, if desired.

◌ Creamy Butter Frosting

(Frosts 9-inch layer cake) Use recipe for Creamy Orange Frosting, substituting 1 teaspoon vanilla for the orange rind.

◌ Creamy Lemon Frosting

(Frosts 9-inch layer cake) Use recipe for Creamy Orange Frosting, substituting 1 ½ teaspoons grated lemon rind for the orange rind.

◌ Date Nut Frosting

Ingredients

1 cup sour cream
2 cups brown sugar
1 cup dates, chopped

1 teaspoon vanilla
1 cup walnuts, chopped

Directions (Frosts 8-inch layer cake)

Beat cream; add sugar and cook over slow fire. Add chopped dates and vanilla. Remove from fire. Add nuts. Spread on cake while warm.

◌ Festive Frosting

Ingredients

4 egg whites
2 teaspoons vanilla
1 cup granulated sugar
1 cup light corn syrup
½ cup water

¼ cup broken walnut meats
¼ cup seedless raisins
¼ cup candied cherries, chopped
¾ cup grated coconut

Directions (Frosts 8-inch layer cake)

Beat egg whites until stiff. Add vanilla.

Boil sugar, syrup, and water in covered saucepan to 240° F. (spin thread stage).

Pour slowly over egg whites, beating constantly.

Divide mixture in half. To one half add walnut meats, raisins, cherries, and ¼ cup coconut. Color mixture delicately pink. Spread filling between cake layers. Spread top with remaining half of frosting, and cover with remaining grated coconut.

ᕁ Seven Minute Frosting

Ingredients

2 egg whites
1 ½ cups sugar
Pinch of salt
½ cup cold water

2 teaspoons light corn syrup
¼ teaspoon cream of tartar
1 teaspoon vanilla

Directions (Frosts a two or three 8-inch layer cake)

Combine first five ingredients in top of double boiler. Beat at medium
    speed of electric mixer 1 minute. Place over boiling water and beat
    at high speed of mixer 7 minutes.
Turn into bowl and add cream of tartar and vanilla. Beat for 1 minute
    longer. Spread on cake.

ᕁ Chocolate Seven Minute Frosting

(Frosts a two or three 8-inch layer cake) Use recipe for Seven Minute
Frosting, folding in 3 squares of unsweetened chocolate, melted and
cooled, to the frosting just before spreading on the cake.

ᕁ Chocolate Frosting

Ingredients

2 eggs
2 lbs. powdered sugar, sifted
½ lb. butter
4 squares unsweetened chocolate

2 teaspoons lemon juice
2 teaspoons vanilla
2 cups chopped nuts
3 tablespoons cream

Directions (Frosts 9-inch layer cake)

Beat the eggs well and gradually work in the sugar.
Melt together butter and chocolate. Add to above. Add lemon juice
    and vanilla and mix well. Add cream and mix. Fold in nuts and
    spread on cake.

ᘒ Chocolate Confectioners' Frosting

Ingredients

2 cups sifted confectioners' sugar
2 tablespoons hot milk (about)
1 teaspoon vanilla

1 square unsweetened chocolate,
   melted

Directions (Makes about 2 cups)

Combine all ingredients. Beat until smooth and of good spreading
   consistency.

ᘒ Creamy Soft Chocolate Frosting

The Derings, Green Lake, Wisconsin

Ingredients

1 cup sugar
⅛ teaspoon salt
¼ cup cornstarch
1 ½ cups water

3 squares unsweetened chocolate
½ cup milk
1 teaspoon butter
1 teaspoon vanilla

Directions (Frosts 8-inch layer cake)

Mix together dry ingredients. Stir in water. Cook and stir until thick
   and clear.
Combine chocolate and milk in top of double boiler. Cook over
   boiling water until chocolate melts. Add to the above mixture.
Add butter and vanilla to above mixture. Cool and spread.

ᘒ Caramel Fudge Frosting

Ingredients

1 ½ cups firmly packed brown
   sugar
1 cup milk

2 tablespoons butter
Pinch of salt
½ teaspoon vanilla

Directions (Frosts 8-inch layer cake)

Combine sugar and milk together in saucepan. Bring to a boil, stirring constantly. Boil, covered 3 minutes and then uncovered until
   the soft-ball stage is reached or to a temperature of 236° F. Stir
   occasionally. Remove from heat.
Add butter, salt, and vanilla to the above mixture. Cool frosting until
   it is lukewarm or has reached 110° F. Beat until thick and creamy.
   Spread on cake.

ᕱ Fudge Frosting

Anchorage-by-the-Sea, Mattapoisett, Massachusetts

Ingredients

2 cups confectioners' sugar
⅓ cup butter
2 squares unsweetened chocolate

Pinch of salt
1 teaspoon vanilla
⅓ cup milk

Directions (Frosts 8-inch layer cake)

Place all ingredients in a saucepan and cook over very low heat for about 3 minutes. Spread on cooled cake. (Marshmallows may be cut in pieces and placed over top of cake and frosting poured over them.)

ᕱ Praline Fudge Frosting

Ingredients

2 ½ cups sugar
1 cup maple syrup
1 cup light cream

Pinch of salt
1 teaspoon vanilla

Directions (Frosts 8-inch layer cake)

Combine first three ingredients in large saucepan. Bring to a boil, stirring constantly; boil covered for 3 minutes. Then boil uncovered until mixture reaches the soft-ball stage or to a temperature of 236° F., stirring occasionally. Remove from heat.

Add salt and vanilla to the above mixture. Cool frosting until it is lukewarm or has reached 110° F. Beat until thick and creamy. Spread on cake.

ᕱ Chocolate Marshmallow Frosting

Ingredients

1 ½ boxes powdered sugar
⅛ teaspoon salt
3 squares unsweetened chocolate
3 tablespoons butter

½ cup cream
1 teaspoon vanilla
18 marshmallows
½ cup chopped pecans

Directions (Frosts 9-inch layer cake)

Sift together sugar and salt. Melt chocolate and butter in double boiler. To the sugar add cream and vanilla and blend. Stir in the hot chocolate mixture and beat well.

Cut marshmallows in small pieces. Stir into frosting along with nuts. Let stand, stirring occasionally until of spreading consistency.

∾ Maple Frosting

Ingredients

2 tablespoons butter	Cream
1 lb. confectioners' sugar, sifted	½ cup pecan halves
1 teaspoon maple flavor	

Directions (Frosts 10-inch square layer cake)

Cream butter and work in sifted sugar.

Add maple flavor and sufficient cream to make it of spreading consistency. Spread on cooled cake. Top with pecan halves.

∾ Mocha Frosting

Ingredients

1 ½ boxes (1 ½ lbs.) powdered sugar	3 tablespoons butter, melted
	½ cup strong cold coffee
3 squares unsweetened chocolate	¼ cup plus 1 tablespoon cream

Directions (Frosts 9-inch layer cake)

Sift sugar. Melt together butter and chocolate. Stir into sugar along with coffee.

Add cream and stir to blend well. If the cream is not enough, add just a bit more to make of spreading consistency.

∾ Rum Butter Frosting

Ingredients

½ lb. butter	4 tablespoons rum
2 lbs. powdered sugar	1 tablespoon cream

Directions *(Frosts 10-inch tube cake)*

Cream butter at high speed in electric mixer. Gradually add all of the
sugar. Scrape down bowl and add rum a tablespoon at a time. Add
cream, and if still too stiff, add a little more until of good spreading
consistency. This will make nice thick icing between the layers, on
top, and on all sides.

ᐯ Mocha Butter Cream Frosting

Ingredients

1 box (1 lb.) sifted confectioners' sugar	½ cup butter
¼ cup cocoa	5 tablespoons cold coffee (about)
Pinch of salt	½ teaspoon vanilla

Directions *(Frosts 9-inch layer cake)*

Sift together sugar, cocoa, and salt.

Cream butter and gradually add part of the sugar mixture. Beat after
each addition until light and fluffy.

Add the remaining sugar mixture alternately with coffee until of
right consistency to spread. Beat after each addition until smooth.
Add vanilla.

ᐯ Seafoam Frosting

Williamsburg Inn, Williamsburg, Virginia

Ingredients

1 ½ cups brown sugar	¼ teaspoon cream of tartar
½ cup water	2 egg whites, beaten

Directions *(Frosts 8-inch layer cake)*

Boil together first three ingredients until mixture spins a thread.

Slowly add the above syrup to egg whites, beating all the time.
    Spread on cooled cake.

～ Sour Cream Frosting

Old Tyme Coffee House, Moose Lake, Minnesota

Ingredients

1 cup heavy sour cream
1 ½ cups granulated sugar
½ teaspoon soda
1 teaspoon vanilla

Pinch of salt
1 tablespoon butter
2 tablespoons fresh cream

Directions (Frosts a loaf cake)

Boil sour cream and sugar slowly over low heat, stirring occasionally. Cook until the soft-ball stage has been reached. This will take about ½ an hour. Remove from heat.

Add soda. Cook over high heat, stirring rapidly all the time, for 1 minute or until it turns a nice caramel color. Remove from stove.

Add vanilla, salt, and butter. Cool slightly; then beat, adding cream until the frosting is the right consistency to spread. Should spread like butter.

～ Spiced Sour Cream Frosting

Ingredients

1 cup sugar
½ cup sour cream

⅛ teaspoon nutmeg

Directions (Frosts 9-inch layer cake)

Combine sugar and sour cream and boil for 1 minute, stirring constantly.

Add nutmeg to the above mixture and cool slightly. Beat until thickened and white in color (about 20 minutes).

～ White Mountain Frosting

Ingredients

½ cup sugar
¼ cup light corn syrup
¼ cup egg whites
½ teaspoon vanilla

Red vegetable coloring
1 pint fresh strawberries, halved, or 1 box frozen thawed strawberries, halved

Directions (Frosts one 10-inch tube cake)

Boil sugar and corn syrup together until a candy thermometer registers 242° or mixture will spin a 6- to 8-inch thread.

Beat egg whites until stiff. Pour above mixture into egg whites, beating constantly.

Add vanilla and enough red coloring to get a deep pink frosting. Frost cake and decorate top and sides with strawberries.

ᴄᴡ White Icing

Lake Breeze Resort, Three Lakes, Wisconsin

Ingredients

2 egg whites   4 tablespoons cold water
1 cup sugar

Directions (Frosts a 9-inch layer cake)

Mix together all ingredients and cook in double boiler until thick. Beat constantly with an egg beater while cooking. Put on cake while hot.

ᴄᴡ Boiled White Icing

Ingredients

2 ¾ cups sugar   1 cup water
2 tablespoons corn syrup   ¾ cup egg whites
1 teaspoon vinegar   ¼ cup sugar
Dash of salt   ¼ teaspoon cream of tartar

Directions (Frosts one 9-inch cake)

Combine first five ingredients and bring to a boil. Cook to 238° F. on a candy thermometer.

Beat together remaining ingredients until frothy. Add ⅓ of above syrup to egg whites mixture, beating all the time. Return syrup to range and let come to a boil. Again add ⅓ of the syrup to egg white mixture and beat well. Bring remaining syrup to a boil and let cook 2 minutes. Fold into mixture and beat icing until cold and ready to spread.

Caramel Icing

Ingredients

2 cups brown sugar
1 cup light cream

3 tablespoons butter
1 teaspoon vanilla

Directions (Frosts 9-inch layer cake)

Combine brown sugar and cream in saucepan. Stir until the sugar
   is dissolved. Then cook, without stirring, to the soft-ball stage,
   238° F.
Add butter. Remove from heat and cool. Then add vanilla. Beat icing
   until thick and creamy. Add a little cream if too thick.

Orange Butter Cream Icing

Damon's, Cleveland, Ohio

Ingredients

¼ cup butter
2 cups confectioners' sugar
1 egg, beaten

1 cup orange marmalade
¼ teaspoon salt

Directions (Frosts a 9-inch layer cake)

Cream together butter and sugar. Stir in egg. Fold in marmalade and
   salt. If the marmalade is thin, reduce amount to ¾ cup, and it may
   be necessary to add a little more sugar.

Fluffy Orange Icing

Ingredients

2 cups sifted confectioners' sugar
1 tablespoon melted butter

1 ½ tablespoons grated orange
   rind
¼ cup orange juice

Directions (Frosts 9-inch layer cake)

Place all ingredients in top of double boiler. Cook and stir over hot
   water for 10 minutes. Beat icing until cool and of right spreading
   consistency.

↝ Maple Sugar Icing

Ingredients

2 cups maple sugar
1 cup light cream

Pinch of salt
½ cup chopped walnuts

Directions (Frosts 8-inch layer cake)

Combine sugar, cream, and salt in a saucepan. Cook and stir until
mixture reaches the soft-ball stage or 234° F. Remove from heat.
Cool slightly. Beat until creamy.
Add nuts. Spread on cooled cake.

↝ Caramel Whip Icing

Cromer's Restaurant, Flint, Michigan

Ingredients

2 cups brown sugar
6 tablespoons butter
1 ⅓ cups water

5 tablespoons cornstarch
1 ⅓ cups whipping cream,
whipped

Directions (Makes about 3 cups)

Combine brown sugar and butter in heavy skillet. Cook and stir until
mixture bubbles and the sugar darkens.
Mix a little of the water with the cornstarch. Add this with remaining
water to the above mixture. Cook and stir until thickened. Chill.
Fold whipped cream into caramel mixture. Spread between cake
layers.

↝ Mocha Icing

Old English Inn, Omaha, Nebraska

Ingredients

½ cup hot coffee
3 tablespoons butter

4 tablespoons cocoa
3 cups powdered sugar

Directions (Frosts one jelly roll)

Pour hot coffee over the butter and add the cocoa and powdered
sugar. Stir well. Ice the roll and keep in refrigerator until ready to
serve.

∾ Quick Brown Sugar Icing

Ingredients

1 ½ cups brown sugar
5 tablespoons cream
3 teaspoons butter

Pinch of salt
½ teaspoon vanilla

Directions (Frosts 8-inch layer cake)

Combine first four ingredients in saucepan. Cook and stir until
mixture comes to a boil. Remove from heat. Cool slightly.
Add vanilla and beat until frosting is of spreading consistency.

∾ Chocolate Filling

Ingredients

2 eggs
½ cup sugar
1 cup milk
1 tablespoon butter

1 square unsweetened chocolate,
grated
Pinch of salt
1 teaspoon vanilla

Directions (Makes about 1 cup)

Beat eggs until thick and lemon colored. Gradually add sugar and
continue beating until smooth and well blended.
Add milk slowly to the above mixture. Then add butter, chocolate,
and salt. Cook in double boiler until thick, stirring frequently.
Cool.
Add vanilla and spread between cake layers.

∾ Clear Orange Filling

Francis Fowler Jr., Los Angeles, California

Ingredients

2 tablespoons butter
4 tablespoons cornstarch
2 tablespoons grated orange rind
1 cup sugar

½ teaspoon salt
1 ½ teaspoons lemon juice
1 cup orange juice and pulp

Directions (Makes enough for 9-inch layer cake)

Mix all ingredients together and cook in double boiler 5 minutes.
Spread between layers and on top and sides of cake.

~ *Lemon Filling*
Lake Breeze Resort, Three Lakes, Wisconsin

Ingredients

2 egg yolks

Juice of 1 lemon

2 tablespoons cornstarch

1 cup scalding water

Pinch of salt

½ cup chopped nuts

Directions (Makes about 1 ½ cups)

Cook first five ingredients until thick. Spread lemon filling between
cake layers.

Sprinkle cake with nuts and top with icing.

~ *Almond Custard Filling*

Ingredients

1 cup sugar

1 cup sour cream

1 tablespoon flour

1 egg, beaten

1 cup blanched, ground almonds

½ teaspoon vanilla

Directions (Makes about 2 cups)

Combine sugar, sour cream, and flour in top of double boiler. Cook
over low heat, but do not let the mixture boil.

Pour above mixture over the beaten egg. Place over boiling water and
cook and stir until custard is thick.

Add nuts to the above mixture. Cool custard and then add vanilla.

~ *Pineapple Filling*

Ingredients

¼ cup sugar

1 tablespoon flour

Pinch of salt

⅔ cup milk

2 egg yolks, slightly beaten

1 ½ tablespoons butter

1 cup canned crushed pineapple,
well drained

Directions (Makes about 2 cups)

Combine sugar, flour, and salt in top of double boiler.

Mix milk with egg yolks and add to above mixture. Cook and stir
over boiling water for 15 minutes or until thickened. Remove
from heat.

Add remaining ingredients. Cool. Spread.

◌ Cream Filling

Ingredients

²⁄₃ cup sugar
5 tablespoons flour
⅛ teaspoon salt

2 cups milk
2 eggs, slightly beaten
1 teaspoon vanilla

Directions (Makes about 2 cups)

Combine dry ingredients in top of double boiler. Stir in milk gradually. Cook over boiling water until mixture thickens, stirring constantly. Cover and cook for 10 minutes longer, stirring occasionally.

Stir a little of the hot mixture into the slightly beaten eggs. Slowly add to the above mixture. Cook over hot water for 2 minutes, stirring constantly. Chill.

Add flavoring. Makes enough filling for three-layer cake, or use in cream puffs or éclairs.

◌ Rum Cream Filling

(Makes about 2 cups.) Use recipe for Cream Filling, omitting the vanilla and substituting 1 tablespoon rum flavoring.

> ➤ *To make a good uncooked icing, thorough beating is necessary. Too much sugar and too little beating makes a brittle hard frosting.*

◌ Cocoa Whipped Cream

Ingredients

2 tablespoons sugar
2 tablespoons cocoa

Pinch of salt
1 cup heavy cream

Directions (Makes about 1 ½ cups)

Mix sugar, cocoa, and salt together. Add to heavy cream. Chill 1 hour. Whip until stiff.

⮞ Coffee Glaze

Ingredients

2 ½ tablespoons water
1 tablespoon butter
1 ⅓ cups sifted confectioners'
   sugar

Pinch of salt
2 teaspoons instant coffee
   powder

Directions (Makes about 1 cup)

Heat water and butter together.
Combine remaining ingredients in bowl and add hot liquid. Stir until
   smooth. Pour over the top of a tube angel food cake.

➤ *For best results with cooked frostings, use an accurate candy and
icing thermometer.*

Biscuit Desserts

(Shortcakes, dumplings, cobblers)

C OBBLERS, for which there are some wonderful recipes in this section, are a concoction from New England. A cobbler is a deep-dish fruit pie with a biscuit mixture, usually on top. This quick fruit pie gets its name from the phrase "cobble up," meaning put together in a hurry. The familiar apple pan dowdy is an early version of the apple cobbler. But cherries, peaches, blackberries, apricots, and huckleberries make excellent cobblers too. Whipped cream or rich heavy cream is marvelous over this dessert, and you have to go a long way to find something as quick and easy for a family meal or for that unexpected company. Other sauces may be used too, depending on the occasion and your particular taste. Custard sauce goes well with blueberry and peach cobblers, and hot lemon sauce with apple cobbler.

Still another dessert that can be made as a biscuit or as a cake is shortcake. This is made of a biscuit mixture and baked either as a large cake or as individual cakes. When ready to be served, shortcakes are split in half and fruit is spooned between the layers and on top. Perhaps strawberries, raspberries, and peaches are the best-known fruits used for shortcake. Shortcakes may be served plain, with heavy cream, or for a really special dessert, with whipped cream.

Today with the modern food processing of canned and frozen fruits and the plentiful selection on your grocer's shelves, short-cakes are no longer limited to the summer season.

Still another type of biscuit dessert I cover in this section is fruit dumplings, which get their name from their irregular shape. Originally all dumplings were steamed. However, some recipes today call for baking. This results in a more uniform shape. Apples, peaches, cherries, blueberries, and apricots can be used for delicious fruit dumplings.

Dumplings are made by rolling a biscuit mixture until it is ¼-inch thick and then cutting the dough into 4-inch squares. Fruit, which has been pared or cored as the need may be, is then placed in the center of a square of dough, and the four corners are drawn up around the fruit. The ends are then pinched together, and the dumplings are ready to bake. Dumplings are usually served with a sauce of some type. A lemon or foamy sauce is good with them, or in some cases a hard sauce.

Biscuit desserts in their many forms can be adapted to any fruit and suited to every taste. Fruit, whether fresh, frozen, crushed, mashed, sliced, or whole, is good when used in a biscuit dessert. Don't forget that you can make a really wonderful treat by just using a simple sauce.

Serve steamed puddings piping hot. Make your sauce with care. It can make or break the pudding. Put the steamed pudding in the oven for a minute or two to dry out the top. Hard sauce flavored with rum or brandy is delicious with steamed puddings.

ᴖ Peach Cobbler

Ingredients

1 cup sugar
1 tablespoon cornstarch
1 cup boiling water
3 cups fresh, sliced, peeled
   peaches
1 tablespoon butter
½ teaspoon cinnamon

1 cup sifted flour
1 tablespoon sugar
1 ½ teaspoons baking powder
½ teaspoon salt
3 tablespoons shortening
½ cup milk (about)

Directions (Serves 6)

Combine sugar and cornstarch in saucepan.
Add boiling water gradually. Boil 1 minute, stirring constantly.
Add peaches to syrup. Pour into a 10 × 6 × 2-inch baking dish.
Dot mixture with butter. Sprinkle with cinnamon.
Sift together flour, sugar, baking powder, and salt.
Cut shortening into flour mixture with pastry blender.
Stir milk into above mixture to make a soft dough. Drop mixture by
   spoonfuls onto fruit mixture in baking dish. Bake in hot oven at
   400° about 30 minutes. Serve warm with cream.

ᴖ Cherry Cobbler

Use recipe for Peach Cobbler, substituting 3 cups sweet pitted cherries for the peaches. (If desired add 2 drops almond extract.) Bake as directed for Peach Cobbler.

ᴖ Blackberry Cobbler

(Serves 6)

Use recipe for Peach Cobbler, substituting 3 cups blackberries for the peaches and reducing the sugar from 1 cup to ¾ cup. Bake as directed for Peach Cobbler.

❧ Apple Dumplings

Richards Treat Cafeteria, Minneapolis, Minnesota

Ingredients

2 cups cake flour
2 teaspoons baking powder
½ teaspoon salt
⅔ cup shortening
⅓ cup milk, or perhaps ½ cup
6 to 8 tart apples
½ teaspoon cinnamon

¼ teaspoon nutmeg
¾ cup brown sugar
6 tablespoons butter
½ cup brown sugar
½ cup granulated sugar
2 cups water
½ cup butter

Directions (Serves 6)

Mix and sift first three ingredients.

Work shortening into flour mixture lightly with the tips of fingers.

Make hole in flour and add milk gradually while mixing lightly.
   Knead lightly into a ball and roll into a rectangular-shaped piece of
   dough about ¼ inch thick, and cut into six pieces.

Peel and slice apples and divide between six squares of dough.

Mix spices with ¾ cup brown sugar and add to the apples.

Dot each square with a tablespoon of butter and bring up the corners
   of the dough and pinch together to make dumpling.

Make a syrup of ½ cup each brown and granulated sugar, 2 cups
   water, and ½ cup butter, and while hot set in dumplings, and bake
   in 350° to 375° oven for 1 hour, or until apples are done. Dumplings are best when made of quick-cooking apples, though winter
   apples may be used if slowly cooked.

❧ Strawberry and Rhubarb Shortcake

Ingredients

1 lb. fresh rhubarb
½ cup water
1 cup sugar

1 package frozen strawberries,
   defrosted

Directions (Serves 4)

Cut rhubarb in ½-inch slices. Simmer in water until tender and while
   hot add sugar and strawberries. Serve over your favorite shortcake.
   Top with whipped cream.

❧ Strawberry Shortcake

Ingredients

1 ½ quarts fresh, stemmed, slightly crushed strawberries
1 cup sugar
2 cups sifted flour
2 tablespoons sugar
3 teaspoons baking powder
1 teaspoon salt
6 tablespoons shortening
⅔ cup milk (about)

Directions (Serves 6)

Combine strawberries and 1 cup sugar and let stand while preparing the shortcake.

Sift together flour, remaining sugar, baking powder, and salt into a bowl.

Cut shortening into the flour mixture with pastry blender until fine crumbs are formed.

Add milk to the above and stir until a soft dough is formed. Knead lightly on lightly floured board. Spread half of the dough into a well-greased 8-inch round layer pan. Dot with butter. Spread remaining dough on top. Bake in hot oven at 450° for 12 to 15 minutes. Separate layers. Spoon sweetened berries between the layers and on top. Serve with whipped cream.

❧ Raspberry Shortcake

(Serves 6)

Use recipe for Strawberry Shortcake, substituting raspberries for the strawberries.

❧ Peach Shortcake

(Serves 6)

Use recipe for Strawberry Shortcake, substituting 1 quart fresh, peeled, sliced peaches for the strawberries.

～ Banana Gingerbread Shortcake

Ingredients

¾ cup shortening (½ butter and ½ shortening or 6 tablespoons of each)
1 cup sugar
2 eggs, slightly beaten
1 cup molasses
1 teaspoon ginger
1 teaspoon cinnamon
½ teaspoon salt
1 teaspoon soda
1 cup warm coffee
2 ½ cups sifted flour
Sliced bananas
Whipped cream

Directions (Serves 16)

Cream shortening with 1 cup sugar. Add eggs.

Add molasses, ginger, cinnamon, and salt to the creamed mixture.

Put soda into warm coffee. Add to above mixture.

Add flour to the above and stir well. Pour into an 8 × 12-inch pan and bake in a 350° oven for 40 to 50 minutes or until done, depending upon the size of the pan used and the thickness of the dough.

When ready to serve, split each serving and put sliced bananas between and on top. Serve with whipped cream.

～ Dutch Apple Cake

Ingredients

1 ½ cups sifted flour
2 ½ teaspoons baking powder
½ teaspoon salt
4 tablespoons sugar
¼ cup shortening
1 teaspoon vanilla
½ cup milk (about)
4 ½ cups sliced tart apples
3 tablespoons butter
⅔ cup sugar
1 tablespoon flour
1 teaspoon cinnamon
1 tablespoon lemon juice

Directions (Serves 6 to 8)

Sift together first four ingredients into a bowl.

Cut shortening into flour mixture with pastry blender or two forks until coarse crumbs are formed.

Add vanilla and milk to above mixture. Stir until a soft dough is formed. Roll out dough on lightly floured board and line a 9-inch pie pan.

Press apple slices into dough.

Cream butter and gradually add the remaining ingredients. Spread on top of apples. Bake in hot oven at 400° for 40 to 50 minutes. Serve warm with cream.

∾ Dutch Peach Cake

(Serves 6 to 8)

Use recipe for Dutch Apple Cake, substituting fresh sliced peaches for the apples. Bake as directed.

∾ Blueberry Shortcake au Kirsch

Ingredients

2 cups blueberries
1 cup sugar
2 teaspoons arrowroot
3 teaspoons water

2 liqueur glasses Kirschwasser
4 slices sponge cake
Vanilla ice cream

Directions (Serves 4)

Wash blueberries; place in saucepan; cover with sugar; stir and heat. Bring to quick boil.

Dissolve arrowroot in water and stir into blueberries. Cook for a few minutes to thicken. Let cool.

When cool, add Kirschwasser; cover tightly and let stand in cool place for several hours.

Serve on slices of sponge cake, and top with vanilla ice cream.

∾ Blueberry Slump

Ingredients

1 quart blueberries
1 cup sugar
4 tablespoons arrowroot or
    cornstarch
Juice of 1 lemon
½ cup sugar

4 tablespoons butter
¼ teaspoon salt
1 egg
½ cup milk
1 ½ cups sifted cake flour
2 teaspoons baking powder

Directions (Serves 8)

Wash berries and drain. Mix sugar and arrowroot and add to berries. Place in greased casserole and sprinkle with lemon juice.

Cream together butter and sugar. Add salt. Beat the egg and add to creamed mixture. Add milk and mix well. Stir in flour and baking powder briskly and spoon over berries. Bake in 425° oven for 20 to 25 minutes. Serve warm with vanilla ice cream. Note: If fresh blueberries are not available, frozen ones may be used. In that case, use two packages and let defrost slightly.

Plum Rolls

Ingredients

1 No. 2 ½ can prune plums or
    1 quart canned damsons
4 tablespoons sugar
2 tablespoons butter
1 teaspoon
Angostura bitters
2 cups flour

½ teaspoon salt
3 teaspoons baking powder
2 tablespoons sugar
4 tablespoons butter
1 egg
½ cup milk

Directions (Serves 8 to 10)

Drain plums thoroughly; remove pits, and cut fruit into coarse
    pieces.

Add 4 tablespoons of sugar, 2 tablespoons of butter, and bitters to
    juice strained from plums; place in baking pan and bring to boil
    on high heat.

Sift dry ingredients together.

Cut butter into dry ingredients as in any pastry.

Beat egg thoroughly; combine with milk, and add pastry to make
    soft dough. Place on floured board and roll to ½-inch thickness.
    Spread with chopped plums and roll up. Slice roll crosswise into
    1 ½-inch lengths and place cut side down, in hot syrup. Bake in
    350° oven for about 30 minutes or until pastry is done.

Peach Pinwheels

Ingredients

2 tablespoons cornstarch
1 cup sugar
¼ teaspoon salt
½ teaspoon cinnamon
4 cups sliced, fresh peaches
1 tablespoon lemon juice
1 cup water

1 cup biscuit mix
2 tablespoons butter, melted
¼ cup milk
2 tablespoons butter, melted
¼ teaspoon cinnamon
2 tablespoons sugar
¼ cup chopped pecans

Directions (Serves 8)

Combine first eight ingredients in an 11 × 7 × 2-inch baking dish.

Add melted butter and milk to biscuit mix. Stir until a soft dough is
    formed. Turn onto lightly floured board and knead 10 times. Roll
    out into a 6-inch square about ¼-inch thick.

Spread dough with melted butter. Combine sugar and cinnamon and sprinkle over the dough. Top with chopped pecans. Roll up as for jelly roll. Moisten edge and press against roll to seal. Cut with sharp knife into 8 slices about ¾ inch thick. Place cut side up on peach mixture. Bake in hot oven at 425° for 25 minutes or until lightly browned. Serve warm with cream.

∾ Apple Pudding

The Ardzli Restaurant, Springfield, Ohio

Ingredients

4 lbs. winesap apples
2 cups granulated sugar
2 cups brown sugar

¾ lb. butter
2 cups flour

Directions (Serves 12 to 14)

Peel apples and slice thin. Place in bottom of buttered 8 × 14-inch baking pan. Sprinkle with sugar.

Cream butter and brown sugar together in mixer. Stir in flour. Pat out dough and cut in cookie shapes. Place close together all over top of apples. Bake until golden brown in preheated oven at 350° for 45 to 50 minutes. Serve warm with cream or ice cream.

∾ Apple Betty Pudding

Ingredients

6 cups sliced apples
⅓ cup granulated sugar
¾ cup hot water
4 tablespoons vegetable
  shortening
2 tablespoons butter

½ cup brown sugar
½ teaspoon ground cinnamon
1 cup sifted flour
1 teaspoon baking powder
¼ teaspoon salt

Directions (Serves 6)

Combine apples, sugar, and water, and simmer, covered, in saucepan for 10 minutes. Put into greased 9-inch pan.

Blend shortening and butter until soft. Add brown sugar and work until creamy.

Sift together remaining ingredients and add to shortening mixture, blending thoroughly. Sprinkle over top of apples. Bake 40 minutes in 350° oven. Serve with rich cream or with vanilla ice cream.

ᴄᴡ Sally Lunn

Althaea, Lewisburg, West Virginia

Ingredients

½ cup butter
1 tablespoon sugar
½ teaspoon salt
2 eggs

1 yeast cake
1 cup milk
3 cups flour

Directions

Cream together first three ingredients.
Beat eggs and add to above and beat well.
Heat milk to lukewarm and dissolve yeast in it. Add to above. Add
flour, mix thoroughly; pour into buttered tube pan. Let rise
1 ½ hours or until doubled in bulk. Bake in 350° oven 45 to 50
minutes. Serve hot with butter.

ᴄᴡ Maple Rag-a-Muffin Dessert

Twist-o' Hill Lodge, Williston, Vermont

Ingredients

1 ½ cups flour
½ teaspoon salt
3 teaspoons baking powder
¼ teaspoon cream of tartar
4 tablespoons shortening
⅓ to ½ cup milk

Butter
1 ½ cups maple syrup
¼ cup chopped nuts
½ cup whipping cream,
    whipped, or 1 pint vanilla ice
    cream

Directions (Serve 6)

Sift dry ingredients. Cut in shortening and add milk to make a soft
dough. Roll out on lightly floured board and cut 12 small biscuits.
Place in well-greased pan and dot generously with butter. Heat
syrup and pour over biscuits. Bake 15 minutes in a 450° oven.
Serve warm with whipped cream or a small scoop of ice cream.
Garnish with nuts.

Custards

I N PLAIN or dressed-up fashion, the custard dessert, like the egg, is a foundation to good eating.

Composed of eggs, milk, and sugar, custards contain ingredients necessary in our daily diet. The plain custard may be varied with chocolate, coffee, maple syrup, wine, or heavy cream. To perk up the flavor of a plain custard, drop fruit, candied cherries, jelly, or nuts into the bottom of the custard cup.

The two most common faults in making custards are cooking too long or cooking at too high a temperature. Custard sauces and puddings must not boil because high heat destroys the flavor and causes the egg to cook, giving the dessert a curdled appearance. If soft custard shows signs of curdling, remove from the boiling water at once and set in a bowl of ice water to cool quickly.

In custard making do not hesitate to use leftover yolks. The whites do not improve the custard. If you want a rich brown crust on your custard, beat the eggs until thick and lemon colored. For a crunchy crust, try spreading leftover cake, cookie, or macaroon crumbs over the custard before baking.

Yes, in plain dress or "glad rags," custard desserts can become a favorite in any season with almost any type of menu.

ᴖ Baked Custard

Ingredients

2 large eggs or 4 egg yolks,   ¼ teaspoon salt
  slightly beaten   ½ teaspoon vanilla
⅓ cup sugar   2 cups milk, scalded

Directions (Serves 6)

Mix first four ingredients together in bowl.

Add milk to egg mixture gradually. Strain into custard cups or a
  1 ½-quart baking dish. Place baking dish in pan of hot water.
  Sprinkle with nutmeg, if desired. Bake in moderate oven at 350°
  for 30 to 35 minutes or until silver knife inserted into custard
  comes out clean. Remove from hot water immediately. Serve
  cool or chilled.

ᴥ *To preserve yolks of eggs for a day, slide them into a bowl without
breaking and cover them with cold water.*

ᴖ Baked Chocolate Custard

Ingredients

2 squares unsweetened chocolate   ⅓ cup sugar
4 cups milk   ¼ teaspoon salt
4 eggs, slightly beaten   1 teaspoon vanilla

Directions (Serves 8 to 10)

Combine chocolate and milk in top of double boiler. Cook and stir
  over boiling water until chocolate melts. Beat with rotary egg
  beater until blended.

Combine eggs, sugar, and salt in bowl. Add above mixture gradually,
  stirring until sugar is dissolved.

Add vanilla to the mixture. Pour into custard cups. Place cups in pan
  of hot water and bake in slow oven at 325° for 45 minutes or until
  knife inserted comes out clean. Chill. Top with cream and a dash
  of cinnamon, or unmold and serve with cream.

ᴖ Baked Caramel Custard

(Serves 6)

In small frying pan melt ½ cup sugar over low heat, stirring constantly. Divide caramelized sugar syrup among the custard cups, turning cups around so that the caramel will coat the insides. Allow to harden. Meanwhile, prepare recipe for Molded Custard.

ᴖ Baked Maple Custard

(Serves 6)

Place 1 tablespoon maple syrup into the bottom of each custard cup. Then prepare recipe for Molded Custard.

ᴖ Caramel Custard

Ingredients

½ cup sugar
1 tablespoon hot water
2 cups scalded milk

3 egg yolks, well beaten
½ teaspoon vanilla
Pinch of salt

Directions (Serves 4)

Place sugar in small heavy skillet. Melt over low heat, stirring constantly.

Add water to the melted sugar. Stir until sugar is dissolved.

Add above mixture to the scalded milk.

Pour milk gradually over eggs.

Add vanilla and salt to the above mixture. Beat custard until blended. Pour into 1-quart baking dish. Place baking dish in pan of hot water. Bake in slow oven 325° about 1 hour or until silver knife comes out clean when inserted.

ᴖ Coconut Custard

(Serves 6)

Use recipe for Baked Custard, adding ¾ cup shredded cut coconut to the custard mixture.

ᘓ Molded Custard

(Serves 6)

Use recipe for Baked Custard except use 3 eggs or 6 egg yolks. Pour into greased molds. Unmold on serving dish.

ᘓ Pecan Custard

(Serves 6)

Use recipe for Baked Custard, adding ⅔ cup finely chopped pecans to custard mixture.

ᘓ Ivory Cream Custard

Ingredients

6 egg whites
⅓ cup sugar
½ teaspoon salt

1 ½ cups cold water
1 ½ cups heavy cream

Directions (Serves 6)

Beat egg whites slightly with fork.

Add remaining ingredients to egg whites and stir until thoroughly mixed. Pour into custard cups. Place cups in pan of hot water. Bake in moderate oven at 350° for 40 to 50 minutes or until silver knife comes out clean when inserted in the center. Remove from water to cool. Chill.

ᘓ Whipped Cream Custard

Ingredients

4 egg yolks
¾ cup sugar
2 tablespoons cornstarch
1 pint light cream, scalded

2 tablespoons butter
Pinch of salt
1 ½ teaspoons vanilla
1 cup heavy cream, whipped

Directions (Serves 6)

Combine egg yolks, sugar, and cornstarch in top of double boiler and beat together until blended.

Stir light cream into above mixture gradually.

Add butter and salt to mixture. Cook over boiling water, stirring frequently, until thick. Cool.

Fold vanilla and whipped cream into cooled mixture. Pour into serving dishes or individual dessert glasses. Chill.

ᕦ Lemon Sponge Custard

Ingredients

¾ cup sugar
2 tablespoons butter
2 teaspoons grated lemon rind
3 egg yolks
1 cup milk

¼ cup lemon juice
3 tablespoons flour
3 egg whites
⅛ teaspoon salt

Directions (Serves 4 to 6)

Cream together sugar, butter, and lemon rind until well blended.

Add yolks to the above mixture, one at a time, beating well after each addition.

Combine milk and lemon juice together.

Add flour, alternately with liquid, to creamed mixture.

Beat egg whites and salt together until stiff peaks are formed. Fold into egg yolk mixture. Pour into greased custard cups. Place cups in pan of hot water and bake in moderate oven at 350° about 45 minutes. Serve hot or cold with heavy cream.

ᕦ Orange Sponge Custard

(Serves 4 to 6)

Use recipe for Lemon Sponge Custard, substituting 1 tablespoon grated orange rind for the lemon rind and ⅓ cup orange juice for the lemon juice.

ᕦ Floating Island

Ingredients

1 pint milk
2 tablespoons sugar
1 teaspoon cornstarch
2 egg yolks

Nutmeg
2 egg whites, beaten
2 tablespoons sugar

Directions (Serves 4)

Scald milk in double boiler.

Stir together 2 tablespoons sugar with cornstarch and egg yolks until
  smooth, and add scalded milk. Return to double boiler and stir
  until smooth. Cool.

Pour custard into sherbet dishes and sprinkle top with nutmeg.

Beat egg whites until stiff and add 2 tablespoons sugar; then beat
  again. Drop from spoon in pan with small amount of water. Bake
  in slow oven at 325° about 15 minutes or until brown. Lift from
  pan with fork and top custard with meringue.

∾ Cabinet Pudding

Ingredients

2 cups milk	2 eggs, slightly beaten
2 tablespoons butter	¼ teaspoon salt
2 tablespoons sugar	½ teaspoon vanilla
2 cups cake or bread crumbs	

Directions (Serves 6)

Combine milk, butter, and sugar in saucepan. Cook over low heat
  until milk reaches the scalding point. Cool slightly.

Add crumbs to the milk mixture.

Combine remaining ingredients and stir slowly into the milk. Pour
  into greased 1-quart casserole and place casserole in pan of hot
  water. Bake in moderate oven at 375° about 1 hour.

∾ Grapenut Pudding

(Serves 6)

Use recipe for Cabinet Pudding, substituting 1 cup grapenuts for
cake crumbs. Heat grapenuts with the milk.

✏ Old-Fashioned Bread Pudding

Ingredients

2 cups stale bread cubes (¼ to ½-inch cubes)	¼ cup sugar
2 cups milk	2 eggs
¼ cup butter	Pinch of salt
	¾ teaspoon vanilla

Directions (Serves 4 to 6)

Place bread cubes in greased 1-quart casserole.

Combine milk, butter, and sugar in saucepan. Cook over low heat until milk reaches the scalding point.

Beat eggs slightly. Add salt. Stir in warm milk. Add vanilla. Pour over bread cubes. Place casserole in pan of hot water. Bake in moderate oven at 350° about 1 hour or until silver knife comes out clean when inserted in center of pudding. Serve hot or cold with plain cream, currant jelly, or hot Caramel, Lemon, Chocolate, or Clear Sauce. (*See* Dessert Sauces section.)

✏ Chocolate Bread Pudding

(Serves 4 to 6)

Use recipe for Old-Fashioned Bread Pudding, adding 1 square unsweetened chocolate to the milk-butter-sugar mixture before heating.

✏ Fruit Bread Pudding

(Serves 4 to 6)

Prepare Old-Fashioned Bread Pudding, adding ½ cup chopped raisins, dates, figs, or nuts before baking.

> ✦ *Store cooked custards or custard puddings, pies, éclairs, and sauces in a cool or refrigerated place (50° F. or lower) to prevent them from spoiling and to prevent possible growth of bacteria (staphylococcus), which, although rarely fatal, can make you "deathly sick."*

∾ Old-Fashioned Lemon Pudding

Ingredients

½ cup bread, zwieback, or cake crumbs
2 cups milk
⅓ cup soft butter
½ cup sugar

3 egg yolks, beaten
3 tablespoons lemon juice
2 teaspoons grated lemon rind
3 egg whites

Directions (Serves 6)

Soak crumbs and milk together; set aside.

Cream butter and sugar together until well blended.

Add yolks to creamed mixture and mix well.

Add juice and rind of lemon with milk mixture to the creamed butter, sugar, and egg yolks.

Beat egg whites until stiff but not dry. Fold into mixture. Pour into greased 1-quart casserole. Bake in slow oven at 325° about 45 minutes.

∾ Crème Brûlée

Mrs. Virginia Safford, *The Minneapolis Star,*
Minneapolis, Minnesota

Ingredients

1 quart light cream
8 egg yolks
5 tablespoons granulated sugar

2 teaspoons vanilla
2 tablespoons brown sugar

Directions (Serves 8)

Scald cream. Beat egg yolks and sugar together. Remove cream from heat and pour very slowly into egg mixture, stirring constantly. Add vanilla; set mixture in baking dish, and place in pan of hot water. Bake in moderate oven at 350° about 1 hour or until silver knife inserted in center comes out clean.

When above is done, sprinkle with brown sugar. Place under broiler until sugar melts and forms a glaze. Serve cold as an ice cube. (Many times the Crème Brûlée is served with fruit or assorted brandied fruit. The Brûlée is placed in a glass pudding dish; this is centered on a large platter encircled with fruit—pears, peaches, black cherries, or green gage plums. Canned fruit, which is brandied in a hurry, may also be used. Follow this simple process: Drain off syrup, cover fruit with brandy or kirsch, and let stand 12 hours covered in the refrigerator.)

ᕙ *Trifle*

Ingredients

1 dozen ladyfingers
½ cup jam (apricot, strawberry,
    raspberry, etc.)
6 large macaroons
⅓ cup sherry or brandy

1 ½ recipes Soft Custard, chilled
½ cup heavy cream, whipped
⅓ cup blanched, slivered,
    toasted almonds
Candied cherries

Directions (Serves 8)

Line sides of dessert bowl with ladyfingers that have been split in half
    and spread on one side with jam. Place macaroons on the bottom
    of the bowl.
Pour sherry or brandy over the macaroons and let stand until
    absorbed.
Pour Soft Custard over the soaked macaroons and chill.
Garnish with whipped cream, almonds, and cherries.

ᕙ *Soft Custard*

Ingredients

2 eggs or 4 egg yolks, slightly
    beaten
3 tablespoons sugar

Pinch of salt
1 ½ cups scalded milk
½ teaspoon vanilla

Directions (Makes 2 cups)

Combine first three ingredients.
Add milk slowly to egg mixture. Strain into the top of a double boiler.
    Cook over hot water (about 5 minutes) stirring constantly or until
    mixture thickens and coats a metal spoon. Remove pan immedi-
    ately from hot water and place in pan of cold water to cool quickly.
    Add vanilla to the above mixture and chill.

ᕙ *Sabayon*

Ingredients

8 egg yolks
1 cup confectioners' sugar
⅛ teaspoon salt

½ cup Madeira
8 egg whites, stiffly beaten

Directions (Serves 6)

Beat egg yolks, sugar, and salt together until very light. Place in top of double boiler. Cook over hot water, beating constantly, until foamy. (Do not allow water to touch the bottom of the top section of the double boiler.)

Add Madeira to the above mixture gradually. Continue to beat until it doubles in bulk. Remove from heat.

Fold in hot custard to egg whites gradually. Serve at once in sherbet glasses. This may also be served as a sauce.

ᨎ *Vanessi's Zabaglione*

Vanessi's Restaurant, San Francisco, California

Ingredients

8 egg yolks
5 tablespoons sugar
10 oz. dry sauterne

¼ teaspoon lemon rind, chopped
fine
1 oz. anisette

Directions (Serves 4)

Put eggs in round saucepan. Add sugar, lemon rind, and wine. Beat rapidly with wire whip over fire. Do not let boil. Whip until thick; then add anisette.

ᨎ *Zabaglione*

Marguerite Vollmer, New York City

Ingredients

6 egg yolks
⅓ cup sugar

⅓ cup Marsala or sherry

Directions

Put yolks in top of double boiler. Beat until thick and add sugar. Put over hot water (not boiling). Cook over low heat; beat constantly. In about 5 minutes slowly add Marsala. Cook and beat until thick. Serve hot or chilled. Note: Use Dry Sack (Williams & Humber), Florio's, or a medium sweet sherry.

Fruit Desserts

F RUITS—fresh, frozen, or canned, raw or cooked, plain or fancy —are a welcome treat any season of the year.

For a light refreshing dessert after a heavy meal (and for those of you who are low-calorie conscious), fruits are a popular choice. As a homemaker you can easily display your skill by transforming the simple fruit into a glamorous dish. Defrost frozen fruits only about halfway. If they are completely defrosted then they will become soft and flabby and lose some of their flavor. If peeled fresh fruits are to be used, wait until the last minute before peeling. Otherwise, they will become spotted and discolored. If you must pare ahead of time, sprinkle lemon juice over the fruit to keep it fresh looking.

A good rule of thumb in buying fruits is to look first at those that are in season. Produce in season tastes better because it is fresher. It is also less expensive at that time. But do not buy the cheapest fruit on the market just because it is the cheapest. Fruit in this category usually turns out to be an expensive bargain. Freshness is your best buy.

ᏬApple Sauce

The House by the Road, Ashburn, Georgia

Ingredients

8 medium apples, tart	1 teaspoon butter
¼ cup water	1 teaspoon nutmeg
½ cup sugar	1 dozen marshmallows

Directions (Serves 8)

Peel, core, and cut apples in large pieces. Cook and drain and put in bowl.

Add sugar, butter, and nutmeg to apples.

Put apples in baking dish and cover with marshmallows. Stick in oven until brown.

ᏬArabian Nights Baked Apples

Charles H. Baker Jr., Coconut Grove, Florida

Ingredients

8 large red tart apples	½ cup finely chopped figs
¾ cup brown sugar	¼ teaspoon cloves
Red color	½ teaspoon cinnamon
Large piece of orange peel	2 teaspoons Jamaica rum
½ cup finely chopped dates	Brown sugar

Directions (Serves 8)

Core apples and remove peeling down ¼ way from stem end. Place in kettle on rack and add ¾ cup hot water. Stuff cavities with sugar, and color the peeled part with a drop or two of red color. Put orange peel in water; put on lid and cook slowly until tender. Remove and let cool.

Mix dates, figs, cloves, cinnamon, and rum well together. Stuff cavities of apples; place in greased baking dish. Dust heavily with brown sugar that has been mixed with cinnamon and cloves. Brown in 375° oven until sugar caramelizes.

ᕫ *Baked Apple Sunshine*

Ingredients

12 red cooking apples
1 (8 oz.) package dry mincemeat
1 ½ cups sugar
2 cups water
½ cup sugar

1 ½ cups orange juice
Little grated orange rind
   (cranberry juice or lemon juice
   is also good)

Directions (Serves 12)

Wash and core apples. Peel halfway down from top. Cut mincemeat
   into 12 equal portions or blocks. Fill centers with mincemeat.
   Place in baking pan.
Mix together 1 ½ cups sugar and 2 cups water, and boil for 5 minutes.
   Pour over apples and bake in 400° oven for 45 minutes, basting
   occasionally with this liquid.
Sprinkle ½ cup sugar over apples and glaze quickly under broiler.
   Lift into serving dishes.
Drain juice from apples, add orange juice and rind, and boil 10
   minutes. Pour over apples, chill, and serve with cream.

ᕫ *Cherries Jubilee*

Cameo Restaurant, Chicago, Illinois

Ingredients

1 pint fresh black cherries
1 pint water
¾ cup sugar
4 teaspoons sugar
1 lemon peel, whole

½ cup cherry syrup
6 oz. brandy
2 oz. Grand Marnier liqueur
6 (3 oz.) scoops of ice cream
6 slices of plain cake

Directions (Serves 6)

Put cherries, water, and ¾ cup sugar into covered pot and cook
   slowly for 10 minutes. Canned black cherries may be used,
   provided they are whole, sweet, and have the pits in them. Drain
   the cherries from the syrup. Put cherries in a chafing dish.
Place 4 teaspoons sugar, lemon peel, and cherry syrup in chafing dish
   with cherries and bring to a boil.
Pour brandy and liqueur over cherries and set aflame.

Put cake in individual dishes, cover with ice cream, and pour blazing cherries over all. Serve immediately.

⟐ *This dish was created for the Jubilee of Queen Victoria of England.*

∾ Killarney Cherries

Ingredients

1 lb. ox-heart or Bing cherries
1 pint claret
1 cup sugar
1 stick cinnamon bark
12 whole cloves

2 tablespoons red currant jelly
3 tablespoons cherry brandy
1 ½ cups whipped cream
1 tablespoon Kirschwasser
1 tablespoon sugar

Directions (Serves 6)

Let first five ingredients come to boil, cover, and then reduce heat and simmer 12 to 15 minutes. Drain the cherries and chill. Cook juice until it reduces to about ⅓ to make the sauce.

Add jelly to sauce, melt, and chill.

Put brandy in sauce just before serving.

Serve cherries in silver dishes, set in bed of ice. Pour sauce over cherries and top with whipped cream, combined with Kirschwasser and 1 tablespoon of sugar. Should be very cold.

∾ Grapefruit Burgundy

Ingredients

1 cup fruit juice
½ cup sugar

¼ cup wine (either red or white)
6 grapefruit halves

Directions (Serves 6)

Simmer fruit juice and sugar until it becomes of medium thickness.

After syrup has cooled, add the wine.

Cover top half of grapefruit with syrup and decorate with half cherry or mint leaves.

ᴥ *Peaches Supreme*

Ingredients

8 to 10 peaches, halved
1 vanilla bean
½ cup sugar

½ cup water
1 quart raspberries, fresh

Directions (Serves 8 to 10)

Cook first four ingredients just enough to tenderize peaches. Set
   aside to chill.

Mash raspberries into a puree. Chill.

ᴥ *Peaches Flambée Royale*

Ingredients

4 peaches
1 pint cold water
½ cup sugar
¼ stick cinnamon
1 lemon peel, whole
½ cup strawberries or
   raspberries, crushed

½ cup syrup (that the peaches
   were cooked in)
4 oz. brandy
2 oz. of curaçao
3 or 4 small pieces of orange peel
4 scoops of vanilla ice cream

Directions (Serves 4)

Cook peaches with skins on in mixture of cold water, sugar,
   cinnamon and lemon peel. Let water come to boiling point and
   boil for 15 minutes, keeping the pot covered all the time. Take out
   the peaches, skin, cut them in half, and remove pits. Place them in
   a chafing dish.

Put berries and syrup in chafing dish with the peaches and let get hot.

Add brandy, curaçao, and orange peel to the above, and set aflame.

Put ice cream in individual dishes and pour the flaming ingredients
   over all.

ᕽ Black Currant Mousse

Ingredients

1 cup black currant jam or fresh
currants
½ cup powdered sugar
2 cups whipping cream, whipped
1 teaspoon vanilla

2 tablespoons Cassis liqueur
1 pint whipping cream, whipped
3 tablespoons currant jam
½ lb. almonds, chopped

Directions (Serves 4 to 6)

Put jam or fresh currants through a strainer or colander. Combine
with powdered sugar.

Fold 2 cups whipped cream and vanilla into mixture and freeze in
refrigerator trays for 2 hours.

Just before serving, blend Cassis liqueur, 1 pint whipped cream, and
currant jam. Put the mousse on a platter and cover with brandy
mixture. Put peaches on top and all around and pour puree over
all.

Top with nuts. Serve at once and have all mixtures ice cold.

ᕽ Pineapple Delight

Mrs. Wallace Rigby, Larchmont, New York

Ingredients

1 large ripe pineapple
1 pint fresh strawberries

1 large banana
½ cup crème de menthe

Directions (Serves 6)

Cut off the top of the pineapple, retaining the top to use as a lid.
Scoop out the meat of the pineapple, leaving only the rind with a
thin inside layer of pineapple.

Cut the scooped-out fruit into small cubes. Put into a bowl with the
strawberries, which have been capped and washed. Chill. Just
before serving, quarter the banana lengthwise and cube. Mix with
other fruits and put all the fruit into the pineapple shell. Pour the
crème de menthe over the fruit in the shell. Replace top. Serve
from the pineapple into dessert dishes. (Pineapple and strawberries may be sprinkled with sugar before chilling if desired.)

❧ Brandied Grapefruit

Waldorf-Astoria, New York City

Ingredients

6 grapefruit halves

12 tablespoons light brown sugar

6 tablespoons brandy

Directions (Serves 6)

Remove core and seeds from grapefruits.

Spread 2 tablespoons of light brown sugar on top of each grapefruit half.

Pour 1 tablespoon of brandy over each half and allow to marinate for ½ hour. Bake in oven at 325° until hot and bubbling. Serve very hot.

❧ Golden Grapefruit

Old Spinning Wheel Tea Room, Hinsdale, Illinois

Ingredients

½ grapefruit

1 tablespoon brown sugar

1 tablespoon sherry

Directions (Serves 1)

Core grapefruit and fill center with sugar and wine. Heat in 350° oven until sugar is melted. Repeat for as many servings as desired.

❧ Fried Peaches

Fred Waring, New York City

Ingredients

1 tablespoon butter

6 to 8 peaches, peeled

1 cup brown sugar

½ cup cream

Directions (Serves 6 to 8)

Place butter in frying pan and let melt.

Place whole peaches in pan.

Put brown sugar over peaches and let simmer for 30 minutes. Keep turning the peaches.

Just before serving, pour cream over peaches and let it boil up. Serve hot.

‿ Baked Pineapple Hawaiian

Charles H. Baker Jr., Coconut Grove, Florida

Ingredients

1 large pineapple
½ cup sugar
4 tablespoons cognac

1 teaspoon cinnamon
1 tablespoon brandy

Directions (Serves 6 to 8)

Cut off the pineapple top down the fruit 1 ½ inches. Reserve this
for use later. Cut out the heart with a curved grapefruit knife, but
do not dig through the shell. Dice the fruit, discarding the pithy
center.

Coat the fruit with sugar and put back in the shell. Add the juice of
the pineapple.

Pour the cognac over the fruit.

Dust the fruit with cinnamon. Put the top back on and skewer in
place. Bake in 350° oven 30 to 40 minutes until the fruit is tender.
Remove top and serve on a silver platter.

Light brandy and bring to the table blazing.

‿ Pineapple Flambée à la Marie

Arnaud's Restaurant, New Orleans, Louisiana

Ingredients

1 fresh pineapple, sliced ½-inch
thick
Flour
Milk

Cherries
Sugar
Cognac
Sherry wine

Directions (Serves 6)

Roll sliced pineapple in flour; then dip in milk; then roll in flour
again. Fry pineapple in oil or shortening until golden brown. Place
cherry in center of pineapple and cover freely with sugar. Bake in
oven 5 minutes or until sugar is bubbly and golden brown; pour
cognac over it. Heat until cognac is warm. Light with match; then
serve, and add sherry wine.

∾ Strawberries Biltmore

Biltmore Hotel, Los Angeles, California

Ingredients

1 quart strawberries

Rum, enough to cover berries

¼ lb. powdered sugar

Directions (Serves 4 to 6)

Stem and wash berries thoroughly. Drain. Place on napkin to further drain off water.

Add rum and sugar to berries and let stand for 2 hours before serving. Not too long, however, as the berries will become soggy. Drain. Add sauce and serve very cold.

Sauce

Ingredients

1 pint vanilla ice cream

2 oz. Kirschwasser

1 cup whipping cream, whipped

½ cup sugar

Directions

Mix ice cream and Kirschwasser, and stir well.

Fold whipped cream and sugar into the above mixture and chill. Serve over the strawberries in glass compote.

∾ Strawberry Lindomar

Ingredients

15 marshmallows

½ pint crushed strawberries

1 cup cream

½ pint sliced strawberries

2 oz. sauterne

Directions (Serves 8 to 10)

Quarter marshmallows and melt in double boiler with the crushed strawberries. Cool.

Whip cream and combine with above mixture. Put in refrigerator tray and let freeze.

Pour sauterne over sliced strawberries. Just before serving put over frozen mixture as a sundae.

ᕽ Ambrosia

Ingredients

3 oranges, peeled
2 bananas

½ cup grated coconut
4 maraschino cherries

Directions (Serves 4)

Section oranges and slice bananas in rounds. Chill together for
1 hour.

Serve in chilled sherbet glasses topped with coconut and a maraschino cherry.

ᕽ Strawberries à la Tsarina

Charles H. Baker Jr., Coconut Grove, Florida

Ingredients

2 cups stemmed strawberries
2 tablespoons powdered sugar
2 tablespoons port wine
2 tablespoons orange curaçao

2 tablespoons cognac
1 teaspoon curaçao
1 cup whipped cream

Directions (Serves 2)

Toss strawberries and sugar and put in bowl. Chill.

Blend port wine, 2 tablespoons curaçao, and cognac, and pour over
berries.

Add remaining curaçao to whipped cream. Place berries in individual dishes, cover with whipped cream, and serve.

ᕽ Strawberry Fruit Cup

The Birches on Moosehead Lake, Rockwood, Maine

Ingredients

1 pint strawberries
3 large oranges, peeled
2 cups fresh squeezed orange
juice

½ cup grated fresh coconut
2 bananas
Light honey

Directions (Serves 4 to 6)

Wash strawberries before capping. Cut berries in half. Put into large
bowl.

Slice oranges with sharp knife; then dice.

Add juice to other ingredients in bowl.

Add grated coconut.

Slice bananas round, not too thin. Put immediately into bowl.

Sweeten with honey to taste. Chill until icy cold. Serve in cold
sherbet glasses.

ᕦ Raspberry Royal

Royal Savage Inn, Plattsburg, New York

Ingredients

1 pint fresh raspberries or 1 box
frozen raspberries, defrosted
and drained

12 graham crackers, crushed
½ pint whipped cream

Directions (Serves 4)

In sherbet glasses, alternate whipped cream, raspberries, crushed
graham crackers. Repeat this twice. Place whipped cream on top.
Serve at once. (Blackberries are equally good.)

ᕦ Pineapple Trifle

Ingredients

1 cup canned crushed pineapple,
drained
10 marshmallows, cut

1 cup macaroon crumbs
1 cup chopped dates
¾ cup heavy cream, whipped

Directions (Serves 6 to 8)

Combine first four ingredients in bowl.

Fold whipped cream into above ingredients. Chill.

ᕦ Fresh Fruit Trifle

Ingredients

24 almond macaroons
¾ cup sherry wine
6 egg yolks, beaten
1 cup sugar

⅛ teaspoon salt
Any fresh fruit, or whipped
cream and almonds

Directions (Serves 8)

Dip macaroons in wine and place in a flat serving dish.

Beat eggs 5 minutes in electric mixer or with rotary beater for 15 minutes, adding sugar and beating a little longer. Add the balance of sherry and salt. Place in double boiler and cook until it thickens, stirring constantly. Pour this mixture over the macaroons and allow to cool.

Just before serving, cover with fresh sliced peaches, figs, or strawberries. Or cover with whipped cream and blanched almonds.

⟳ Cherry-Nut Trifle

Use recipe for Pineapple Trifle, substituting ⅔ cup maraschino cherries, cut in pieces, for the pineapple. Substitute 1 cup chopped nuts for the macaroons.

⟳ Macédoine of Fruits

Waldorf-Astoria, New York City

Ingredients

Take some fresh fruit of the season (bananas, pineapple, orange, grapefruit)

Directions

Peel and slice fruit. Mix together and set bowl on ice. Add some syrup (Kirsch or maraschino) and let them macerate for two hours.

⟳ The Wonder Dessert

O. B. Wright, Long Beach, California

Ingredients

1 cup oranges

1 cup walnuts

1 cup fresh marshmallows

¼ cup sugar

1 pint whipping cream, whipped

¼ teaspoon vanilla

Directions (Serves 5)

Cut oranges in small pieces and squeeze out some of the juice. This is important, or the dessert will be soft and run.

Break walnuts in pieces, not too small.

Cut marshmallows with scissors and add sugar to prevent them from sticking together.

If possible whip cream with an electric whipper to make stiff. Add vanilla and mix in other ingredients. Serve in fruit cup, piled high. Will keep for a few hours in refrigerator but is better if served at once.

⌒ *Hedelmakeitto (Cold Fruit Soup)*

Ingredients

½ lb. prunes

½ lb. apricots and pears (dried)

½ cup sugar

3 fresh apples, cored and sliced ⅛-inch thick

1 cinnamon bark

1 to 2 tablespoons potato starch

Directions (Serves 6)

Wash dried fruit in warm water and let soak overnight with the sugar added to 1 ½ quarts water.

Add apples to the above and boil. Strain.

Mix cinnamon bark and starch with 1 ½ tablespoons of cold water and thicken the fruit juice. Boil again for a few minutes and add the fruit. Serve cold.

Cheese Desserts

ONE of the most romantic of all foods is cheese. No man can say how long cheese has been a staple food of mankind, but we can safely assume that people have been eating cheese for at least 2,000 years.

There is a legend about the first cheese. According to the tale, an ancient Arabian trader poured milk into his sheepskin canteen before starting out on a long journey. All day the bag swung and jostled at his saddle-bows. At night when he stopped to make camp and to eat, he opened the bag of milk and found that it had become a curious mass of white curd. The action of certain enzymes under ideal conditions had curdled the milk, and the world had its first cheese.

The ancient Greeks believed that cheese was of divine origin and offered it as a fitting sacrifice to the gods on Mount Olympus. The Bible tells us that the boy David carried ten cheeses to his captain.

We also know that cheese was used as money by the nomads of Asia centuries ago. During the Crusades, when Christian knights fought the Mohammedans, cheese was regarded as a desirable booty of war, and when captured was divided like jewelry and other valuable spoils.

But cheese is as American as any food on our tables. It can boast of a wonderful ancestry. It came over on the *Mayflower* along with some of our first citizens. The first cheese factory in the United States was built in 1851 in Rome, New York, where today a bronze plaque stands on the site to commemorate this important event.

Today, cheese is an important part of our meals, and the American housewife can choose from literally hundreds of different kinds. The cheese dessert may range from cream cheese on crackers to the elegant cheese cake, but whatever the choice, serving cheese will surely enhance your reputation as a hostess.

For the unexpected guests here are a few suggestions for a quick, last-minute cheese dessert:

A cheese and cracker tray consisting of crackers and an assortment of cheeses, served along with a large bowl of fresh polished fruit. Serving can be simple: individual dessert plates and knives for cutting the fruit and for spreading or slicing the cheese. Finger bowls are appropriate to save your linen napkins from fruit stains.

A tray of lightly toasted flaky crackers spread with cream cheese and a choice of preserves or jams (currant, guava, elderberry, or cranberry) and a bowl of salted nuts also makes a delightful "passing" tray.

Use your imagination and serve any combination you desire.

Another "quicky" cheese dessert is to sieve 1 cup cottage cheese and thin to desired consistency with milk or cream. Sweeten to taste with sugar and vanilla. Place in bowl and sprinkle with cinnamon. Chill. Serve with crushed sweetened strawberries, raspberries, peaches, or any fresh fruit in season.

ᴄ᷎ Pineapple Cheese Pudding

The Clark Restaurant Company, Test Kitchen,
Cleveland, Ohio

Ingredients

1 No. 2 can pineapple, crushed
2 tablespoons cornstarch
¼ cup water
1 cup creamy cottage cheese
1 cup granulated sugar

¼ cup butter, softened
½ cup cake flour, unsifted
2 eggs
¾ cup milk
1 teaspoon vanilla

Directions (Serves 8)

Heat pineapple in pan over direct heat. Dissolve cornstarch in a little
cold water and add to pineapple. Cook until clear. Spread evenly in
bottom of 10-inch Pyrex pie plate and set aside to cool.

Mix cottage cheese and sugar together.

Add butter to the above and mix.

Add cake flour to butter–cottage cheese mixture and blend well.

Add eggs, one at a time, and mix well after each addition.

Mix milk and vanilla together and slowly add to the batter. Pour
batter over pineapple and bake in 450° oven for 10 minutes. Then
turn oven down to 350° and bake for 30 minutes or until silver
knife inserted in center comes out clean. Serve cold.

Note: All ingredients for this pudding should be at room temperature before using.

➤ *For the lunch box or picnic, cheese cake makes an excellent
dessert. It is filling and not messy to eat.*

ᴄ᷎ Strawberries and Cottage Cheese

Ingredients

Strawberries
Sugar

Cottage cheese

Directions

Wash strawberries and remove stems. Place into individual serving
dishes and sprinkle with sugar. Serve with cottage cheese.

∾ Cottage Cheese Currant Jelly Whip

Ingredients

3 egg whites
¼ cup sugar
Pinch of salt

½ cup currant jelly
1 cup cottage cheese

Directions (Serves 4 to 5)

Beat egg whites until foamy. Add sugar gradually and salt; continue
  beating until stiff.

Combine jelly and cottage cheese, and fold into above. Serve with
  Plain Custard Sauce (*see* Dessert Sauces section), if desired.

∾ Cottage Cheese Parfait

Ingredients

1 cup cottage cheese
1 egg white
2 tablespoons sugar
½ teaspoon salt
1 cup heavy cream

½ teaspoon almond extract
1 box frozen strawberries,
  defrosted, or fresh strawberries, crushed and
  sweetened

Directions (Serves 6)

Beat cottage cheese until smooth.

Combine egg white, sugar, and salt, and beat until stiff. Fold into
  cottage cheese.

Whip cream, adding extract. Fold into mixture.

Alternate spoonfuls of cottage cheese mixture and fruit into individual serving dishes.

∾ Fromage à la Crème

Ingredients

1 cup heavy cream
3 (3 oz.) packages cream cheese
2 tablespoons heavy cream

1 box frozen strawberries,
  defrosted, or sweetened fresh
  strawberries, crushed

Directions (Serves 3 to 4)

Beat 1 cup cream until stiff.

Combine cream cheese and 2 tablespoons cream, and beat until soft.

Fold into above whipped cream. Pour into individual molds and chill.

Unmold and serve with strawberries over the top.

∿ Molded Cream Cheese with Fruit

Ingredients

2 (3 oz.) packages cream cheese
1 tablespoon confectioners' sugar
1 tablespoon milk

1 box frozen strawberries or raspberries, defrosted, or crushed, sweetened, fresh strawberries or raspberries

Directions (Serves 4)

Beat cheese until smooth. Add sugar and blend. Thin to a smooth consistency with milk. Pour into individual molds and chill.

Unmold and serve with fruit over the top.

➥ *A simple cheese and fruit dessert is wonderful for those watching their "spread."*

∿ Pear à la Fromage

Ingredients

Fresh pears
Cottage cheese

Sugar
Cinnamon

Directions

Pare pears and slice thinly.

Sweeten cottage cheese with sugar and cinnamon. Serve over the pears.

⌒ Cheese Cakes ⌒

CHEESE CAKES, one of my favorite desserts, are a superlative ending to any light meal. In the following section I have chosen some of my best-liked cheese cake recipes. The ingredients in all are very much alike, but with some slight changes a different cake results.

In general, there are two kinds—baked cheese cakes and refrigerator cheese cakes. Refrigerator cheese cakes are made with gelatin and require no baking because when the mixture is chilled it becomes firm. Cheese cakes are made with cottage cheese or cream cheese or both kinds of cheese. They are made in various shapes, sizes, flavors, and textures depending upon the recipe.

Contrary to the opinion of most people, cheese cake is easy to make. It is deluxe and "gourmet," yet it can be made in your own kitchen with little trouble and not have to be bought at the neighborhood pastry shop. By following one of my recipes you will surprise yourself with perfect results—and how easy!

⌒ Lindy's Cheese Cake

Lindy's, New York City

Ingredients

1 cup sifted flour
½ cup sugar
1 teaspoon grated lemon rind
1 egg yolk
¼ cup butter, melted
¼ teaspoon vanilla
2 ½ lbs. cream cheese
1 ¾ cups sugar

3 tablespoons flour
1 ½ teaspoons grated orange rind
1 ½ teaspoons grated lemon rind
¼ teaspoon vanilla
5 eggs
2 egg yolks
¼ cup heavy cream

Directions (Serves 10 to 12)

Combine dry ingredients, including lemon rind, in bowl. Make a well in center.

Add egg, butter, and vanilla; work together quickly until well blended. Add a little cold water if necessary to make hold together. Wrap in waxed paper and chill thoroughly in refrigerator for about 1 hour.

Roll out ⅛-inch thick and place over greased bottom of 9-inch springform pan.

Trim off extra dough. Bake in hot oven at 400° for 15 to 20 minutes or until a light gold color. Cool. Butter sides of pan and place over base. Roll remaining dough ⅛-inch thick and line sides of pan. Fill with following mixture.

Put cheese in electric mixer and beat at second speed. Add 1 ¾ cups sugar gradually, then remainder of ingredients in order given. Eggs should be added one at a time. When thoroughly blended and smooth, pour into lined pan, place in oven preheated to 550°, and bake from 12 to 15 minutes. Reduce heat to 200° and continue baking for 1 hour. Cool before cutting.

ᴖ Cheese Cake

Hody's, Los Angeles, California

Ingredients

¼ lb. graham crackers	3 eggs
2 tablespoons sugar	½ teaspoon vanilla
1 ½ teaspoons cinnamon	1 pint sour cream
6 tablespoons melted butter	3 tablespoons sugar
1 ½ lbs. cream cheese	½ teaspoon vanilla
1 cup sugar	

Directions (Serves 6 to 8 people)

Roll crackers very fine. Add sugar, cinnamon, and butter, mixing well. Line 10-inch springform pan.

Place cheese in electric beater and beat well. Add 1 cup sugar gradually and then eggs one at a time. Add vanilla last. Pour into pan and bake 20 minutes at 375°.

Whip sour cream lightly; add remaining sugar and vanilla. Pour carefully over baked pie. Bake in 500° oven for 5 minutes. Cool and place in refrigerator.

❧ Refrigerator Cheese Cake

Ingredients

½ cup graham cracker crumbs
1 package lemon-flavored gelatin
½ cup sugar
1 ¼ cups boiling water
2 egg yolks, slightly beaten

¼ cup concentrate lemonade
½ cup heavy cream
12 oz. cream cheese
2 egg whites

Directions (Serves 8 to 9)

Reserve ¼ cup crumbs. Sprinkle remaining crumbs into bottom of a 1 ½-quart greased springform pan.

Dissolve gelatin and sugar in boiling water. Add gradually to egg yolks. Add lemonade and cream.

Beat cream cheese until smooth. Add gelatin mixture. Chill until slightly thickened.

Beat egg whites until stiff. Fold into slightly thickened gelatin mixture. Pour into pan. Sprinkle with remaining crumbs. Chill until firm (about 2 hours). To serve, loosen sides carefully with spatula and remove from pan.

❧ Cottage Cheese Cake

Ingredients

1 ¾ cups zwieback pieces, finely crushed
½ cup butter, melted
½ cup sugar
24 oz. cottage cheese
4 eggs

1 cup sugar
½ cup heavy cream
½ teaspoon salt
¼ cup flour
2 tablespoons lemon juice
2 teaspoons grated lemon rind

Directions (Serves 12)

Combine zwieback pieces, butter, and sugar. Reserve ½ cup of the mixture. Press remaining crumbs with fingers (or use bottom of cup) into the bottom and sides of a greased 9-inch springform pan.

Sieve the cottage cheese.

Beat eggs. Add 1 cup sugar gradually and beat until thick and creamy. Add remaining ingredients and cottage cheese. Beat well. Turn into pan and sprinkle with remaining crumbs. Bake in slow oven at 325° for 1 hour. Turn off heat and leave in oven 1 hour longer. Cool and chill 5 to 6 hours or overnight.

❧ Creamy Cottage Cheese Cake

Ingredients

12 zwieback pieces, finely
crushed
2 tablespoons sugar
¼ cup butter, melted
24 oz. cottage cheese
2 eggs

⅔ cup sugar
⅛ teaspoon salt
1 teaspoon vanilla
½ pint sour cream
¼ cup sugar
2 teaspoons vanilla

Directions (Serves 10)

Combine zwieback pieces, 2 tablespoons of sugar, and butter. Press
mixture with fingers into the bottom and sides of loose-bottom
9-inch cake pan. Chill.

Beat cottage cheese in blender at high speed until consistency of very
heavy cream (about 3 minutes). Add eggs, ⅔ cup sugar, salt, and
1 teaspoon vanilla, and beat at high speed for about 5 minutes.
Pour mixture into prepared pan and bake in moderate oven at 350°
for 30 minutes.

Mix sour cream, ¼ cup sugar, and vanilla well. Spread carefully over
cheese cake. Return to oven and bake 8 to 10 minutes. (Topping
does not brown.) Cool and chill.

❧ Graham Cracker Cheese Pie

Pals Cabin, West Orange, New Jersey

Ingredients

1 lb. cream cheese
1 lb. cottage cheese
1 pint sour cream
1 lemon, rind and juice
Vanilla flavor
Salt to taste

5 egg yolks
1 cup sugar
20 graham crackers, finely
crushed
½ cup butter, melted

Directions (Makes two 9-inch pies)

Cream cottage cheese, sour cream, and cream cheese.

Add lemon, vanilla, and salt to cheese mixture. Beat yolks and sugar
well, and fold together with cheese mixture.

Line pie tins with crushed graham crackers mixed with melted
butter. Pour in cheese mixture. Bake in 375° oven for 30 minutes.
Chill in refrigerator before cutting.

᷎ Fort Hayes Cheese Cake

Hotel Fort Hayes, Columbus, Ohio

Ingredients

¼ lb. butter, melted	¼ cup sugar
24 graham crackers	¼ cup milk
1 lb. cottage cheese	1 envelope (1 tablespoon)
¼ cup sugar	unflavored gelatin
½ teaspoon vanilla	¼ cup cold water
Juice and rind of 1 lemon	½ pint cream
2 egg yolks	2 egg whites
½ teaspoon salt	½ cup graham cracker crumbs

Directions (Makes 1 springform cake pan)

Combine butter with 24 graham crackers that have been crushed fine and line springform cake pan. (Hold back ½ cup cracker crumbs for top of cake.) Bake 10 to 15 minutes.

Mash cottage cheese through strainer and combine with ¼ cup sugar, vanilla, grated rind, and lemon juice.

Combine egg yolks, salt, ¼ cup sugar, and milk, and make a cooked custard.

Soak gelatin in cold water. Beat into custard while still hot. Cool custard.

Beat cream and egg whites together and fold into above mixture.

Pour above mixture into baked springform. Sprinkle remaining crumbs on top and leave in refrigerator overnight.

᷎ *Pie without cheese is like a kiss without a squeeze! Cheese with pie is not new, but you may be surprised to find how good it tastes with fresh peaches, apples, or other fruit.*

᷎ Pennsylvania Dutch Cheese Pie

Hotel Brunswick, Lancaster, Pennsylvania

Ingredients

4 eggs	Pinch of salt
½ lb. cottage cheese	A little lemon and vanilla
½ lb. sugar	flavoring
1 tablespoon flour	1 10-inch unbaked pie shell

Directions (Makes one 10-inch pie)

Separate egg yolks and whites.

Press cottage cheese through a sieve.

Cream together the cottage cheese, sugar, egg yolks, flour, salt, and flavoring. Beat the egg whites until stiff and fold into mixture.

Bake in unbaked pie shell in 400° oven for 25–30 minutes.

➥ *Cheese cake is best the second day because it mellows in flavor.*

Gelatin Desserts

THE PURPOSE of gelatin is to set up colorful and deliciously flavored mixtures so that they can be molded into attractive shapes. Gelatin is the base for those familiar sponge, jelly, whip, cream, and other refrigerator desserts. These desserts will lend sparkle and color to your meals.

In the early days women made their own gelatin by following a long and tedious recipe. Today both flavored and unflavored gelatins are available for quick and easy use.

To be good, a gelatin dessert should be firm without being too stiff. The flavors used should blend well with the other ingredients (and even with the meal itself) to furnish just the right "finishing touch."

Gelatin desserts also offer the hostess an opportunity for a special holiday touch. A bright green lime flavor is appropriate for St. Patrick's Day, something in cherry flavor for Father Washington's Birthday, or an orange flavor for Halloween. Possibilities for creative adventures are unlimited.

Above all do not get into a "flavor rut." If you use a variety of flavors, different recipes, and some of your own ideas then your family will never tire of a gelatin treat for dessert.

∼ Bavarian Cream

Ingredients

1 envelope (1 tablespoon) unflavored gelatin	¼ teaspoon salt
2 tablespoons cold water	2 egg yolks, slightly beaten
1⅓ cups milk	2 egg whites, stiffly beaten
½ cup sugar	1 cup heavy cream, whipped
	1 teaspoon vanilla

Directions (Serves 6)

Soak gelatin in cold water about 5 minutes.

Scald milk in top of double boiler. Add sugar, salt, and gelatin to the scalded milk. Stir until dissolved.

Stir a little of the hot milk mixture into the egg yolks; then stir into the remaining hot milk. Cook over hot water until slightly thickened, stirring constantly. Chill until almost set.

Fold egg whites, heavy cream, and vanilla into the above mixture. Pour into individual molds and chill until firm.

∼ Berry Bavarian Cream

Ingredients

1 package raspberry or strawberry-flavored gelatin	1 cup crushed raspberries or strawberries
1 cup boiling water	½ cup heavy cream, whipped
¼ cup sugar	

Directions (Serves 10 to 12)

Pour boiling water over gelatin and stir until dissolved.

Sprinkle sugar over fruit in bowl and let stand 20 minutes. Drain off juice into cup and add water to make 1 cup. Reserve fruit. Add juice to dissolved gelatin mixture. Chill until slightly thickened. Set the bowl of slightly thickened gelatin mixture in a larger bowl partly filled with ice and water. Whip gelatin mixture with a rotary egg beater or at a high speed of electric mixer until thick and fluffy, like whipped cream.

Fold fruit and whipped cream into the gelatin mixture. Pour into serving dish or individual molds. Chill until firm. Garnish with whole berries.

♠ *To hasten the thickening of a gelatin mixture, place the bowl of gelatin mixture in a larger bowl filled with ice and water. (It is best to use metal bowls.) Stir occasionally to prevent a stiff layer forming on the bottom.*

∿ Coconut Bavarian Cream

Ingredients

1 pint coffee cream	Pinch of salt
2 envelopes (2 tablespoons) unflavored gelatin	1 teaspoon almond flavor
	2 cups shredded coconut
1 cup sugar	1 ½ pints whipped cream

Directions (Serves 8)

Let coffee cream come to a boil.

Dissolve gelatin in small amount of cold water. Add sugar, salt, and gelatin to cream and let cool.

Add almond flavor, coconut, and whipped cream to above and chill in ring mold. When ready to serve, turn out on platter; top with more shredded coconut and serve with Caramel Sauce.

Caramel Sauce

Ingredients

1 tablespoon butter	2 egg yolks
1 lb. brown sugar	Pinch of salt
1 cup coffee cream	1 teaspoon vanilla

Directions

Combine butter and sugar in double boiler. Add beaten egg yolks, cream, and salt.

When smooth and thick, let cool. Add vanilla.

∿ Grenadine Bavarian Cream

Ingredients

1 envelope (1 tablespoon) unflavored gelatin	⅓ cup sugar
	¼ teaspoon salt
¼ cup cold milk	4 egg yolks, slightly beaten
1 ½ cups light cream	1 to 2 tablespoons Jamaica rum
1 cup milk	Grenadine syrup

Directions (Serves 6)

Soak gelatin in ¼ cup cold milk about 5 minutes.

Scald milk in top of double boiler. Add light cream, 1 cup milk, sugar, salt, and gelatin. Stir until all is dissolved.

Stir a little of the above mixture into the eggs. Stir into remaining hot milk mixture. Cook over hot water, stirring constantly, until mixture coats a metal spoon. Remove from heat.

Stir rum into the above mixture. Pour into serving dish and chill until firm.

Serve with grenadine syrup.

ᑌ Strawberry Bavarian Cream

Ingredients

1 envelope (1 tablespoon) unflavored gelatin	1 tablespoon lemon juice
2 tablespoons cold water	½ cup sugar
1½ cups crushed strawberries	Pinch of salt
	1 cup heavy cream, whipped

Directions (Serves 6)

Soak gelatin in cold water about 5 minutes. Place over boiling water and stir until dissolved.

Add strawberries, lemon juice, and sugar to the above mixture and stir until blended. Chill until almost set.

Fold salt and whipped cream into the gelatin mixture. Pour into mold and chill until firm. Serve plain or with whipped cream and top with fresh berries, if desired.

ᑌ Chocolate Marshmallow Cream

Ingredients

1 envelope (1 tablespoon) unflavored gelatin	1 square unsweetened chocolate
¼ cup milk	¼ lb. marshmallows, quartered
2 cups milk	¼ cup finely chopped walnuts
½ cup sugar	2 egg whites, stiffly beaten
	1 cup heavy cream, whipped

Directions (Serves 8)

Soak gelatin in ¼ cup milk about 5 minutes.

Combine 2 cups milk, sugar, and chocolate in saucepan. Cook and stir over low heat until mixture just comes to a boil. Beat with

rotary egg beater. Remove from fire. Add above gelatin mixture
and beat until smooth. Chill until slightly thickened.

Stir marshmallows and nuts into the above mixture.

Fold in egg whites and whipped cream. Pour into sherbet glasses.
Chill until firm.

∾ *Maple Cream*

Ingredients

1 envelope (1 tablespoon) unflavored gelatin	3 egg yolks, slightly beaten
2 tablespoons cold water	⅔ cup maple syrup
2½ cups milk	1 teaspoon vanilla
¼ teaspoon salt	3 egg whites, stiffly beaten

Directions (Serves 6)

Soak gelatin in cold water about 5 minutes.

Scald milk in top of double boiler. Add above gelatin mixture and salt
and stir until dissolved.

Stir a little of the above hot milk mixture into eggs. Stir this into
remaining hot milk mixture. Cook in double boiler until slightly
thickened, stirring constantly. Cool.

Stir maple syrup and vanilla slowly into the cooled custard mixture.

Fold in egg whites. Pour into mold or individual molds. Chill until
firm. Serve with whipped cream.

∾ *Rum Cream*

Ingredients

1 envelope (1 tablespoon) unflavored gelatin	2 egg yolks, slightly beaten
¼ cup cold milk	2 egg whites, stiffly beaten
1½ cups milk	1 teaspoon rum or vanilla extract
⅓ cup sugar	(1 to 2 tablespoons Jamaica
⅛ teaspoon salt	rum may be substituted)

Directions (Serves 6)

Soak gelatin in cold milk about 5 minutes.

Scald 1½ cups milk in top of double boiler. Add sugar and salt and
above gelatin mixture. Stir until dissolved.

Stir a little of the above hot milk mixture into eggs. Stir this into remaining hot milk. Cook in double boiler until slightly thickened, stirring constantly. Chill until almost set.

Fold egg whites and rum or vanilla into the above mixture. Pour into serving dish. Chill until firm. Serve with crushed fruit.

❧ Spanish Cream

Ingredients

½ cup sugar	2½ cups scalded milk
1 envelope (1 tablespoon) unflavored gelatin	3 egg yolks, slightly beaten
	1 teaspoon vanilla
Pinch of salt	3 egg whites, stiffly beaten

Directions (Serves 6 to 8)

Combine sugar, gelatin, and salt in top of double boiler. Mix well.

Add scalded milk to the above mixture. Cook directly over medium heat, stirring until gelatin dissolves. Remove from heat.

Slowly stir egg yolks into the hot milk mixture. Return to top of double boiler and cook over hot water until mixture coats a metal spoon. Remove from hot water.

Add vanilla to the above mixture.

Fold hot custard mixture very gradually into beaten egg whites. Pour into individual molds. Chill until firm. Serve with whipped cream.

❧ Macaroon Spanish Cream

(Serves 6 to 8)

Use recipe for Spanish Cream, folding in ¾ cup macaroon crumbs with the egg whites and vanilla.

❧ Chocolate Spanish Cream

(Serves 6 to 8)

Use recipe for Spanish Cream, adding 2 squares unsweetened, shaved chocolate to the milk before scalding. When chocolate is melted, beat with rotary egg beater until blended. Increase sugar to ¾ cup.

∾ Turkish Cream

Ingredients

1 envelope (1 tablespoon)
  unflavored gelatin
¼ cup hot dry sherry wine

1 pint heavy cream, whipped
3 tablespoons sugar
12 nut macaroons, crushed

Directions (Serves 8 to 10)

Pour hot sherry wine over gelatin and stir until dissolved.
Combine remaining ingredients. Add above gelatin mixture and
  mix well. Pour into sherbet glasses and chill. Serve with whipped
  cream.

∾ Festive Jellied Dessert

Ingredients

2 envelopes (2 tablespoons)
  unflavored gelatin
½ cup cold water
½ cup boiling water
¾ cup sugar
¼ teaspoon salt

½ cup orange juice
2 tablespoons lemon juice
1½ cups dry sherry
1 cup pitted dates, finely chopped
⅔ cup walnuts, broken

Directions (Serves 8)

Soak gelatin in cold water about 5 minutes.
Add boiling water, sugar, and salt to the above mixture. Stir until
  dissolved. Cool to room temperature.
Add orange juice, lemon juice, and sherry to gelatin mixture and stir.
  Chill until slightly thickened.
Fold dates and walnuts into gelatin mixture. Pour into mold and chill
  until firm. Unmold and serve with whipped cream on top.

∾ Coffee Rum Jelly

Ingredients

1 envelope (1 tablespoon)
  unflavored gelatin
½ cup cold water

1½ cups strong hot coffee
1 tablespoon Jamaica rum
¼ cup sugar

Directions (Serves 4)

Soak gelatin in cold water about 5 minutes. Add hot coffee and rum and stir until gelatin is dissolved. Add sugar and stir until well mixed and dissolved. Pour into serving dish. Chill until firm. Serve with sour cream on top, if desired.

➤ *Fresh pineapple and its juice must be scalded before using in gelatin; otherwise the gelatin will not thicken.*

∿ Strawberry Charlotte

(Serves 10)

Use recipe for Strawberry Bavarian Cream. Pour mixture into a 1½-quart mold that has been lined on the bottom and sides with about 2 dozen ladyfingers, split in half. Chill until firm.

∿ Charlotte Russe

Ingredients

2 envelopes (2 tablespoons) unflavored gelatin	4 egg yolks, slightly beaten
¼ cup cold water	4 egg whites, stiffly beaten
2 cups milk	1 pint heavy cream, whipped
½ cup sugar	1 teaspoon vanilla, or 1 table-
⅛ teaspoon salt	spoon brandy
	Ladyfingers—split

Directions (Serves 10 to 12)

Soak gelatin in cold water about 5 minutes.

Scald milk in top of double boiler. Add sugar, salt, and above gelatin. Stir until all is dissolved.

Stir a little of the hot milk mixture into egg yolks. Then stir this into remaining hot milk. Cook in double boiler until slightly thickened, stirring constantly. Chill until almost set.

Fold in beaten egg whites, whipped cream, and flavoring.

Line mold with ladyfingers. Turn in gelatin mixture. Chill until firm. Serve with whipped cream on top.

ᴄᴡ Fruit Whip

Ingredients

1 package flavored gelatin
1 cup boiling water
1 cup cold water, or fruit juice
and water
2 egg whites

1 cup fruit, drained (crushed
strawberries, raspberries,
diced peaches, sliced bananas,
cherries, etc.)

Directions (Serves 8 to 10)

Pour boiling water over gelatin and stir until dissolved.

Add water or juice to the above mixture. Chill until slightly
thickened.

Add egg whites to gelatin mixture. Set the bowl of slightly thickened gelatin in a larger bowl partly filled with ice and water. Whip
gelatin mixture with rotary egg beater or at high speed of electric
mixer until fluffy and thick, like whipped cream.

Fold fruit into gelatin mixture. Pour into mold or individual serving
dishes. Chill until firm.

ᴄᴡ Fruited Lime Sour Cream Whip

Ingredients

1 package lime-flavored gelatin
1 cup hot water
¼ cup cold water
2 tablespoons lemon juice

1 cup sour cream
½ teaspoon salt
1½ cups drained, crushed
pineapple tidbits

Directions (Serves 4 to 6)

Dissolve gelatin in hot water. Add cold water and lemon juice and
blend well with rotary beater. Pour into refrigerator tray and chill
15 to 20 minutes or until firm about 1 inch from edge but soft in
center. Pour mixture into a bowl. Place in a larger bowl filled with
ice water. Whip above gelatin mixture with rotary beater until
fluffy.

Fold sour cream, salt, and pineapple into gelatin mixture. Pour into
1-quart mold or individual serving dishes and chill until firm.

ᖇᓈ *Lemon Fluff Dessert*

Ingredients

2 teaspoons unflavored gelatin	⅔ cup sugar
3 tablespoons cold water	4 egg whites
4 egg yolks	⅛ teaspoon salt
⅓ cup lemon juice	¼ cup sugar

Directions (Serves 4 to 6)

Soak gelatin in cold water, about 5 minutes.

Combine egg yolks and lemon juice in top of double boiler. Beat with rotary egg beater or with electric mixer until light in color.

Beat ⅔ cup sugar into above mixture gradually. Add gelatin. Continue beating over boiling water until mixture thickens. Cool.

Beat egg whites and salt together until foamy throughout the mixture. Add ¼ cup sugar gradually and continue beating until peaks are formed. Fold into custard. Pour into serving dish or sherbet glasses. Chill until firm.

ᖇᓈ *Bavarian Date Loaf*

Hotel Florence, Missoula, Montana

Ingredients

1 envelope (1 tablespoon) unflavored gelatin	Few grains salt
¼ cup cold water	5 drops vanilla
¼ cup boiling water	3 drops almond extract
4 eggs	½ pint whipping cream
3 tablespoons sugar	20 dates (remove pits)
	Sponge cake

Directions (Serves 4 to 6)

Soak gelatin in cold water and add boiling water to dissolve. Let get cold.

Beat eggs; add sugar, salt, and flavorings, and cook over boiling water until set. Remove and beat until cold.

Whip cream; mix with egg mixture; add gelatin and dates. Mix well.
Line loaf pan with slices of sponge cake; pour in the date mixture.
Place in refrigerator to set for 6 hours. Serve with whipped cream.

ᕲ Chocolate Sponge

Ingredients

2 envelopes (2 tablespoons) unflavored gelatin	1 cup sugar
	⅛ teaspoon salt
½ cup cold water	3 cups scalded milk
3 squares unsweetened chocolate	1 teaspoon vanilla
½ cup boiling water	2 egg whites, stiffly beaten

Directions (Serves 6)

Soak gelatin in cold water about 5 minutes.

Combine chocolate, boiling water, sugar, and salt in saucepan and bring to a boil. Cool slightly.

Add soaked gelatin to scalded milk and stir until dissolved. Then stir in chocolate mixture. Cool.

Fold in vanilla and egg whites. Pour into ring mold. Chill until firm. Unmold and fill center with whipped cream and garnish with chopped nuts.

ᕲ Lemon Bisque

Blosser's Restaurant, Logan, Ohio

Ingredients

1 package lemon-flavored gelatin	1 tablespoon lemon juice
2 cups hot water	½ cup sugar
¾ cup heavy cream, whipped	⅛ teaspoon salt
Grated rind of 1 lemon	1 cup rolled vanilla wafers

Directions (Serves 6 to 8)

Dissolve gelatin in hot water and chill until thickened but not firm. Beat until fluffy.

Fold heavy cream, lemon rind and juice, sugar, and salt into above.

Cover bottom of 9-inch square pan with half of wafers; pour in filling and sprinkle remaining wafers on top. Chill until firm.

ᕽ Macaroon Pudding

Miss Katharine L. Little, Chicago, Illinois

Ingredients

4 egg yolks, beaten
½ cup sugar
1 envelope (1 tablespoon)
    unflavored gelatin
1 cup milk

4 egg whites, beaten
Vanilla to taste
12 almond macaroons
1 cup whipped cream

Directions (Serves 6 to 8)

Mix together egg yolks and sugar.

Dissolve gelatin in milk and add to the above. Let come to a boil, just to the boiling point.

Stir egg whites and vanilla into mixture and put into a large or individual molds.

Break macaroons into small pieces and fill the molds.

Put in refrigerator until it sets. Serve with whipped cream. Sprinkle with glazed cherries and chopped nuts, if desired. If a circle mold is used, fill the center with whipped cream.

ᕽ Snow Pudding

Ingredients

1 envelope (1 tablespoon)
    unflavored gelatin
¼ cup cold water
1 cup boiling water
¾ cup sugar

¼ cup lemon juice
¼ teaspoon salt
1¼ teaspoons grated lemon rind
2 egg whites, stiffly beaten

Directions (Serves 6)

Soak gelatin in cold water about 5 minutes. Pour over boiling water and stir until gelatin is dissolved.

Add sugar, lemon juice, salt, and lemon rind, and stir until blended thoroughly. Chill until slightly thickened.

Fold egg whites into slightly thickened gelatin. Whip together until mixture is fluffy and holds its shape when the beater is raised. Pour into individual serving dishes and chill. Serve with Plain Custard Sauce. (*See* Dessert Sauces section.)

ᐁ Cabinet Pudding

Ingredients

1½ tablespoons unflavored gelatin
⅓ cup cold water
6 egg yolks
⅓ cup sugar
⅛ teaspoon salt

6 egg whites, stiffly beaten
1 teaspoon vanilla
18 macaroons
½ cup Jamaica rum or sherry wine
Cherries

Directions (Serves 8)

Soak gelatin in water about 5 minutes. Dissolve over hot water to melt gelatin.

Combine yolks, sugar, and salt, and beat until thick and lemon colored. Add above gelatin mixture and beat until blended.

Fold egg whites and vanilla into the above mixture.

Soak macaroons in rum. Line mold with macaroons. Alternate layers of custard and macaroons, topping with custard. Chill until firm. Unmold and garnish with cherries. Serve with whipped cream on top.

ᐁ Rice Pudding with Whipped Cream

Ingredients

2 teaspoons unflavored gelatin
¼ cup cold water
1 cup cooked rice
⅓ cup sugar

½ cup blanched, slivered almonds (optional)
1 pint heavy cream, whipped
2 teaspoons vanilla

Directions (Serves 10)

Soak gelatin in cold water about 5 minutes. Heat to dissolve gelatin. (Heating the gelatin after it has soaked helps to gel the final mixture.)

Add rice to above mixture and blend well. Chill.

Fold in remaining ingredients. Pour into wet mold and thoroughly chill. Unmold and serve with crushed, sweetened strawberries or raspberries, or Butterscotch Sauce. (*See* Dessert Sauces section.)

➤ *To unmold gelatin molds, put them in hot water for a second, and then cut around the inside of the mold with a sharp knife. Shake out over serving dish.*

∾ Sherry Pudding

Chef, Hotel Florence, Missoula, Montana

Ingredients

2 cups milk	3 tablespoons powdered sugar
2 egg yolks	½ pint whipping cream
½ cup sugar	1 jigger whiskey
2 envelopes (2 tablespoons) unflavored gelatin	½ cup sherry wine
	Almond macaroons, crumbled
½ cup cold milk	Candied cherries, sliced
2 egg whites	

Directions (Serves 8)

Scald milk in double boiler. Beat egg yolks and ½ cup sugar. Add to hot milk; cook until it coats a spoon.

Mix gelatin in cold milk; add to hot custard, mixing well. Let set in cool place until slightly thickened.

Beat egg whites stiff; add powdered sugar. Beat cream. Mix all together.

Add whiskey and wine to egg whites and cream, and fold into custard mixture, stirring well.

Combine crumbled macaroons and sliced cherries. Place alternately in pudding mold with custard mixture. Let stand in refrigerator until firm. Serve with whipped cream sauce to which has been added 3 tablespoons powdered sugar and 1 tablespoon sherry wine.

∾ Stephanie Pudding

Marjorie Mills, Boston, Massachusetts

Ingredients

1 envelope (1 tablespoon) unflavored gelatin	½ cup sugar
	¼ cup lemon juice
¼ cup cold water	3 egg whites, beaten
1 cup grape or loganberry juice, hot	

Directions (Serves 4)

Soak gelatin in cold water.

Dissolve gelatin with hot juice.

Add sugar and lemon juice to dissolved gelatin and strain. Set in a cool place. Stir mixture occasionally and, when thick, whisk until frothy.

Add egg whites to above mixture and beat until stiff enough to hold its own shape. Serve cold with Boiled Custard Sauce.

➤ *Keep unmolded gelatin desserts in the refrigerator until you serve them.*

∿ Syllabub

Ingredients

2 egg yolks	¼ cup cold water
½ cup sugar	½ pint whipping cream
¼ teaspoon salt	2 tablespoons rum
1 cup milk	2 tablespoons cherries
1 envelope (1 tablespoon) unflavored gelatin	

Directions (Serves 4)

Beat egg yolks thoroughly; add sugar and salt and beat well.

Add milk to above and cook in top of double boiler over boiling water until mixture is of thin custard consistency. Stir constantly while cooking.

Soften unflavored gelatin in cold water and stir into hot custard until dissolved.

Allow mixture to cool until it just begins to set.

Whip cream until stiff. Chop cherries and fold into whipped cream along with rum. Fold into above mixture.

∾ Peppermint-Chocolate Dessert
Chateau Hutter, Sturgeon Bay, Wisconsin

Ingredients

½ lb. peppermint stick candy
½ cup light cream
1 envelope (1 tablespoon)
   unflavored gelatin

2 tablespoons cold water
1½ cups heavy cream, whipped
½ lb. chocolate sandwich
   cookies

Directions (Serves 9)

Crush candy; add cream and heat until candy dissolves.
Dissolve gelatin in cold water and add to the above. Chill until
   partially set.
Fold in whipped cream. Crush cookies and place ½ of the crumbs
   into the bottom of pan; then add layer of peppermint mixture.
   Repeat. Chill 12 hours.

➨ *Egg whites beat best at room temperature.*

∾ Chocolate Ice Box Cake

Ingredients

3 squares unsweetened chocolate
½ cup sugar
Pinch of salt
¼ cup hot water
1½ teaspoons unflavored gelatin
1 tablespoon cold water

4 egg yolks
1 teaspoon vanilla
4 egg whites, stiffly beaten
½ cup heavy cream, whipped
24 ladyfingers

Directions (Serves 8 to 10)

Melt chocolate in top of double boiler. Add sugar, salt, and hot water.
   Stir until sugar is dissolved and mixture blended.
Soak gelatin in water about 5 minutes. Add to hot chocolate mixture
   and stir until gelatin is dissolved. Cook in double boiler until
   mixture is smooth and well thickened. Remove top section from
   boiling water.
Add yolks to the above mixture, one at a time, beating thoroughly
   after each addition. Place top section over boiling water and cook
   2 minutes, stirring constantly. Add vanilla and cool.
Fold chocolate mixture into egg whites. Chill.

Fold whipped cream into chocolate mixture.

Line bottom and sides of mold with waxed paper. Arrange ladyfingers on bottom and sides of mold. Add a small amount of the chocolate mixture; then add ladyfingers and chocolate mixture in alternate layers, topping with chocolate. Cut off ladyfingers around sides of mold and arrange cut pieces on chocolate mixture. Chill 12 to 24 hours. Unmold. Serve with whipped cream, if desired.

➤ Save the juices from canned pineapple, peaches, and other fruits. Put them in glass bottles; set them away in the refrigerator, and use these juices in your breakfast fruit cup, or add a little lemon to make some refreshing hot weather "ades."

∾ Chocolate Ice Box Cake

Stage Coach Inn, Salado, Texas

Ingredients

4½ squares chocolate
¾ cup sugar
6 tablespoons hot water
Pinch of salt
1½ tablespoons cold water
1½ teaspoons unflavored gelatin

6 egg yolks
1 teaspoon vanilla
6 egg whites
¾ cup whipping cream
16 ladyfingers, split

Directions (Serves about 14)

Melt chocolate in top of double boiler; then add sugar, salt, and hot water, stirring until sugar is dissolved.

Dissolve gelatin in cold water and add to hot chocolate mixture. Cook in double boiler until smooth and thick. Remove from heat.

Add egg yolks, one at a time, beating mixture after adding each egg. Return to boiling water and cook 2 minutes, stirring constantly. Add vanilla and let cool.

Fold in beaten egg whites and whipped cream. Chill. Line bottom and sides of angel cake pan with waxed paper and arrange split ladyfingers on bottom and sides of pan. Add alternate layers of chocolate mixture and ladyfingers. Chill 12 to 24 hours.

⌒ Orange Ice Box Cake

Hotel Fort Hayes, Columbus, Ohio

Ingredients

2 cups milk
2 tablespoons cornstarch
1 cup sugar
2 eggs or 4 yolks
1 envelope (1 tablespoon)
  unflavored gelatin

2 tablespoons cold water
¾ cup orange juice
1 teaspoon grated orange rind
1 pint whipping cream
1½ dozen ladyfingers
½ pint whipping cream

Directions (Serves 4 to 6)

Heat milk in double boiler.

Mix cornstarch, sugar, and eggs thoroughly. Pour the hot milk over the egg mixture and return to double boiler and continue to cook 10 minutes, or until thickened.

Soak gelatin in the cold water and add orange juice and rind. Place this mixture in refrigerator until cool and slightly thickened.

Beat cream until stiff and fold into orange mixture.

Split the ladyfingers and cut about ¼ inch from end of each half. Stand these around edge of a springform pan, and line the bottom with the small pieces of ladyfingers. Pour the whipped cream mixture into the lined mold and let stand several hours until thickened.

Just before serving, cover top with whipped cream, using a pastry decorator. Garnish with maraschino cherries. Serve.

> ➥ *For satisfying results in anything you cook, take precautions from beginning to end. Follow recipes carefully, use exact level measurements, and know your oven temperature. Don't proceed by guess.*

⌒ Angel Food Mold

Mrs. Voijt Frank Mashek, Chicago, Illinois

Ingredients

1 envelope (1 tablespoon)
  unflavored gelatin
½ cup cold milk
2 cups milk
2 egg yolks, slightly beaten

1 cup sugar
1 teaspoon vanilla
2 egg whites, beaten
1 pint whipping cream, whipped
Bits of angel food cake

Directions (Serves 6 to 8)

Soak gelatin in cold milk.

Cook 2 cups milk, egg yolks, and sugar in double boiler; pour over gelatin and milk; stir to dissolve. Let cool.

Add vanilla, egg whites, and whipped cream to cooled mixture.

Put bits of angel food in mold and pour mixture over them. Serve with whipped cream into which cut and sugared strawberries have been added.

✎ Almond Cream Mold

Ingredients

6 tablespoons sugar	¼ cup cold water
3 tablespoons cornstarch	2 teaspoons almond extract
2 whole eggs	1 pint whipped cream
1 quart milk	3 tablespoons sugar
1 envelope (1 tablespoon) unflavored gelatin	14 graham crackers

Directions (Serves 12)

Stir together sugar, cornstarch, and eggs in double boiler into a smooth mixture and add to milk. Cook until smooth.

Soak gelatin in water for 5 minutes. Add to hot mixture and stir until thoroughly dissolved. Cool.

Add almond extract to custard.

Add sugar to whipped cream. Stir part of whipped cream into custard, leaving only enough to cover top. Pour into 9 × 12-inch pan and line top with crackers. Smooth rest of whipped cream on top. Chill until set, and cut into squares.

➤ *One of the common faults in American cooking is the too generous use of sugar; thus the delicate flavor of many dishes is overshadowed by too sweet a taste.*

Pastry

ALTHOUGH PIE HAS OFTEN been called "the great American dessert," especially apple pie, it has been known since the days of Chaucer in the fourteenth century. Originally in England "pie" meant a substantial entree of meat or fish with a top crust.

The French, on the other hand, specialized in pies or tarts with the crust on the bottom and the filling on top. For a long time there was a great deal of controversy in Europe as to whether the crust should go on the bottom or the top of a pie. In America the problem ended, for the early settlers put a crust on the bottom as well as on the top. That was America's contribution, and that is how "pie" (referring to dessert pie) earned the title "the great American dessert."

When the pioneers came to America, they found that apples, pumpkin, and squash would grow in abundance. Displaying Yankee ingenuity, they put them in pies. To this day in New England, pumpkin and squash pies are as traditional as corn on the cob and baked beans.

I have not the slightest idea how the saying "as easy as pie" came about. However, if one follows a few basic rules, making a pie is easy. Here are some rules to keep in mind:

Measure ingredients accurately, use as little water as possible, handle dough quickly and lightly, and bake in a preheated oven.

If your crust should break, make a small patch of dough, moisten the edges lightly, and place the patch over the broken area; run over lightly with the rolling pin. If you need more crust for a fluted edge, this also can be done by moistening the edges slightly and adding a new piece of dough.

You can make a nice trimming around your pie by fluting the crust with your thumb and forefinger, or pressing the edges down firmly with a fork. For a more elaborate pie trim, braid three strips of crust together and arrange neatly around edge of pie.

Be sure to cut vents for a two-crust pie, especially in the case of fruit pies. Bake fruit pies in a hot oven at 425° for 15 minutes, and then lower heat to 325°. This will help seal the crust and keep the pies from running over.

Follow these simple rules, and with a little experience you too will be a good pastry baker.

➤ Pastry Shells

Lowell Inn, Stillwater, Minnesota

Ingredients

½ cup lightly salted butter   5 teaspoons cold water
1 cup sifted pastry or all-purpose
   flour

Directions

Cream butter as for cake. (Do not melt by heat.)
Next add flour and cold water. Mix lightly. Roll out as pie crust. Cut
   to fit individual pastry shell pans. Bake at 450° for 8 to 10 minutes.

➤ Pie Crust for Two 9-Inch Double-Crust Pies

Lowell Inn, Stillwater, Minnesota

(Three to One Formula) Three parts of flour to one of shortening by
volume.

Ingredients

1⅓ cups (⅔ lbs.) shortening   To 12 tablespoons cold water,
4 cups (1 quart) all-purpose flour   add 2 teaspoons salt
   (sifted)

Directions

Carefully combine, using pastry blender, ½ of the shortening with
   the flour to a cornmeal consistency. Add remaining shortening
   and blend to the size of large peas. All flour must be completely
   absorbed in the shortening.
If pastry flour is used, either the shortening may be slightly reduced,
   or the flour increased. This blended shortening and flour may be
   prepared the day before and set in the refrigerator.
Add cold water, a little at a time while stirring, until dough forms a
   loose ball in the bowl. Cut dough in 4 equal parts for our crusts.
   We use pastry canvas and rolling pin cover that have been perme-
   ated with the same type of flour used in the dough. Lightly roll out
   dough to ⅛-inch thickness. Use trimmings only in lower crust,
   which can be rolled a little thicker than the top crust. Place pie tin
   on dough and trim, allowing ½-inch around the tin. Fit dough
   into pie tin and fold edge to form a rim; flute. Prick bottom and
   sides well with a fork. Bake in 450° oven till brown. Check oven
   temperature often with oven thermometer. Well-browned pie tins
   or Pyrex give good results. Do not use new pie tins.

∽ Graham Cracker Crust

Ingredients

20 graham crackers (1½ cups crumbs)

½ cup melted butter
1 tablespoon sugar

Directions (Makes one 9-inch shell)

Mix butter and sugar with crumbs and line the inside of a pie tin. Press crumbs firmly into place and bake in a hot oven 8 to 10 minutes. This can be made the day before using.

∽ Coconut Crust

Ingredients

2 tablespoons soft butter

1½ cups shredded coconut, cut

Directions (Makes one 8-inch pie shell)

Spread butter evenly in an 8-inch pie pan.

Press coconut into the bottom and sides of the buttered pie pan. Bake in a slow oven at 300° for 15 to 20 minutes or until golden brown. Cool before filling. Fill with ice cream, a cream filling, or a chiffon filling.

∽ Chocolate Coconut Pie Crust

Ingredients

2 squares unsweetened chocolate
2 tablespoons butter
2 tablespoons hot milk

⅔ cup sifted confectioners' sugar
1½ cups shredded coconut, cut

Directions (Makes one 9-inch pie shell)

Melt chocolate and butter in the top of a double boiler, stirring until blended.

Combine milk and sugar, and add to chocolate mixture, stirring until blended.

Add coconut to the above mixture and mix well. Press mixture into the bottom and sides of a well-buttered 9-inch pie pan. Chill until firm. Fill with ice cream or a chiffon filling.

∽ Meringue Pie Crust

Ingredients

2 egg whites

¼ teaspoon salt

¼ teaspoon cream of tartar

½ cup sugar

Directions (Makes one 9-inch shell)

Beat egg whites until foamy; add salt and cream of tartar and beat until stiff but not dry peaks are formed. Gradually add sugar, 2 tablespoons at a time, beating after each addition. Continue beating until meringue will stand in stiff peaks and is smooth and glossy. Spread in bottom and sides of a greased 9-inch pie plate. Bake in slow oven at 250° for about 60 minutes or until lightly browned. Cool and fill with fresh sweetened berries or ice cream.

∽ Macaroon Pie Crust

Ingredients

1 egg white

2 tablespoons sugar

1 tablespoon light corn syrup

½ teaspoon vanilla

2 cups coconut, finely cut

Directions (Makes one 9-inch pie shell)

Beat egg white until foamy. Add sugar and beat until mixture will stand in soft peaks. Add corn syrup and flavoring. Fold in coconut. Using the back of a spoon, press macaroon mixture firmly into the bottom and sides of a greased 9-inch pie pan. Bake in moderate oven at 350° for 15 minutes or until lightly browned. Cool. Fill with ice cream, cream filling, or sweetened fresh berries.

∾ Apricot and Peach Turnovers

Ingredients

½ lb. dried apricots
½ lb. dried peaches
1½ cups water
1 cup sugar

⅓ cup butter
½ grated nutmeg
1 tablespoon flour
1 recipe of pastry

Directions (Makes 8)

Add water to fruit and cook until the consistency of mush.
Add remaining ingredients to the above.
Cut pastry into saucer-shaped rounds and put in ample filling. Fold
over and seal the edges. With a fork, prick the top so the steam
can escape. Place on a baking sheet and bake in 350° oven for
15 minutes; then lower to 300° and bake until a golden brown
and the crust seems crisp on both sides.

∾ Raspberry Tart

Alcona Beach, Harrisville, Michigan

Ingredients

1 quart raspberries, fresh or
 frozen
1 cup sugar
¼ teaspoon salt

1 tablespoon cornstarch
1 baked 9-inch pie shell or
 8 baked tart shells

Directions (Serves 8)

Combine sugar and raspberries; let stand until they make a cup
of juice. Drain, reserving the berries. Thicken the 1 cup of juice
with cornstarch and cook until clear; add salt, and then pour over
berries. Pour into baked pie shell or baked tart shells. Serve with
whipped cream or ice cream.

∾ Apple Tart, French Style

Ingredients

2 cups sifted flour
½ teaspoon salt
2 tablespoons sugar
½ cup soft butter
1 egg, well beaten
2 tablespoons cold water (about)

3 tablespoons cornstarch
¾ cup sugar
Pinch of salt
¾ teaspoon cinnamon
¼ teaspoon nutmeg
5 cups peeled, sliced tart apples

Directions (Makes one 9-inch)

Sift together dry ingredients. Cut in the butter until the mixture is like coarse crumbs.

Stir in the egg and water to make a pie dough. Take ⅔ of the dough and roll about ⅛-inch thick, and fit into a 9-inch cake pan.

Combine remaining ingredients in a bowl. Then arrange the apple mixture in the shell. Roll remaining dough out to fit the top, making a slit in the center. Fit over the apple mixture. Bake in a hot oven 425° for 40 minutes or until brown. While warm, spread with confectioners' sugar icing. Remove warm tart from cake pan by inverting on a wire rack. Serve warm.

❧ Filling for Small Pastries, Tarts, etc.

Ingredients

¼ lb. butter	All juice from above
¾ lb. lump sugar	6 egg yolks, beaten
2 lemons, grated rind only	4 egg whites, beaten

Directions

Melt together butter and sugar.

Add lemon rind and juice to above.

Add beaten yolks and whites to mixture and stir until it thickens. Pour into tart shells.

❧ Apple Pie Deluxe

Filling

Ingredients

1½ tablespoons cornstarch	3½ cups peeled and thinly
¾ cup sugar	sliced, fresh, tart apples
Pinch of salt	1 tablespoon lemon juice
¾ teaspoon cinnamon	1 cup heavy cream
¼ teaspoon nutmeg	1 unbaked 9-inch pie shell

Directions (Makes one 9-inch pie)

Combine the ingredients in a large bowl. Then turn into unbaked pie shell. Bake in hot oven at 425° for 30 minutes. Then sprinkle the Walnut Crumb Topping over the top of the pie. Spoon ⅓ cup melted butter over the crumb topping. Bake 20 to 25 minutes longer or until done.

Walnut Crumb Topping

Ingredients

½ cup sugar
½ cup fine graham cracker
  crumbs
¼ cup flour

¼ cup chopped walnuts
1 teaspoon cinnamon
⅛ teaspoon nutmeg

Directions

Combine all ingredients.

> ➥ *When an unbaked pie crust is to be filled with a very moist filling, it is best to brush its surface with a small amount of lightly beaten egg white, and then to chill the crust. This precaution will prevent the moisture of the filling from penetrating into the lower crust.*

ᕫ Dutch Apple Pie

Elizabeth Parker's Restaurant, Richmond, Indiana

Ingredients

1 unbaked 10-inch pie shell
Winesap apples
½ cup sugar
1 tablespoon cornstarch

¼ teaspoon nutmeg
¼ teaspoon cinnamon
⅔ cup coffee cream
1 tablespoon butter

Directions (Makes one 10-inch pie)

Prepare unbaked pie shell.

Peel, core, and cut apples in eighths and fill shell.

Mix sugar, cornstarch, nutmeg, and cinnamon, and blend through apples.

Pour cream over apples.

Dot butter over top. Preheat oven. Bake for 30 minutes at 375° and then cover and reduce heat to 350°. Bake until apples are tender.

ᴖ English Apple Pie

Daven Haven Lodges, Grand Lake, Colorado

Ingredients

1 egg
¾ cup sugar
½ cup flour
1 teaspoon baking powder

¼ teaspoon salt
1 cup finely chopped apples
⅓ cup nut meats

Directions (Makes one 8-inch pie)

Beat together egg, sugar, flour, baking powder, and salt.

Add apples and nut meats to the above. Mix well. Put in Pyrex pie pan. Bake at 350° for 25 to 30 minutes. Serve with cream or ice cream.

ᴖ Apple Pie

Ingredients

1 ¼ cups flour
2 tablespoons poultry fat or
   shortening
2 tablespoons butter
3¾ tablespoons ice water

Pinch of salt
1 stick butter
1 cup sugar
1 heaping tablespoon flour
Winesap apples

Directions (Makes one 9-inch pie)

Sift flour and salt. Cut in butter and poultry fat; add ice water and mix gently.

Roll out thin and line pie pan, which has been heavily buttered. Use leftover pastry for strips to cover top of pie. (If poultry fat is not available, use shortening.)

Slice half the stick of butter over the crust in the pie tin. Mix together sugar and tablespoon of flour and put half over butter. Peel and chop enough apples to fill pie tin heaped up. Cover with remainder of sugar and flour mixture. Top with strips of crust and slice remainder of butter over top. Place in 450° preheated oven for 10 minutes, lower heat to 350°, and bake for 25 to 30 minutes or until done and pastry is brown on top.

⌒ Apple Pie

Ingredients

2 unbaked 8-inch pie crusts
1 cup sugar
2 tablespoons flour
½ grated nutmeg
½ cup orange juice

3 tablespoons light corn syrup
⅓ cup melted butter
Winesap apples cut into thin
    slices (enough to fill a pie pan)

Directions

Mix first six ingredients all together.

Add apples to the above and thoroughly mix together. Butter a pie
pan heavily before putting in the bottom pastry; then fill with the
apple mixture and make strips from the remaining crust for the
top. Preheat oven. Bake at 400° for 15 minutes; then reduce oven
to 250° and bake for 35 to 40 minutes.

⌒ Strawberry Pie

Ingredients

1 baked 9-inch pie shell
1½ quarts fresh strawberries
1 cup sugar

6 tablespoons cornstarch
¾ cup whipping cream, whipped
1 tablespoon sugar

Directions (Makes one 9-inch pie)

Place best berries points up, around edge of shell. Mix other berries
with 1 cup sugar and cornstarch, and cook in double boiler until
thick.

When cool, place strawberry mixture in pie shell and cover with
whipped cream sweetened with tablespoon of sugar. Serve.

⌒ Fried Apple Pie

The Park View Inn, Berkeley Springs, West Virginia

Ingredients

2 cups sifted flour
3 teaspoons baking powder
1 teaspoon salt
¼ cup shortening

⅓ cup of milk, approximately
1½ cups thick, sieved applesauce
1 cup sugar
3 teaspoons ground cinnamon

Directions (Makes 8 to 10 individual pies)

Mix and sift flour, baking powder, and salt.

Cut in shortening until well mixed.

Add milk gradually to make a soft dough. Put on lightly floured board and knead with a light touch. Roll very thin. Lay on saucer and cut eight or ten circles with a sharp knife.

Place on one side of each circle 3 tablespoons of thick applesauce. Fold in half, and then moisten and seal edges with a fork. Fry in 1½ inches hot fat at 350° in heavy-bottom frying pan. When brown on one side, turn and brown the other.

Have ready a flat pan, the bottom covered with sugar and cinnamon. Lift pie from fat, drain, and then place in sugar. Turn, giving both sides a good sugar coating. Serve while hot with ice cream or plain cream.

∾ Fresh Apple Crumb Cake

Ingredients

½ cup soft butter	5 cups peeled, sliced, tart apples
½ cup sugar	2 tablespoons cornstarch
1½ cups sifted flour	½ cup sugar
Pinch of salt	¾ teaspoon cinnamon

Directions (Makes one 9-inch cake)

Crumb together the butter, ½ cup sugar, flour, and salt with pastry blender, fork, or fingers until well mixed. Set aside ¾ cup of the crumbs. Press remaining crumbs into the bottom of a 9-inch springform pan and about ¾ inch up the sides.

Combine apples, cornstarch, ½ cup sugar, and cinnamon in bowl and mix well. Then arrange apple mixture in crumb shell. Bake in hot oven at 425° for 20 minutes. Remove from oven and sprinkle the top with the reserved crumbs. Return to oven and continue baking 20 to 30 minutes longer or until shell is brown.

ᴄᴡ *Riverside Lodge Fresh Strawberry Pie*

Riverside Lodge and Ranch, Lyons, Colorado

Crust

Ingredients

1 cup flour
¼ teaspoon salt
¼ teaspoon baking powder

⅙ cup lard
⅙ cup butter
2 tablespoons ice water (about)

Directions (Makes one 9-inch pie)

Mix flour, salt, and baking powder by sifting together. Work in lard
and butter; then add water drop by drop until mixture is right
consistency to roll. Roll ¼-inch thick. Place 9-inch tin on pastry,
cut 1 inch larger than tin; place crust in tin; flute and prick. Bake
12 to 15 minutes in 450° oven.

Filling

Ingredients

1 quart fresh strawberries
½ cup sugar
2 tablespoons sugar

½ pint whipping cream
4 drops vanilla

Directions

Wash, stem, and quarter strawberries. Sprinkle with ½ cup sugar and
let stand in refrigerator for 1 hour. Shortly before time to serve put
in baked pie shell.

Whip cream with vanilla; add 2 tablespoons sugar, and top pie with
sweetened whipped cream.

ᴄᴡ *Open Fresh Strawberry Pie*

Lowell Inn, Stillwater, Minnesota

Pie Shell

Ingredients

1 cup flour
½ cup shortening

½ teaspoon salt
1 tablespoon cold water

Directions

Cut shortening into flour. Mix salt and cold water together and stir
into the flour-shortening mixture. Form into a ball. Roll out on
lightly floured board. Fit into 9-inch pie pan. Bake in 425° oven for
15 minutes.

Filling

Ingredients

1 cup crushed fresh strawberries
1 cup sugar
1 tablespoon cornstarch

Fresh strawberries, enough to fill
the pie shell

Directions

Boil crushed berries, sugar, and cornstarch together until
transparent.
Put fresh strawberries in pie shell, pour the hot berry syrup over
them, and chill.

∾ Blueberry Pie

Lowell Inn, Stillwater, Minnesota

Ingredients

2 unbaked 9-inch pie crusts
1 quart blueberries

1 ¼ cups sugar
4 tablespoons melted butter

Directions (Makes one 9-inch pie)

Line greased pie tin with bottom pastry. Combine berries, sugar, and
butter, and pour into pastry shell. (Do not add thickening agents.)
Cover with top crust. Bake in 450° oven for 10 minutes. Reduce
heat to 350° and bake for about 30 minutes longer or until crust is
golden brown. Serve runny in a fairly deep dish.

∾ Blueberry Pie

Ingredients

1 No. 2 can blueberries, syrup
pack
3 tablespoons sugar
¼ teaspoon salt
2 tablespoons cornstarch

1 tablespoon lemon juice
1 tablespoon butter
1 baked 8-inch pie shell
3 egg whites, beaten stiff
6 tablespoons sugar

Directions (Makes one 8-inch pie)

Drain juice from blueberries and add water, if necessary, to make
1 cup of liquid.
Mix dry ingredients and combine with liquid. Cook over low heat
until thickened and clear, stirring constantly. Remove from heat.

Add lemon juice and butter to the above mixture and fold in the berries. Fill pie shell with the blueberry mixture.

Beat 6 tablespoons sugar gradually into the beaten egg whites. Beat until peaks are formed. Spread over the blueberry filling. Bake 15 to 20 minutes in a 325° oven or until meringue is lightly browned.

ᴄᴡ Raspberry Pie

John Ebersole's Restaurant, White Plains, New York

Ingredients

2 cups frozen raspberries	Pinch of salt
¼ cup cold water	3 tablespoons cornstarch
2 tablespoons butter	¼ cup cold water
½ cup sugar	1 baked 9-inch pie shell
1 teaspoon lemon juice	

Directions (Makes one 9-inch pie)

Defrost and drain raspberries; reserve juice.

Combine berry juice with cold water and butter, sugar, lemon juice, and salt. Place over low heat.

Dissolve cornstarch with cold water and add to above. Cook until thick, stirring constantly. Remove from fire; add berries; let cool. Pour into 9-inch baked pie shell. Serve with whipped cream.

ᴄᴡ Riverside Lodge Fresh Raspberry Pie

(Makes one 9-inch pie)

Use recipe for Riverside Lodge Fresh Strawberry Pie, except substitute 1 quart fresh raspberries, which have been washed and stemmed, for the strawberries.

➤ *Serve hot fruit pies with cream.*

❦ Cherry Pie

Stagecoach Inn, Manitou Springs, Colorado

Crust

Ingredients

2½ cups sifted flour
1 teaspoon salt

¾ cup shortening
¼ cup water

Directions (Makes one 9-inch pie)

Mix flour and salt. Cut shortening into it until pieces are size of bean. Mix well with water until dough comes together and can be shaped into a ball. Divide into two parts. Roll out into two 9-inch pie crusts. Line a 9-inch pie plate with pastry.

Filling

Ingredients

2 cups fresh or frozen sour pitted
  cherries
1 tablespoon flour

1½ cups sugar
1 tablespoon butter
¼ teaspoon almond extract

Directions

Mix flour and sugar; then stir in with the flavor and cherries. Pour into pastry shell; dot with butter. Cover with pastry top. Bake slowly for 45 minutes in a 350° oven.

❦ Apricot Pie

Mrs. John R. Shields, Bogota, New Jersey

Ingredients

1 lb. apricots, canned or fresh
1 cup apricot juice
½ cup sugar
1 tablespoon cornstarch

Drop of yellow coloring
1 baked 9-inch pie shell
1 pint whipping cream, whipped

Directions (Makes one 9-inch pie)

Drain juice from canned apricots. Combine juice, sugar, and cornstarch. Mix. Cook until thick and clear; add a drop of yellow coloring. Chill until partially set. In a good rich 9-inch baked pie shell, fill as follows: First, ½ pint whipped cream. Second, canned or fresh apricots. Third, ½ pint whipped cream. Cover with chilled cooked apricot juice.

Peach Praline Pie

Ingredients

4 cups sliced fresh peaches
¾ cup sugar
1½ teaspoons cornstarch
1½ teaspoons lemon juice
¼ cup flour

⅓ cup firmly packed brown
  sugar
½ cup chopped pecans
3 tablespoons butter
1 unbaked 9-inch pie shell

Directions (Makes one 9-inch pie)

Combine first four ingredients in large bowl and mix well.
Combine flour, brown sugar, and pecans in small bowl.
Mix butter into the above mixture until it is crumbly. Sprinkle ⅓ of
  this mixture in the bottom of the pie shell. Cover with the peach
  mixture. Then sprinkle the remaining pecan mixture over the top.
  Bake in hot oven at 425° for about 45 minutes.

Fresh Peach Crumb Pie

Ingredients

½ cup soft butter
½ cup sugar
1½ cups sifted flour
Pinch of salt

4 cups sliced fresh peaches
2 tablespoons cornstarch
½ cup sugar
1 tablespoon lemon juice

Directions (Makes one 9-inch pie)

Crumb together the first four ingredients with pastry blender, fork,
  or fingers until well mixed. Set aside ¾ cup of the crumbs. Press
  remaining crumbs into the bottom of a 9-inch springform pan and
  about ¾ inch up the sides.
Combine in a bowl the peaches, cornstarch, sugar, and lemon juice,
  and mix well. Then arrange peach mixture in crumb shell. Bake in
  hot oven at 425° for 20 minutes. Remove from oven and sprinkle
  top with reserved crumbs. Return to the oven and continue to
  bake 20 to 30 minutes longer or until the shell is browned.

Riverside Lodge Fresh Peach Pie

(Makes one 9-inch pie)

Use recipe for Riverside Lodge Fresh Strawberry Pie, except substitute 1 quart fresh peaches, which have been peeled and sliced, for the
strawberries.

～ *Peach Plum Pie*

Ingredients

1 recipe pastry
6 medium peaches, pitted, pared,
   and sliced
4 red plums, pitted and sliced
1 cup sugar

3 tablespoons cornstarch
Pinch of salt
½ teaspoon grated orange rind
1 ½ tablespoons butter

Directions (Makes one 9-inch pie)

Line a 9-inch pie pan with half of the pastry.

Fill pie shell with fruit. Combine sugar, cornstarch, and salt, and
   pour over the fruit. Add rind and dot with butter. Using remaining
   pastry, cover with lattice top. Bake in hot oven at 425° for 50 to 60
   minutes.

～ *Deep Dish Plum Pie*

Ingredients

1 uncooked pastry shell
1 pastry top
2 lbs. blue prune plums
⅓ cup cold water
1 cup sugar
½ teaspoon salt

2 tablespoons plus 1 teaspoon
   cornstarch
3 tablespoons cold water
½ cup chopped walnuts
6 tablespoons orange marmalade

Directions (Makes one 9-inch deep pie)

Line a deep 9-inch pie pan with pastry and chill. Have ready a pastry
   top.

Wash and pit plums. If they are large, quarter; if small, halve. Put
   plums in saucepan, add sugar, salt, and water, and bring to a boil.
   Lower heat at once and simmer for 4 minutes.

Dissolve cornstarch in 3 tablespoons water and add to plums. Cook
   slowly, stirring constantly from the bottom of the pan until the
   mixture is thick and clear. Remove from fire and let get cold.

When mixture is cold stir in walnuts. Spread bottom of pie pastry
   with marmalade and cover with plum filling. Put on top crust
   and slit to allow steam to escape. Bake in 450° oven for 25 to 30
   minutes, or until crust is done and lightly browned.

❧ Apricot Cream Pie

Mills Restaurants of Ohio
(Cincinnati, Columbus, and Cleveland)

Ingredients

¾ cup sugar	½ teaspoon salt
3½ cups milk	1 teaspoon vanilla
4 tablespoons cornstarch	1½ tablespoons butter
½ cup cold milk	1 cup cooked apricots
2 egg yolks, beaten slightly	1 baked 9-inch pie shell

Directions (Makes one 9-inch pie)

Put sugar and 3½ cups milk in double boiler and bring to scalding point.

Soak cornstarch in ½ cup cold milk and add to above. Cook until mixture thickens.

Add a small amount of the above hot mixture to the eggs, mix, and pour back into the double boiler. Cook until thick.

Add salt, vanilla, and butter to above and blend well.

Cut apricots in pieces and add to above. Stir well. Cool. Put in baked pie shell and cover with meringue.

❧ Apricot Meringue

Ingredients

6 egg whites	¾ cup cooked apricots
¾ cup sugar	

Directions

Whip egg whites until stiff and dry; add sugar gradually.

Drain apricots well and add to above. Spread on pie and serve.
DO NOT BROWN IN OVEN.

❧ Rhubarb Pie

Sunset Farm, Whittier, North Carolina

Crust

Ingredients

1 cup flour	⅓ cup shortening
1 teaspoon baking powder	2 tablespoons cold water (about)
¼ teaspoon salt	

Directions (Makes one 9-inch pie)

Sift dry ingredients together. Work in shortening quickly with fingers until of crumb consistency. Add just enough cold water to make stiff dough. Roll out and line 9-inch pie pan.

Filling

Ingredients

4 cups rhubarb	2 eggs
1 ½ cups sugar	2 tablespoons butter
½ cup flour	

Directions

Cut rhubarb in ½-inch cubes. Place in uncooked pastry shell.
Mix together sugar and flour, and sprinkle over rhubarb.
Beat whole eggs well and put by spoonfuls over rhubarb.
Break butter in small pieces and sprinkle over pie. Stripe pie with thin strips of pastry. Bake in oven at 350° until done.

➜ *Egg whites, several days old, will beat up better than those that are strictly fresh. A watery egg white gives better volume than a thick white.*

～ Baked Cream Pie

Ingredients

1 pint coffee cream	2 egg whites
1 tablespoon cornstarch	1 uncooked pie crust
1 box (1 lb.) powdered sugar	

Directions (Makes one 9-inch pie)

At breakfast time combine cornstarch and sugar. Pour cream over sugar; mix well and let stand until an hour before lunch.
Beat egg whites stiff and stir into cream and sugar mixture. Place in uncooked pie crust and bake in 450° oven for 15 minutes. Reduce heat to 300° and bake until done.

⌒ Coconut Cream Pie

El Encanto Tea Shop, Los Angeles, California

Ingredients

1 cup milk
1⅓ cups sugar
Pinch of salt
2 egg yolks, beaten
2 tablespoons cornstarch
1 tablespoon milk
2½ teaspoons unflavored gelatin

1 tablespoon milk
½ cup coconut
1 cup whipped cream
1 teaspoon vanilla
2 egg whites, beaten
1 baked 10-inch pastry shell

Directions (Makes one 10-inch pie)

Combine first three ingredients in saucepan. Bring to a boil.

Blend cornstarch and 1 tablespoon milk and mix with eggs. Add to hot milk above and cook slightly.

Dissolve gelatin in 1 tablespoon milk and pour hot mixture over it. Let set until firm. Put in electric beater and beat well.

Add coconut, whipped cream, and vanilla to above mixture and put in refrigerator for 10 minutes.

Fold in stiff egg whites; pour in baked pastry shell; cover with whipped cream and sprinkle with coconut.

⌒ French Cream Coconut Pie

Ingredients

1 pint milk
1 cup sugar
4½ tablespoons cornstarch
5 egg yolks
⅔ cup milk
4⅔ tablespoons butter

1 pinch salt
1 tablespoon vanilla
½ can coconut or ½ fresh
    coconut, grated
½ pint whipping cream, whipped

Directions (Serves 6 to 8)

Scald 1 pint milk.

Mix together sugar, cornstarch, egg yolks, and ⅔ cup milk, and add slowly to above, stirring constantly until mixture thickens. Remove from fire.

Add butter and salt to above mixture and stir until butter is dissolved.

Stir vanilla into mixture and pour immediately into baked pie shell.

Put coconut on top of filling.

Put whipped cream on top of coconut.

To vary this pie, stir into finished cream filling 3 half-squares unsweetened melted chocolate, or top with fresh fruit such as red raspberries, before topping with whipped cream. Place in refrigerator before serving.

᷍ Custard Pie

Stone's Restaurant, Marshalltown, Iowa

Ingredients

3 eggs, beaten lightly
2½ cups milk
1 cup sugar
Pinch of salt

2 tablespoons melted butter
1 9-inch unbaked pie shell
Grapenuts or graham cracker
    crumbs

Directions (Makes one 9-inch pie)

Mix together all ingredients and put in uncooked pie shell. Sprinkle top with grapenuts or graham cracker crumbs. Do not stir. Bake in 400° oven for 12 to 15 minutes. Then reduce heat to 300° and cook until custard is set in the center of the pie.

᷍ Continental Cream Pie

Hilton Hotel, El Paso, Texas

Crust

Ingredients

14 ginger cookies or graham
    crackers

5 tablespoons butter, melted

Directions (Makes one 9-inch pie)

Roll cookies or crackers fine.

Mix butter well with above. Pat evenly in a 9-inch springform pan. Bake in 300° oven for 10 minutes or until lightly brown.

Filling

Ingredients

4 egg yolks, beaten
2 cups milk, scalded
1½ tablespoons cornstarch
½ cup sugar
1 envelope (1 tablespoon)
    unflavored gelatin

4 tablespoons cold water
4 egg whites, beaten
½ cup sugar
Candied fruit

Directions

Slowly add milk to egg yolks.

Combine sugar and cornstarch and stir into the above. Cook over
simmering water for 20 minutes, or until custard generously coats
spoon. Remove from the fire.

Soak gelatin in cold water for about 5 minutes. Add to the custard
while it is still hot. Let cool.

Beat egg whites very stiff; gradually beat in sugar and add to custard
while it is still soft and smooth. Fill the pie crust and set it in the
refrigerator. Sprinkle with candied fruit.

⤳ *Special Continental Cream Pie*

(Makes one 9-inch pie)

Use recipe for Continental Cream Pie, adding 2 tablespoons brandy
when the egg white meringue is folded into the cooled custard.

> ⤳ *Our favorite American man's dessert is good apple pie with a flaky
> crust and coffee to go with it. There are three ways to improve that
> apple pie. One is to add a scoop of rich, creamy ice cream. Another is
> to serve a piece of good, strong cheese with it—the kind that bites back
> at you. And the third—and least known—is to place a thin slice of
> ham on top of it.*

⤳ *Chocolate Cream Pie*

Ingredients

2 squares unsweetened chocolate	2 egg yolks, slightly beaten
2½ cups milk	2 tablespoons butter
6 tablespoons flour	1½ teaspoons vanilla
¼ teaspoon salt	1 baked 9-inch pie shell
1 cup sugar	½ cup whipping cream, whipped

Directions (Makes one 9-inch pie)

Combine chocolate and milk in top of double boiler. Cook and stir
over boiling water until the chocolate is melted. Beat with rotary
egg beater until the mixture is blended.

Combine flour, salt, and sugar, and add gradually to the chocolate
   mixture. Cook until the mixture is thickened (about 10 minutes
   longer), stirring occasionally.
Pour a small amount of the chocolate mixture over the egg yolks,
   stirring vigorously. Return to the double boiler and cook 5 minutes
   longer.
Add butter and vanilla to the chocolate mixture. Turn into baked pie
   shell. Cool.
Garnish with whipped cream.

◌ Sour Cream Pie

Mrs. A. W. Boswell, Monmouth, Illinois

Ingredients

3 egg yolks
¾ cup sugar
1 teaspoon cinnamon
1 cup sour cream
1 cup seedless raisins

½ cup chopped pecans
1 unbaked 9-inch pie shell
3 egg whites
6 tablespoons sugar

Directions (Makes one 9-inch pie)

Beat the yolks of 3 eggs; add ¾ cup sugar to the cinnamon, sour
   cream, raisins, and nuts. Mix well and pour into unbaked crust.
   Bake in 400° oven for 10 to 15 minutes. Reduce heat to 325° and
   bake ½ hour or until well set.
Cover with meringue by whipping the egg whites stiff, and adding
   6 tablespoons sugar gradually. Brown slowly in low oven.

◌ Pumpkin Pie

Derby's Cafe, Chamberlain, South Dakota

Ingredients

3 cups pumpkin
1½ cups granulated sugar
4 eggs, beaten
1 teaspoon salt
2 teaspoons cinnamon

1 teaspoon ginger
1 cup cream
2 cups milk
2 unbaked 8-inch pie shells

Directions (Makes two 8-inch pies)

Beat all ingredients together thoroughly and pour into 8-inch
   unbaked pie shells. Bake at 350° for 45 minutes or until set.

∾ Pumpkin Pie

Twist-O-Hill Lodge, Williston, Vermont

Ingredients

1 cup pumpkin
1 cup sugar
1½ tablespoons flour
1 teaspoon cinnamon
½ teaspoon nutmeg

½ teaspoon salt
1½ cups hot milk
1 egg
1 unbaked 9-inch pie shell

Directions (Makes one 9-inch pie)

Mix pumpkin with dry ingredients.

Separate egg. Beat yolk and add with milk to dry ingredients. Beat
egg white and fold carefully into mixture.

Pour into pie shell. Bake for 10 minutes at 450°. Reduce heat and
bake for 35 minutes at 350° until firm. May be topped with
whipped cream and chopped Brazil nuts when served.

➥ *To vary pumpkin pie add cider, good brandy, or sherry to the
custard.*

∾ Orange Pumpkin Pie

Ingredients

1½ cups milk
2 eggs, beaten
2 tablespoons orange juice
1 teaspoon orange rind
1¼ cups pumpkin
¾ cup brown sugar
1 teaspoon cinnamon

½ teaspoon ginger
½ teaspoon nutmeg
½ teaspoon salt
1 unbaked 9-inch pie shell
½ cup walnuts
½ teaspoon orange rind
1 cup whipped cream

Directions (Makes one 9-inch pie)

Combine milk, beaten eggs, orange juice, and rind.

Mix pumpkin, brown sugar, cinnamon, ginger, nutmeg, and salt well,
and add to above mixture. Pour into unbaked 9-inch pie shell.
Bake in 420° oven for 10 minutes. Reduce temperature to 350° and
bake for 40 minutes.

When cool cover with whipped cream and sprinkle with nut meats
and orange rind.

ᴄ᷎ Lemon Chiffon Pie

Stone's Restaurant, Marshalltown, Iowa

Ingredients

4 egg yolks, beaten	1 envelope (1 tablespoon)
½ cup sugar	unflavored gelatin
½ cup lemon juice	¼ cup cold water
1 lemon rind, grated	4 egg whites, beaten
Pinch of salt	½ cup sugar

Directions (Serves 6 to 8)

Cook egg yolks, sugar, lemon juice, lemon rind, and salt in double
 boiler, stirring constantly until consistency of custard.
Soak gelatin in cold water for about 5 minutes. Then add to hot
 custard.
Beat sugar into egg whites. Fold hot custard into egg whites carefully.
 Put in baked 8-inch pie shell and chill 3 hours.

ᴄ᷎ Lime Chiffon Pie

Brook Farm Restaurant, Chevy Chase, Maryland

Ingredients

4 egg yolks, slightly beaten	½ cup lime juice
¾ cup sugar	2 tablespoons grated lime rind
¼ teaspoon salt	2 drops green vegetable coloring
1 envelope (1 tablespoon)	4 egg whites
unflavored gelatin	¼ cup sugar
¼ cup cold water	1 baked 10-inch pie shell

Directions (Makes one 10-inch pie)

Combine egg yolks, ¾ cup sugar, and salt in top of double boiler and
 stir constantly.
Soak the gelatin in the cold water about 5 minutes; then add this to
 the above hot custard, stirring until dissolved.
Add lime juice and rind and food coloring to the above mixture and
 remove from heat.
While custard is cooling, beat egg whites dry and stiff; fold sugar
 into egg whites. Fold the beaten egg whites and cooled custard
 together. Pour into baked pie shell and place in refrigerator. Spread
 with whipped cream before serving.

Florida Lime Chiffon Pie

Johnston's Coffee Shop, Daytona Beach, Florida

Ingredients

1 can sweetened condensed milk	3 egg yolks
Grated rind of 1 lime	3 egg whites
½ cup lime juice	1 baked 9-inch pie shell

Directions (Makes one 9-inch pie)

Beat condensed milk, lime rind, and lime juice together with an egg
beater until thick.

Whip the whites of the eggs stiff and fold into this mixture. (If you
wish, you may use the whipped egg whites as a meringue, adding
3 tablespoons of sugar. Brown in oven.) Pour filling into baked pie
shell and cool.

Butterscotch Chiffon Pie

Ingredients

¾ cup brown sugar	1 envelope (1 tablespoon)
4 egg yolks	unflavored gelatin
½ teaspoon salt	¼ cup cold water
½ cup milk	4 egg whites, beaten stiff
	¼ cup sugar

Directions (Makes one 9-inch pie)

Cook brown sugar, egg yolks, salt, and milk in double boiler until
thick.

Soak gelatin in cold water and add to the above mixture. Let cool.

Add sugar to beaten egg whites and beat well. Fold into the above
mixture. Place in 9-inch pie shell and cover with whipped cream.

Pumpkin Chiffon Pie

Ingredients

1 cup brown sugar	1 envelope (1 tablespoon)
3 egg yolks	unflavored gelatin
1 ¼ cups pumpkin	¼ cup cold water
2 teaspoons cinnamon	3 egg whites, beaten
½ teaspoon ginger	2 tablespoons sugar
¼ teaspoon allspice	1 baked 10-inch pie shell
½ teaspoon salt	

Directions (Makes one 10-inch pie)

Put first seven ingredients in double boiler and cook until it begins to thicken.

Soak gelatin in water for 5 minutes. Add to hot mixture and stir until thoroughly dissolved. Cool.

Beat sugar into whites and fold into mixture. Pour into baked pie shell and chill. Serve garnished with whipped cream.

∾ Pecan Chiffon Pie

Ingredients

1 cup milk	1 teaspoon vanilla
¼ cup water	1 teaspoon butter
½ cup sugar	4 egg whites
Pinch of salt	¼ cup sugar
¼ cup cornstarch	¼ cup chopped, toasted pecans
¼ cup milk	1 baked 9-inch pie shell

Directions (Makes one 9-inch pie)

Combine first four ingredients in saucepan and bring just to a boil.

Dissolve cornstarch in milk. Add to the above mixture. Cook and stir until thick. Remove from fire.

Add vanilla and butter to the above.

Beat egg whites stiff; add sugar gradually, beating until stiff peaks are formed.

Fold in chopped pecans. Fold this meringue easily into the hot cooked mixture. Place in baked pie shell and chill thoroughly. Garnish with whipped cream and sprinkle with chopped nuts. (A few drops of brown coloring gives mixture the color of pecans.)

∾ Lemon Fluff Pie

Stoddard's atop Butler Hall, New York City

Ingredients

4 egg yolks, beaten	1 teaspoon sugar
Juice of 2 lemons	1 baked 8-inch pie shell
Rind of 1 lemon, grated	2 egg whites, beaten
¾ cup sugar	¼ cup sugar
2 egg whites, beaten	

Directions (Makes one 8-inch pie)

Cook egg yolks, lemon juice, and lemon rind in double boiler for about 12 minutes, stirring constantly. If it gets lumpy, beat with egg beater after removing from fire. It is better not to let it get lumpy.

Beat 1 teaspoon sugar into 2 egg whites and fold into mixture. Pour into baked pie shell.

Beat 2 egg whites until foamy and then add ¼ cup sugar gradually. Beat until stiff peaks are formed. Spread over filling and brown in moderate oven 350° for about 15 minutes.

-❧ *Spread whipped cream over the top of chiffon and cream pies, provided you're not counting calories.*

ᴕ Sherry Chiffon Pie

The Derings, Green Lake, Wisconsin

Ingredients

1 cup milk	1 envelope (1 tablespoon)
½ cup sugar	unflavored gelatin
3 egg yolks	4 tablespoons cold milk
¼ teaspoon nutmeg	3 egg whites
¼ teaspoon salt	1 cup heavy cream, whipped
½ cup sherry wine	1 baked 9-inch pie shell
	Grated bitter chocolate

Directions (Makes one 9-inch pie)

Combine 1 cup milk and ½ cup sugar in the top of a double boiler and heat. Add the well-beaten egg yolks, nutmeg, and salt, and stir constantly until thickened. Add the wine slowly and the gelatin, which has been softened in the cold milk. Cool.

Fold in the stiffly beaten egg whites and finally the stiffly whipped cream. Pour into a baked pie shell; top with a layer of sweetened whipped cream; chill. Add grated bitter chocolate just before serving.

∾ Sunny Silver Pie

High Hampton, Cashiers, North Carolina

Ingredients

4 egg yolks
2 or 3 tablespoons lemon juice
Rind of 1 lemon, grated
⅛ teaspoon salt
½ cup sugar
1½ teaspoons unflavored gelatin

⅓ cup cold water
4 egg whites, beaten
½ cup sugar
1 baked 9-inch pie shell
1 cup whipping cream

Directions (Makes one 9-inch pie)

Combine first five ingredients and cook in double boiler until thick, stirring constantly. Remove from fire.

Soak gelatin in cold water and add to the above.

Beat egg whites and ½ cup sugar together well. Fold into the above mixture.

Place in baked pie shell and set in refrigerator for 2 or 3 hours.

Whip cream and spread on top of pie.

∾ New Year Eggnog Pie

Ingredients

2 teaspoons unflavored gelatin
¼ cup cold water
3 egg yolks
1 cup milk
½ cup sugar

¼ teaspoon salt
3 tablespoons rum
3 egg whites, beaten stiff
1 baked 9-inch pie shell
1 cup heavy cream

Directions (Makes one 9-inch pie)

Soften gelatin in cold water about 5 minutes.

Make a custard of egg yolks, milk, sugar, and salt, and stir in the gelatin while custard is hot.

When mixture is cool, add rum. When it begins to thicken, fold in egg whites.

Pour into either a baked pie crust or a graham cracker crust.

Whip cream, but do not sweeten. Spread over pie and sprinkle with nutmeg. Chill until ready to serve.

❧ Eggnog Pie

The Carr House, Wolfeboro, New Hampshire

Ingredients

1 envelope (1 tablespoon)
   unflavored gelatin
¼ cup cold water
4 egg yolks, beaten
½ cup sugar
½ teaspoon salt

½ cup hot water
4 egg whites, beaten
¼ cup sugar
3 teaspoons rum
1 baked 9-inch pie shell

Directions (Makes one 9-inch pie)

Soak gelatin in cold water for 5 minutes.

Put egg yolks, ½ cup sugar, salt, and hot water in double boiler and
   cook until custard consistency. Add gelatin and cool.

Add ¼ cup sugar gradually to beaten egg whites, beating until
   smooth and glossy. Fold in egg white meringue and rum and fill
   baked pie shell. Place in refrigerator to set. Serve with thin layer of
   whipped cream and grated nutmeg over top.

❧ Eggnog Pie

Santa Maria Inn, Santa Maria, California

Ingredients

3 envelopes (3 tablespoons)
   unflavored gelatin
2 tablespoons cold water
2 cups boiling water
8 egg whites, beaten stiff

2½ cups sugar
4 oz. rum
1 pint whipped cream
2 baked 9-inch pie shells

Directions (Makes two 9-inch pies)

Soak gelatin in cold water; then add boiling water. Allow to cool and
   to begin setting before proceeding with the following.

Add sugar gradually to beaten egg whites, beating until smooth and
   glossy. Add rum and then fold into gelatin.

Fold whipped cream into above mixture and pour into previously
   baked pie shells. Place in a cool place and allow to set. Top with
   additional whipped cream.

∿ Lime Pie

Brown's, Fort Lauderdale, Florida

Ingredients

2 tablespoons sugar	1 baked 9-inch pie shell
3 egg yolks	3 egg whites
1 can condensed milk	3 tablespoons sugar
½ cup lime juice	

Directions (Makes one 9-inch pie)

Beat together sugar and egg yolks.

Beat condensed milk into the egg mixture.

Add lime juice and stir thoroughly. DO NOT COOK.

Pour mixture into pie shell.

Whip up egg whites, adding the 3 tablespoons of sugar gradually. Spread over the pie and put in 350° oven for a few minutes to brown the top.

-● *The secret for that mile-high effect in lemon chiffon pie: first, let the egg whites warm to room temperature before beating—this gives more volume. Second, fold the egg meringue into the custard mixture—not the custard into the meringue. Finally, use the correct pie pan.*

∿ Frozen Lime Pie

Ingredients

½ cup lime juice	Grated rind of 2 limes
24 marshmallows	2 or 3 drops green vegetable color
2 whole eggs	2 cups graham cracker crumbs
¼ cup sugar	⅓ cup melted butter
Pinch of salt	1 cup heavy cream, whipped

Directions (Makes one 9-inch pie)

Melt marshmallows in double boiler with lime juice.

Beat eggs until light in color. Gradually add sugar and salt, beating until thick. Pour into this the above mixture, beating during the addition. Add lime rind and green color and mix thoroughly. Let get cold.

Combine crumbs and butter and mix well. Line a 9-inch pie tin with ¾ of the mixture. Set in refrigerator to chill.

When filling is cold and crust is chilled, add whipped cream to filling and mix well. Pour into pie shell; top with remaining crumbs and cover with aluminum foil. Set in freezing compartment for at least 6 hours.

∽ Frosted Lime Pie

Vera Kirkpatrick, San Mateo, California

Ingredients

1½ cups hot water	⅓ to ½ cup fresh lime juice,
1¼ cups sugar	depending on strength and
7 tablespoons cornstarch	taste
7 tablespoons cold water (or ½ scant cup)	1 teaspoon grated lime rind
	1 tablespoon butter
2 large egg yolks (or 3 small ones)	A few drops of green coloring

Directions (Makes 6 individual pies or one 10-inch pie)

Put sugar and water in top of double boiler and bring to a boil over direct heat.

Mix cornstarch and cold water to a thin paste, add to the above, and cook over hot water until thick and smooth, stirring frequently.

Beat yolks slightly and add to above. Cook a few minutes longer. Remove from fire.

Mix remaining ingredients and add to the above. Chill slightly and pour in baked pie shells; top with meringue.

Meringue

Ingredients

¼ lb. marshmallows	¼ cup sugar
2 large egg whites (or 3 small ones)	1 tablespoon lime juice

Directions

Melt marshmallows in double boiler. Beat egg whites stiff and combine with sugar, lime juice, and marshmallows. Pile gently on top of the pie filling. Pies may be browned slightly under the broiler but are nicest chilled and garnished with springs of fresh mint leaves dipped in egg white and bar sugar.

ᴄᴡ Nell Palmer's Pecan Pie

Lowell Inn, Stillwater, Minnesota

Ingredients

3 eggs
¾ cup sugar
¼ lb. butter, melted

1 cup dark corn syrup
1 uncooked 9-inch pie shell
1 cup pecan halves

Directions (Makes one 9-inch pie)

Beat eggs until light.

Slowly beat sugar, butter, and corn syrup into the eggs.

Pour above into uncooked pie shell and bake slowly in 300° oven for
40 minutes. Completely cover the pie with whole pecan halves and
return to a 350° oven and bake for another 10 to 15 minutes. May
be served with whipped cream.

-ᴥ *Pick tart, juicy apples such as Winesaps, Jonathans, and
Wealthies for pie making.*

ᴄᴡ Mrs. Murphy's Pecan Pie

Mrs. Thomas J. Murphy, Cincinnati, Ohio

Ingredients

½ cup sugar
2 eggs, beaten
2 tablespoons flour
2 tablespoons butter

1 teaspoon vanilla
1 cup white corn syrup
1 cup pecan halves
1 unbaked 8½-inch pie shell

Directions (Makes one 8½-inch pie)

Cream together first five ingredients.

Stir syrup into the above and add pecans. Put into unbaked pie shell
and bake at 325° for 40 minutes or until brown on top.

ᴄᴡ Pecan Pie

The Derings, Green Lake, Wisconsin

Ingredients

3 eggs
1 cup granulated sugar
1 cup maple syrup
1 cup pecans, chopped

½ teaspoon salt
1 teaspoon vanilla
1 unbaked 9-inch pie shell

Directions *(Makes one 9-inch pie)*

Beat eggs slightly; add sugar, syrup, nuts, salt, and vanilla. Pour into unbaked pie shell and bake in slow oven at 325° for 40 minutes or until done.

➧ *Use heat-resistant glass or enamelware pans for browned undercrusts.*

ᕙ *Pecan Pie*

Pine Tree Inn, Lynnhaven, Virginia

Ingredients

3 eggs, slightly beaten
1 cup dark corn syrup
⅛ teaspoon salt
1 cup granulated sugar

1 teaspoon vanilla extract
1 unbaked 9-inch pie shell
⅔ cup pecan meats

Directions *(Makes one 9-inch pie)*

Mix together all ingredients except nuts. Pour into unbaked pie shell. Place nut meats carefully over top of mixture in attractive patterns. Bake in hot oven at 450° for 10 minutes. Then reduce heat to 350° and bake for about 30 minutes or until a clean knife blade inserted into center of pie comes out clean.

ᕙ *Pecan Pie*

New Perry Hotel, Perry, Georgia

Ingredients

3 eggs
1 cup sugar
1 cup white corn syrup
¼ lb. melted butter

1 teaspoon vanilla
1 cup chopped pecans
1 uncooked 9-inch pie shell

Directions *(Makes one 9-inch pie)*

Beat eggs well.
Add remaining ingredients, in order given, to eggs. Pour in uncooked pie shell and cook in preheated oven at 350° for 30 to 45 minutes.

> *Pie à la mode is all right if it is good pie and the ice cream is top-grade vanilla—but heaven forbid using chocolate.*

Spiced Nut Pie

Ingredients

3 eggs, separated
½ cup sugar
¼ lb. butter
1 cup mixed nuts—pecans and
    walnuts
1 cup steamed seedless raisins
½ teaspoon cinnamon

½ teaspoon cloves
1 teaspoon nutmeg
¼ teaspoon salt
2 tablespoons cider vinegar
3 egg whites
½ cup sugar
1 uncooked 9-inch pie shell

Directions (Makes one 9-inch pie)

Cream together egg yolks, butter, and ½ cup sugar.

Mix nuts, raisins, cinnamon, cloves, nutmeg, salt, and vinegar, and
    add all to above.

Beat egg whites stiff and slowly beat ½ cup sugar into whites. Fold
    into above.

Bake in moderate oven at 350° in uncooked pastry shell about
    40 minutes.

Date Nut Pie

Villula Tea Garden, Seale, Alabama

Ingredients

12 dates, chopped fine
1 cup pecans, chopped fine
1 cup sugar
12 premium crackers, rolled fine

½ teaspoon baking powder
1 teaspoon almond extract
3 egg whites, stiffly beaten

Directions (Makes one 8-inch pie)

Mix all ingredients except egg whites and extract. Fold in egg whites
    and extract. Put in 8-inch pie pan, which has been greased. Bake
    30 minutes at 350° or until light brown. Let cool before cutting.

Hazelnut Pie

Plentywood Farm, Bensenville, Illinois

Ingredients

1 unbaked 9-inch pie crust
3 eggs
1/2 cup sugar
1/4 teaspoon salt

1 cup dark corn syrup
1/2 teaspoon vanilla
1 cup toasted chopped hazelnuts

Directions (Makes one 9-inch pie)

Beat eggs slightly and add other ingredients in order. Mix well. Line
pie tin with pastry; pour in filling and bake 45 minutes in 300°
oven. Serve with whipped cream.

1 cup golden table syrup instead of dark corn syrup makes a
maple-flavored pie.

Treasure Chest Pie

Ingredients

1 8-inch pie shell, unbaked
1/2 cup butter
1 cup sugar
3 egg yolks, beaten
1 egg white, beaten
1/2 cup cooked raisins
1/2 cup mincemeat

1/2 cup walnuts, broken
1/2 cup pecans, broken
2 tablespoons orange juice
1 teaspoon vanilla
1/2 teaspoon salt
2 tablespoons Apple Jack brandy

Directions

Make a rich flaky crust, but do not bake it first.

Cream butter and sugar together.

Stir egg yolks and egg white into mixture until it foams.

Add remaining ingredients to mixture and pour into pie shell,
uncooked. Put a crisscross crust on top and bake in 400° oven for
12 to 15 minutes, or until the filling sets, and then cover the pie
with an inverted pie pan; lower the temperature to 350° and bake
until the top crust becomes brown and the filling is well set. May
be served with whipped cream, but that is not necessary.

❧ Black Walnut Pie

Ingredients

¼ lb. butter
1 cup sugar
1 cup dark corn syrup
3 eggs

1 teaspoon cinnamon
¼ cup black walnut meats
2 tablespoons boiling water
1 uncooked 9-inch pie shell

Directions (Makes one 9-inch pie)

Melt butter; add sugar and corn syrup and stir to dissolve. Beat eggs and add to mixture. Put walnut meats in cloth and beat to pulp. Add to mixture with cinnamon and stir in boiling water. Bake in uncooked pie shell in 350° oven for 50 minutes.

❧ Sour Cream Raisin Pie

Ingredients

1 10-inch baked pastry shell
½ cup seedless raisins
½ cup nut meats
1 cup sugar
2½ tablespoons flour
1 teaspoon cinnamon

¼ teaspoon ground cloves
1½ cups sour cream
3 egg yolks
3 egg whites
6 tablespoons sugar

Directions (Makes one 10-inch pie)

Chop raisins and nuts and mix together.

Mix together dry ingredients and add to raisins and nuts.

Pour sour cream over above mixture and stir all together thoroughly. Place in double boiler and bring to a boil.

Beat egg yolks together and add gradually to above mixture, stirring constantly to prevent lumping. Cook all together until thick. Let cool and pour into pastry shell.

Beat the egg whites together and add 6 tablespoons of sugar gradually. Top the pie with the meringue and brown in a slow oven.

∾ Brownie Pie

Ingredients

2 squares unsweetened chocolate
2 tablespoons butter
3 eggs, well beaten
½ cup sugar
¾ cup dark corn syrup
⅔ cup pecan halves
1 unbaked 9-inch pie shell

Directions (Makes one 9-inch pie)

Melt chocolate and butter together over hot water.
Add chocolate, sugar, and corn syrup to the beaten eggs and beat
thoroughly. Stir in pecan halves. Pour mixture into unbaked pie
shell. Bake in moderate oven at 375° for 40 to 50 minutes.

∾ English Toffee Pie

Pendarvis House, Mineral Point, Wisconsin

Ingredients

2 cups heavy sour cream
2¼ cups sugar
1 teaspoon ground cloves
3 eggs
2 egg yolks
3 cups seedless raisins
½ cup chopped walnuts
½ cup quartered blanched
   almonds
½ cup chopped hazelnuts
1 teaspoon vanilla
¼ cup sherry
2 unbaked 9-inch pie shells

Directions (Makes two 9-inch pies)

Combine sugar, cream, and cloves. Blend well. Beat together whole
eggs and egg yolks and stir into the sugar mixture.
Stir raisins, nuts, vanilla, and sherry into above mixture and blend
well. Pour into the unbaked pie shells and bake in 400° oven for
15 minutes. Reduce heat to 350° and bake 35 to 40 minutes or
until a silver knife inserted in center comes out clean. Serve with
vanilla ice cream if you like. Note: If two pies are not wanted,
one might be wrapped in aluminum foil and put in the freezer for
a short time. When wanted, let defrost and warm in the oven at
about 350°, just long enough to get warm through.

∾ *Grandma Obrecht's Lemon Pie*

Lowell Inn, Stillwater, Minnesota

Ingredients

1 ½ cups sugar
5 tablespoons cornstarch
½ teaspoon salt
1 ½ cups boiling water
2 teaspoons butter

4 egg yolks, slightly beaten
½ cup lemon juice
Grated rind of 1 lemon
1 baked 9-inch pie shell

Directions (Makes one 9-inch pie)

Mix sugar, cornstarch, and salt together.

Add boiling water to above; cook over direct heat, stirring constantly until mixture boils. Then place in double boiler; cover and cook until thick.

Remove from fire; add butter and egg yolks; return to fire and cook two minutes.

Add lemon juice and rind to above. Cook until thick. Pour into baked pie shell.

Meringue

Ingredients

4 egg whites
8 tablespoons granulated sugar

¼ teaspoon cream of tartar

Directions

Beat egg whites very stiff; add sugar and cream of tartar gradually and beat until blended. Spread over pie; sprinkle with a little sugar before baking. Bake in preheated 350° oven until brown.

∾ *Chess Pie*

Mrs. Earle Forbes, Greenville, North Carolina

Ingredients

3 eggs
1 cup sugar
¼ teaspoon salt
¼ teaspoon nutmeg

½ cup butter
¼ tablespoon tart jelly
1 unbaked 8-inch pie crust

Directions (Makes one 8-inch pie)

Beat eggs lightly.

Mix dry ingredients together and add slowly to eggs, beating all the while.

Melt butter and add to above.

Stir jelly into above, mixing well. Pour into unbaked pie crust and place in 350° oven for 10 minutes and then reduce heat to 300° for 20 minutes, or until it sets.

⌒ Chess Pie

Mrs. R. G. Price, Bowling Green, Kentucky

Ingredients

¼ lb. butter
1½ cups sugar
1½ teaspoons mild white vinegar

1½ teaspoons cornmeal
3 eggs
1 uncooked 9-inch pie shell

Directions (Makes one 9-inch pie)

Melt butter; stir and add sugar slowly; remove from fire.

If vinegar is strong, reduce amount of vinegar a bit and dilute with water. Add to above with cornmeal. Cool slightly.

Beat eggs slightly and add to above. Pour into uncooked pastry shell and bake for 10 minutes at 425°. Lower heat to 300°, or 275° is better, for almost an hour. Take from oven when pie still shakes slightly.

⌒ Lemon Pie

Ingredients

2 tablespoons flour, scant
1 cup sugar
¼ cup lemon juice
Rind of 1 lemon, grated
4 egg yolks
2 egg whites

1 cup water
1 pinch salt
1 tablespoon butter
1 baked 8-inch pie shell
2 egg whites
¼ cup sugar

Directions (Makes one 8-inch pie)

Add flour to 1 cup sugar; mix well.

Mix thoroughly the lemon juice, lemon rind, egg yolks and whites, water, and salt, and add to the above. Cook over boiling water until thick.

Add butter to the above mixture. Cool. Pour into baked pie shell.

Beat egg whites until foamy and then add ¼ cup sugar gradually. Beat until stiff peaks are formed. Spread over filling and brown in moderate oven at 350° for about 15 minutes.

➤ *An 8-inch pie cuts into 5 or 6 servings, and a 9-inch pie cuts into 7 or 8 pieces. It all depends upon how big one's appetite is.*

∽ Jelly Pie

Ingredients

½ cup butter
2 cups sugar
4 eggs
½ cup tart jelly

1 cup light cream
Pinch of salt
1 unbaked 8-inch pie shell

Directions (Makes one 8-inch pie)

Cream butter until soft; add sugar gradually and cream together until light and fluffy. Add salt, then add eggs, one at a time, and beat well. Add jelly and continue to beat until smooth. Turn into unbaked pie shell. Bake in hot oven at 450° for 10 minutes; reduce temperature to 325° and continue to bake for 50 minutes longer. Cool and garnish with whipped cream, if desired.

∽ French Chocolate Mint Pie

Lamkin Lake Shore Lodge, Good Hart, Michigan

Ingredients

1½ cups powdered sugar
¼ lb. butter (half margarine
    and half butter may be used,
    although butter is better)
2 eggs

2 squares melted unsweetened
    chocolate
6 drops oil of peppermint
1 baked vanilla wafer pie shell or
    plain pastry shell

Directions (Makes one 9-inch pie)

Cream butter and sugar together.
Beat eggs well. Add melted chocolate. Mix thoroughly.
Add peppermint to mixture and beat until light and fluffy. Put into vanilla wafer pie shell or thin pastry shell and let stand in refrigerator overnight. Note: The secret of the success in this dessert is in the beating; beat thoroughly, and the mixture will be light and fluffy and delicate.

→ *Custard pies should be stored in a cool place as soon as they have cooled naturally.*

◑ Pineapple-Mint Parfait Pie

Ingredients

1 package lime-flavored gelatin
1¼ cups hot pineapple juice
   (if not enough juice, add water
   to make 1¼ cups)
Few drops mint extract

1 pint vanilla ice cream
1 cup drained canned, crushed
   pineapple
1 baked 9-inch pie shell
1 cup whipping cream, whipped

Directions (Makes one 9-inch pie)

Dissolve gelatin in hot liquid in a 2-quart saucepan. Add mint extract. Add ice cream by spoonfuls, stirring until melted. Chill mixture until thickened but not set (25 to 35 minutes).

Fold drained pineapple into the above mixture. Turn into pie shell. Chill until firm, about 15 to 25 minutes.

Garnish with whipped cream.

◑ Frozen Chocolate Peppermint Pie

Hotel Anderson, Wabasha, Minnesota

Ingredients

4 egg whites
½ teaspoon cream of tartar
1 cup sugar
2¾ cups whipping cream

2 cups fudge sauce
½ teaspoon oil of peppermint
1 quart vanilla ice cream

Directions (Makes one 12-inch pie)

Beat egg whites until frothy. Add cream of tartar. Beat until whites are stiff. Add sugar slowly, a tablespoon at a time, beating until mixture is thick and glossy. Line a deep 12-inch pie pan with meringue and bake in preheated 300° oven for 50 to 60 minutes. Cool.

Whip cream until stiff. Slowly add fudge sauce and oil of peppermint.

Soften ice cream a bit in electric beater. Spoon into cooled meringue shell. Do not let ice cream get too soft, just enough to manage. Pour over this the chocolate whipped cream mixture. Freeze until firm. Note: If you do not have a 12-inch pan, use two 9-inch pie pans.

❧ Fudge Pie with Peppermint Ice Cream

Mrs. Ashby, Bowling Green, Kentucky

Ingredients

2 squares semisweet baking
   chocolate
3 eggs
1 cup sugar
¼ cup flour
½ cup melted butter
½ cup pecans

1 teaspoon vanilla
¼ teaspoon salt
½ pint vanilla ice cream
¼ cup crushed peppermint
   candy
Couple of drops of red coloring

Directions (Makes one 9-inch pie)

Melt chocolate in double boiler. Beat eggs; add sugar and flour to
   the beaten eggs and mix well. Add this mixture to the melted
   chocolate.

Add the butter, pecans, vanilla, and salt to the above. Grease a 9-inch
   pie pan with shortening; pour in mixture and bake in slow oven at
   275° for about 30 minutes or until set. Cool.

Whip vanilla ice cream and blend in crushed peppermint candy. Add
   a little coloring to the ice cream to make it pink enough. (Do not
   put too much candy into the ice cream, as it will make it syrupy.)
   Refreeze the ice cream and serve on top of the Fudge Pie.

❧ Strawberry Parfait Pie

Ingredients

1 package strawberry-flavored
   gelatin
1¼ cups boiling berry juice (add
   water to make 1¼ cups)
1 pint vanilla ice cream

1 box (12 oz.) frozen
   strawberries, defrosted and
   drained
1 baked 9-inch pie shell
1 cup whipping cream, whipped

Directions (Makes one 9-inch pie)

Dissolve gelatin in boiling liquid in a 2-quart saucepan. Add ice
   cream by spoonfuls, stirring until melted. Chill mixture until
   thickened but not set (15 to 20 minutes).

Fold drained strawberries into the above mixture. Turn into pie shell.
   Chill until firm, about 20 to 30 minutes.

Garnish with whipped cream.

Holiday Pie

Ye Old College Inn, Houston, Texas

Pumpkin Custard

Ingredients

2 cups sugar
4 eggs
4 cups custard pumpkin, canned
1 teaspoon salt
2 teaspoons cinnamon
2 teaspoons allspice
3 cups milk

Directions (Makes two 9-inch pies)

Cream together sugar and eggs.
Add remaining ingredients in order given to the sugar and egg mixture.

Mincemeat Base Filling

¾ lb. prepared mincemeat
8 oz. chopped tart apples
Pastry for two 9-inch pie shells

Directions

Line two 9-inch pie pans with your favorite crust. Build up sides as high as possible, and crimp around edges. Spread half of the mincemeat filling in each pie shell. Then pour pumpkin custard on top. Bake in 350° oven for approximately 45 minutes. This results in a two-layer pie of unusual taste.

Prick pastry with a fork to prevent puffing during baking. If the pastry still puffs, reach quickly in the oven and prick again.

White Christmas Pie

Ingredients

1 package (1 tablespoon) unflavored gelatin
½ cup sugar
¼ cup flour
¼ teaspoon salt
1¾ cups milk
¾ teaspoon vanilla
¼ teaspoon almond extract
½ cup whipping cream, whipped
3 egg whites
½ cup sugar
1 cup shredded coconut, cut
1 baked 9-inch pie shell

Directions (Makes one 9-inch pie)

Combine first four ingredients in saucepan.

Stir milk into the above mixture. Cook over low heat, stirring
constantly, until the mixture comes to a boil. Remove from heat
and cool. When slightly thickened, beat with rotary egg beater
until smooth.

Fold extracts and whipped cream into the above mixture.

Beat egg whites until foamy. Add ½ cup sugar gradually, beating
until mixture stands in stiff peaks. Fold the meringue and coconut
into the gelatin mixture. Pour into baked pie shell. Chill until set.

∽ Christmas Pie

Brevard Hotel, Cocoa, Florida

Crust

Ingredients

1½ cups ground Brazil nuts	3 tablespoons sugar

Directions (Makes one 9-inch pie)

Mix nuts and sugar thoroughly. Line bottom and sides of pie tin and
bake in 400° oven for 8 minutes or until lightly browned. Watch
carefully, for it scorches easily.

Filling

Ingredients

1 envelope (1 tablespoon) unflavored gelatin	½ cup glacéed cherries
¼ cup cold water	2 tablespoons light rum
3 egg yolks	3 egg whites
¼ cup sugar	¼ cup sugar
⅛ teaspoon salt	½ pint cream
1½ cups scalded milk	Sliced Brazil nuts

Directions

Soak gelatin in cold water about 5 minutes.

Beat egg yolks slightly with a fork; add salt. Add ¼ cup sugar gradually. Then stir in gradually and carefully the hot milk. Place in
double boiler and cook over boiling water until it coats a metal
spoon. Remove at once and stir in gelatin. Cook; then chill custard
until it mounds when dropped from a spoon. Beat with an egg
beater until smooth.

Stir in cherries, which have been sliced thin. Beat in carefully the
rum. Beat egg whites until stiff. Add gradually ¼ cup sugar and
beat until stiff and dry. Fold into the custard. Pour into cooled
baked Brazil nut crust. Place in the refrigerator until the following
day or for at least 4 hours, until firm.

Whip at least a half pint of cream and spread over the pie. Top with
sliced Brazil nuts.

❧ Chocolate Angel Pie

Ingredients

½ cup sugar
⅛ teaspoon cream of tartar
2 egg whites
½ cup nuts

¾ cup semisweet chocolate
3 tablespoons hot water
1 teaspoon vanilla
1 cup heavy cream, whipped

Directions (Makes one 9-inch pie)

Sift sugar and cream of tartar. Beat egg whites stiff, not dry. Add
sifted sugar gradually while beating until smooth and glossy. Line
well-buttered 9-inch pie pan with mixture. Keep center hollowed
out to ¼-inch thickness. Do not spread on rim of pan. Sprinkle
with nuts. Bake in slow oven at 275° for 1 hour or until delicate
brown. Cool thoroughly.

Melt chocolate in double boiler. Stir in water. Cook until thick. Cool
slightly. Add vanilla. Fold in whipped cream. Fill shell and chill in
refrigerator for 3 or 4 hours.

❧ Heavenly Pie

Ingredients

3 egg whites, beaten
½ cup sugar

⅓ cup confectioners' sugar
1 cup whipping cream

Directions

Beat egg whites stiff and dry. Add ½ cup sugar gradually.

Fold confectioners' sugar into mixture. Bake in ungreased glass pie
plate in 275° to 325° oven for 1 hour. About 2 hours before serving,
crush the top slightly.

Whip cream and spread over the pie. Place in the refrigerator until
ready to serve. Shred bitter chocolate over the top.

ᜐ Butterscotch Pie

Ingredients

1¼ cups firmly packed brown
    sugar
¼ teaspoon salt
2 tablespoons water
2 cups milk
4½ tablespoons cornstarch

3 egg yolks, slightly beaten
2 tablespoons butter
½ teaspoon vanilla
1 baked 9-inch pie shell
½ cup pecans, chopped
1 cup whipping cream, whipped

Directions (Makes one 9-inch pie)

Combine first three ingredients in top of double boiler and cook over
direct heat for 5 minutes, stirring constantly.

Blend a small amount of the milk with the cornstarch. Add this
with the remaining milk to the above mixture. Cook over boiling
water for about 20 minutes or until thick and smooth, stirring
constantly.

Stir a small amount of the hot mixture over the beaten egg yolks and
mix well; return to the double boiler and cook 5 minutes longer.
Add butter and vanilla. Pour into baked pie shell and chill.

Just before serving, sprinkle top with nuts and garnish with whipped
cream.

ᜐ Lemon Angel Pie

Vera Kirkpatrick, San Mateo, California

Ingredients

4 egg whites
1 teaspoon cream of tartar
1 cup sugar
4 egg yolks

½ cup sugar
1½ lemons, juice and rind
1 cup heavy cream
⅔ teaspoon vanilla

Directions (Makes one 9- or 10-inch pie)

Beat egg whites stiff, add cream of tartar and 1 cup sugar, and beat
until smooth and glossy. Put in buttered pie tin and bake for
60 minutes at 200°. Cool when done.

Beat egg yolks with ½ cup sugar; add juice of the lemons and grated
rind of the lemons. Cook in top of double boiler over boiling water
until thick. Let cool.

Whip cream, sweeten to taste, and add vanilla. Spread half of
whipped cream on cold meringue; put custard filling on cream,
then remainder of cream on top. Chill 3 hours before serving.
Garnish with mint leaves and fresh strawberries.

Angel Pie

Quaker House, Orchard Park, New York

Ingredients

3 egg whites
½ teaspoon vinegar
½ cup sugar
3 egg yolks
½ cup sugar

1 lemon—juice and grated rind
1½ cups whipping cream
¼ cup sugar
1 teaspoon vanilla

Directions (Serves 6 to 8)

Beat whites with vinegar until stiff but not dry.

Add ½ cup sugar gradually. Spread this meringue in a buttered 9-inch pie plate in the shape of a pie shell. Bake at 300° for 1 hour. Cool.

Beat yolks until light and thick. Add ½ cup sugar gradually. Add juice and cook this mixture in top of double boiler until thick. Add lemon rind. Cool and spread on baked meringue shell.

Whip cream until thick. Add ¼ cup sugar and vanilla to whipped cream. Spread on top of lemon mixture in meringue. Chill in refrigerator 6 to 24 hours.

Maid of the Mist Pie

Crust

Ingredients

14 graham crackers

¼ cup butter, melted

Directions

Crush graham crackers with rolling pin. Blend butter with crumbs and pat into pie pan.

Filling

Ingredients

3 egg yolks
1 cup sugar
Juice of two large lemons

3 egg whites
½ pint whipping cream

Directions

Beat sugar and egg yolks well together; add lemon juice; place in double boiler and cook to custard consistency.

Beat egg whites very stiff; fold into custard; blend thoroughly; put into crust and bake in very moderate oven, about 325°, until set. Whip cream until stiff; cover pie when cool, just before serving.

ᴄᴡ *Banana Butterscotch Pie*

Dorothy Brehmer Klassen, Fond du Lac, Wisconsin

Ingredients

1 cup brown sugar
4 tablespoons flour
1 cup milk
2 egg yolks, beaten
4 tablespoons butter
$\frac{1}{2}$ teaspoon vanilla

1 baked 8-inch pie shell
2 large bananas, sliced
2 egg whites, beaten
2 tablespoons sugar
1 cup whipped cream

Directions (Makes one 8-inch pie)

Mix brown sugar and flour and put in top of double boiler.

Add milk slowly to the above. Cook, stirring constantly until it thickens.

Add egg yolks to mixture and cook 3 minutes longer. Remove from fire.

Add butter to mixture. Cool.

Add vanilla to mixture.

Line pie shell with banana slices and pour the mixture over the slices.

Make a meringue with egg whites and sugar. Cover pie and brown in oven, or cover pie with whipped cream.

ᴄᴡ *Graham Cracker Pie*

Crust

Ingredients

30 graham crackers, crushed
2 tablespoons flour
2 tablespoons cinnamon

$\frac{1}{2}$ cup sugar
1 cup melted butter
$\frac{1}{2}$ cup lard, melted

Directions (Makes two 8-inch pies)

Mix all ingredients and press in pie pan.

Filling

Ingredients

1 quart milk
8 egg yolks, beaten
4 tablespoons cornstarch
2 teaspoons vanilla
Pinch of salt
2 tablespoons melted butter

½ cup sugar
8 egg whites, beaten
½ cup sugar
1 pinch of salt
1 teaspoon vanilla

Directions

Heat milk.

Mix egg yolks, cornstarch, vanilla, salt, butter, and ½ cup sugar; add the heated milk and cook until thick. Then fill the pie shells.

Make a meringue of remaining ingredients and cover pies. Brown in 350° oven.

ᴄ⁓ *Boiled Cider Pie*

Ingredients

1 cup sugar
2 tablespoons cornstarch
½ cup boiled cider
2 eggs yolks, slightly beaten
¾ cup boiling water

1 tablespoon butter
1 baked 8-inch pie shell
2 egg whites
¼ cup sugar

Directions (Makes one 8-inch pie)

Combine 1 cup sugar with cornstarch in saucepan. Add boiled cider gradually, mixing well. Stir in the egg yolks and then add boiling water. Cook over low heat until clear and thick, stirring constantly. Add butter and remove from heat. Cool slightly and pour into baked pie shell.

Beat egg whites until very soft peaks are formed. Add ¼ cup sugar, a tablespoon at a time, beating after each addition. Beat until meringue will stand in stiff peaks. Spread over filling and bake in 350° oven for about 10 minutes or until lightly browned.

ᶜᵕ᷄ *Barbara Fritchie Sugar House Pie*

Water Gate Inn, Washington, D.C.

Ingredients

1 pie shell, unbaked
2 tablespoons flour
¼ cup evaporated milk
½ cup brown sugar
½ cup light corn syrup
2 egg yolks

1 tablespoon melted butter
½ teaspoon flavoring, vanilla,
   lemon, or rum
½ teaspoon salt
2 egg whites
Nutmeg

Directions (Makes one 9-inch pie)

Make your favorite pie crust and line pie tin. Put into refrigerator to
chill while you make the filling.

Mix flour with a portion of the milk to make a smooth paste. Add
sugar, syrup, beaten egg yolks, remainder of milk, and butter. Mix
well. Cook in upper part of double boiler over hot water, stirring
constantly until thick and smooth. Remove from fire.

Add flavoring and salt to above mixture. Beat egg whites stiff and
fold into mixture. Pour into uncooked pie shell and sprinkle with
nutmeg. Bake in 425° oven for 10 minutes. Reduce heat to 300°
and bake about 45 minutes longer or until a knife blade inserted
in center comes out clean. Serve cold. If you like, you may garnish
each piece as it is served with a tablespoon of rum-flavored
whipped cream.

ᶜᵕ᷄ *Cavalier Pie Supreme*

Beach Plaza Hotel, Virginia Beach, Virginia

Ingredients

2 envelopes (2 tablespoons)
   unflavored gelatin
1 pint warm water
1 quart whipping cream
6 egg yolks, beaten
1 cup powdered sugar
Pinch of salt

1 teaspoon vanilla
2 baked 8-inch pie shells
1 pint whipping cream
⅓ cup powdered sugar
½ teaspoon vanilla
4 oz. bittersweet chocolate

Directions (Makes two 8-inch pies)

Dissolve gelatin in warm water and let cool.
Whip 1 quart cream until stiff.

Add egg yolks, 1 cup powdered sugar, salt, and vanilla to cream and whip again for 1 minute. Add gelatin and whip well again. Pour into baked pie shells and put into refrigerator to congeal.

Whip 1 pint cream until stiff.

Add ⅓ cup powdered sugar and vanilla to whipped cream, and spread over pies above.

Grate chocolate and spread over pies and return to refrigerator until ready to serve.

ᘓ *Black Bottom Pie*

Dolores Restaurant, Oklahoma City, Oklahoma

Crust

Ingredients

14 crisp gingersnaps   5 tablespoons melted butter

Directions (Makes one 9-inch pie)

Roll snaps out fine. Add butter to cookie crumbs and pat evenly into a 9-inch pan. Bake 10 minutes in 300° oven. Allow to cool.

Filling

Ingredients

2 cups milk, scalded   1 teaspoon vanilla
4 egg yolks, beaten   1 envelope (1 tablespoon)
½ cup sugar   unflavored gelatin
1¼ tablespoons cornstarch   4 tablespoons cold water
1½ squares chocolate

Directions

Add egg yolks slowly to hot milk.

Combine sugar and cornstarch and stir into above. Cook in double boiler for 20 minutes, stirring occasionally until mixture generously coats a spoon. Remove from flame and take out 1 cup.

Add chocolate to the cup of custard and beat well.

As chocolate custard cools, add vanilla; pour into pie crust and chill.

Soak gelatin in cold water and add to remaining hot custard. Let mixture get cool, but not thick.

Meringue

Ingredients

4 egg whites
½ cup sugar
¼ teaspoon cream of tartar

2 tablespoons rum
1 cup whipped cream
½ square chocolate

Directions

Beat egg whites, sugar, and cream of tartar into a meringue and fold into custard.

Add rum. As soon as chocolate custard has set in crust, cover with rum custard. Chill again until custard sets.

Spread whipped cream on top of pie.

Shave chocolate, sprinkle over pie, and serve.

∾ Shoofly Pie

Mrs. Edwin Bowen, Shillington, Pennsylvania

Ingredients

2 unbaked pie shells
1 ½ cups flour
½ cup light brown sugar
½ cup dark brown sugar
¼ cup butter

¾ teaspoon baking soda
¾ cup hot water
¾ cup dark corn syrup
¼ teaspoon salt

Directions (Makes two 7-inch pies)

Prepare pie shells.

Blend flour, sugars, and butter together to make crumbs.

Mix soda with hot water; add syrup and salt and blend thoroughly. In pie shells, place layer of crumbs, layer of liquid, layer of crumbs, layer of liquid, and top with layer of crumbs. Bake at 475° for 10 minutes, then reduce heat to 375° and bake for 30 minutes.

∾ Jefferson Davis Pie

Mrs. McKenzie Moss, Bowling Green, Kentucky

Ingredients

2 unbaked 9-inch pie crusts
3 cups sugar
1 cup butter
4 eggs, beaten lightly

1 cup milk
1 tablespoon flour
¼ teaspoon salt
1 teaspoon vanilla

Directions (Makes two 9-inch pies)

Cream butter and sugar together.

Add eggs to the above.

Stir milk into mixture.

Blend remaining ingredients into mixture. Then beat all the above like the devil. Line 2 pie pans, which have first been well buttered, with pie crust. Pour in the filling and bake in 450° oven for 10 minutes; then reduce heat to 350° for another 30 to 35 minutes.

Soufflés, Fondues, Sponges, and Whips

To MAKE perfect soufflés there are certain rules that you should follow. The egg yolks should be beaten until thick and lemon colored. The egg whites should be beaten only to the point where the peaks are slightly rounded. A quick, deft hand is necessary in mixing a soufflé in order to get the greatest volume and yet not break down the air cells. Last of all, butter only the bottom of the baking dish and not the sides, as this method allows the soufflé to rise more. If these few rules are followed, success will be yours, and you will never again fret for fear of a flat, soggy failure.

◆ *Soufflés should be served at once because they fall very quickly.*

∾ Chocolate Soufflé

Mrs. W. B. Taylor, Bowling Green, Kentucky

Ingredients

2 tablespoons butter
2 tablespoons flour
¾ cup milk
1½ squares chocolate, melted
⅓ cup sugar

2 tablespoons hot water
3 egg yolks, beaten
3 egg whites, beaten
½ teaspoon vanilla

Directions

Blend together butter and flour.
Gradually add milk to the above. Cook until it reaches the boiling
point.
Mix together chocolate and sugar, add to the above mixture, and stir
until smooth.
Add hot water to above mixture. Let cool.
Fold remaining ingredients into mixture. Turn into baking dish and
bake in 350° oven for 25 minutes, or until done. Serve hot with
hard sauce.

∾ Lemon Soufflé

L. S. Ayres and Company, Tea Room, Indianapolis, Indiana

Ingredients

1¼ cups sugar
⅛ teaspoon salt
2½ tablespoons flour
2½ tablespoons butter

2½ lemons and rind, grated
3 eggs, separated, plus one extra
  white
1¼ cups milk

Directions (Serves 8)

Mix sugar, salt, and flour. Add butter, lemon juice, rind, and beaten
egg yolks, blended with the milk. Beat well. Fold in stiffly beaten
egg whites. Pour into a buttered casserole; place in a pan of boiling
water and bake for 30 minutes in an oven at 350°. Be accurate as
to baking time as bottom remains a thick liquid, which serves as a
sauce.

➥ *"Of all books produced," said Joseph Conrad, "since the most
remote ages by human talents and industry, those only that treat of
cooking are, from a moral point of view, above suspicion."*

❧ Date Soufflé

Ingredients

2 tablespoons butter	¾ cup milk
3 tablespoons sugar	3 egg whites, beaten
3 egg yolks	1 teaspoon salt
2 tablespoons flour	1 package dates, chopped (14 oz.)

Directions (Serves 8)

Cream together butter and sugar.

Add yolks to above.

Add flour to the above, alternately with milk.

Beat together egg whites and salt, and fold into mixture.

Fold dates into mixture. Pour into greased 1½- or 2-quart casserole dish. Set in pan of hot water and bake in 350° oven for 35 minutes. Serve with Orange Sauce.

Orange Sauce

Ingredients

1 cup sugar	1 teaspoon cornstarch
1 cup orange juice	1 tablespoon butter
1 orange rind, grated	1 egg yolk
1 lemon, juice	

Directions

Mix together all ingredients and cook in a double boiler until it coats a spoon.

❧ Orange Soufflé

Chalet Suzanne, Lake Wales, Florida

Ingredients

6 egg whites	4 tablespoons orange marmalade
6 tablespoons sugar	1 teaspoon orange extract

Directions (Serves 6)

Beat egg whites stiff and beat in sugar gradually.

Mix marmalade into the above. Put in a double boiler that holds 3 quarts. Cook slowly for 1 hour. Turn out on a round platter. (It should stand up like a man's silk hat.) Pour sauce around it and serve.

Sauce

Ingredients

6 egg yolks, beaten

1 cup sugar

Pinch of salt

1 pint whipped cream

2 tablespoons curaçao

Candied kumquats, sliced

Directions

Beat yolks, sugar, and salt together until smooth.

Add whipped cream and curaçao to the sauce just before serving.

Decorate each portion with kumquats.

> ➣ *For a soufflé with a "top hat," cut a circle around the top of the mixture with a sharp knife about 2 inches from the edge before putting in the oven.*

∾ Rum Soufflé

Ingredients

4 egg yolks

¼ cup sugar

½ teaspoon vanilla

Pinch of salt

4 egg whites, stiffly beaten

¼ cup Jamaica rum

Directions (Serves 4)

Combine yolks and sugar and beat until thick and lemon colored.

Add vanilla and salt to the above mixture.

Fold egg whites into egg yolk mixture. Pour into flat baking dish.
(Mixture should be about 1 inch high.) Bake in slow oven at 325°
for 25 minutes or until firm.

Pour rum over soufflé. Ignite and serve immediately.

∾ Vanilla Soufflé

Ingredients

¼ cup butter

¼ cup flour

¼ teaspoon salt

¾ cup milk

3 egg yolks

½ cup sugar

1 teaspoon vanilla

3 egg whites

¼ teaspoon cream of tartar

Directions (Serves 8)

Melt butter in saucepan.

Add flour, salt, and milk to the above mixture and blend together.
Cook over low heat, stirring constantly, until thick and smooth.
Remove from heat.

Beat egg yolks until thick and lemon colored. Add sugar gradually
and continue beating.

Add vanilla to milk mixture and blend into egg yolk mixture.

Combine egg whites and cream of tartar, and beat until stiff. Gently
fold in egg yolk mixture. Pour into greased 2-quart baking dish.
Place baking dish in pan of hot water. Bake in moderate oven at
350° about 45 minutes or until golden brown. Serve immediately
with whipped cream and sliced toasted almonds.

∾ *Party Soufflé*

Ingredients

9 egg whites	3 teaspoons vanilla
¾ teaspoon cream of tartar	1 quart crushed, sweetened
⅛ teaspoon salt	strawberries
9 tablespoons sugar	

Directions (Serves 12)

Combine first three ingredients and beat until stiff peaks are formed.
Beat in sugar very gradually.

Add vanilla and strawberries, and mix thoroughly. Pour into greased
10-inch tube pan. Place tube pan in pan of hot water (1 inch deep).
Bake in slow oven at 275° about 1½ hours. Carefully invert onto
hot serving dish. Spread with Eggnog Sauce.

Pour over the top and around soufflé. Serve immediately.

Eggnog Sauce

Ingredients

2 egg yolks	½ cup heavy cream, whipped
½ cup sifted confectioners' sugar	2 tablespoons Jamaica rum

Directions

Beat egg yolks until thick and lemon colored. Add sugar gradually
and continue to beat until thick.

Fold whipped cream and rum into above.

🐟 *Do not open the oven when baking a soufflé.*

〜 Chocolate Sponge Pudding

Ingredients

4 oz. sweet chocolate	Pinch of salt
3 egg yolks	2 tablespoons sugar
2 tablespoons sugar	1 teaspoon vanilla
3 egg whites	

Directions (Serves 5)

Melt chocolate in top of double boiler.

Beat yolks until thick and lemon colored. Add 2 tablespoons sugar and continue beating until very thick. Set aside.

Beat egg whites with salt until mixture will stand in soft moist peaks. Add 2 tablespoons sugar gradually, then vanilla, and beat until stiff but not dry. Add hot melted chocolate slowly to egg yolk mixture, mixing well. Fold into egg whites. Pile lightly into sherbet glasses with ladyfingers, macaroons, or vanilla wafers, cut in quarters, or strips of sponge cake. Fill glasses with chocolate mixture. Top with whipped cream and serve.

〜 Chocolate Fondue

Ingredients

2 squares unsweetened chocolate	¼ teaspoon salt
1 cup milk	3 egg yolks
½ cup fine bread crumbs	1 teaspoon vanilla
1 tablespoon butter, melted	3 egg whites, stiffly beaten
½ cup sugar	

Directions (Serves 5 to 6)

Heat chocolate and milk together in saucepan, stirring constantly, until chocolate is melted and mixture blended.

Add bread crumbs, butter, sugar, and salt, and mix well.

Beat yolks slightly in bowl. Gradually add chocolate mixture, stirring constantly. Add vanilla and blend.

Fold above mixture into egg whites. Pour into greased 1½-quart casserole. Place casserole in pan of hot water. Bake in moderate oven at 350° about 40 minutes or until silver knife inserted comes out clean. Serve with cream, whipped cream, Foamy Sauce, or Plain Custard Sauce. (*See* Dessert Sauces section for sauces.)

ᨆ *Chocolate Custard Sponge Pudding*

Ingredients

2 squares unsweetened chocolate	¼ teaspoon salt
2 cups milk	2 tablespoons butter, melted
¼ cup flour	3 egg yolks, slightly beaten
½ cup sugar	3 egg whites

Directions (Serves 6 to 8)

Combine chocolate and milk in top of double boiler. Cook and stir over hot water until chocolate is melted. Beat with rotary egg beater until smooth and blended.

Combine flour, sugar, and salt together in bowl.

Add butter and yolks to above mixture. Then gradually add hot chocolate mixture, blending well.

Beat egg whites to soft peaks. Fold gently into chocolate mixture. Pour into greased 8-inch round baking dish. Place baking dish in pan of hot water. Bake in moderate oven at 350° for 45 to 50 minutes. Serve warm or cold, with whipped cream.

ᨆ *Date-Applesauce Whip*

Ingredients

2 egg whites	1 tablespoon lemon juice
¼ teaspoon salt	¾ cup chopped dates
¼ cup sugar	⅔ cup chopped walnuts
1¼ cups thick sweetened applesauce	Ladyfingers or vanilla wafers

Directions (Serves 6)

Beat egg whites with salt until foamy throughout. Add sugar, 2 tablespoons at a time, beating after each addition. Continue beating until stiff peaks are formed.

Combine applesauce, lemon juice, dates, and walnuts. Fold gently into beaten egg whites. Blend well.

Arrange ladyfingers along the inside of sherbet glasses. Place mixture into sherbet glasses.

❧ Prune Whip

Ingredients

2 egg whites
⅛ teaspoon salt
¼ cup sugar

1½ cups prune pulp
2 tablespoons lemon juice

Directions (Serves 4)

Beat egg whites with salt until foamy throughout. Add sugar, 2 tablespoons at a time, beating after each addition. Continue beating
until stiff peaks are formed.

Combine prune pulp and lemon juice, and fold into beaten egg
whites. Blend well. Place mixture into sherbet glasses and chill.
Serve plain or with Plain Custard Sauce. (*See* Dessert Sauces
section.)

❧ Prune Whip

Ingredients

5 egg whites
⅛ teaspoon salt

¼ teaspoon cream of tartar
1 cup sweetened prune pulp

Directions (Serves 4 to 6)

Combine egg whites and salt, and beat until foamy throughout.
Add cream of tartar and continue beating until stiff.

Fold in prune pulp. Pour into greased 9-inch baking dish. Place
baking dish in pan of hot water. Bake in slow oven at 300° about
1 hour. Serve hot with Plain Custard Sauce. (*See* Dessert Sauces
section.)

❧ Quick Strawberry Fluff

Ingredients

1 cup fresh strawberries, capped
1 egg white
1 cup sugar

2 teaspoons lemon juice
½ cup heavy cream, whipped

Directions (Serves 5)

Combine first four ingredients in bowl and beat at high speed of
electric mixer until light and fluffy.

Fold whipped cream into fruit mixture. Pour into sherbet glasses
and chill.

⟋ Strawberry Marshmallow Cream

Ingredients

1 egg white
Pinch of salt
1 cup heavy cream, whipped
1 cup marshmallows, cut in small
  pieces

1 cup fresh strawberries or 1 box
  frozen strawberries, defrosted
  and drained

Directions (Serves 6)

Beat egg white with salt until stiff.
Fold whipped cream and marshmallows into beaten egg white and
  chill.
Crush berries and fold in just before serving.

Baked and Steamed Puddings

PUDDINGS are a subtle blend of flavors. They may be fragrant and spicy or mild and delicate. When served with the right sauce, they become luxurious desserts.

For generations, steamed puddings have been associated with the three winter holidays: Thanksgiving, Christmas, and New Year's. Plum pudding is as traditional as turkey and cranberry sauce at holiday time. The first plum pudding was very different from our present pudding. It consisted of a mixture of mashed plums mixed with butter, rice, and barley. Whole grains of rice and barley were included as it was believed that these would guarantee an abundant harvest for the coming year. Later, plum pudding was made of a mixture of meat broth, spices, and dried raisins. By the early nineteenth century the familiar English plum pudding of flour, spices, raisins, currants, ground suet, sugar, eggs, and brandy had evolved. The only major difference between the puddings of the early days and those of today is that formerly the pudding was wrapped in a cloth and placed in boiling water to cook, while today our plum pudding is steamed.

The colonial settlers, forced to be thrifty and resourceful, made a new variation of plum pudding. Their adaption, called suet pudding, was made of flour, spices, fruit, and molasses, and although it was not as rich as the original English pudding, it filled the need for such a dessert. Since the time of the suet pudding, many steamed fruit variations have been developed.

From the early settlers we also derive another steamed pudding —the Indian pudding. As the name implies, this recipe was taught to the Puritans by the Indians. It consists of a mixture of cornmeal, molasses, milk, and spices. Indian pudding has a very unusual flavor and texture, and the secret of its preparation is long slow baking or steaming.

In the South, especially in Virginia, colonial women competed with one another in serving elegant puddings. To this day, we still have desserts that were developed as a result of this competition. The Duke of Gloucester and the Queen Charlotte are examples of the fine puddings that came from this era.

Puddings as a group really fall into no special social class. They can be highfalutin' or plain Jane. They can be used to bolster a simple meal or can keep company with the most lavish dinner. They can be heavy and hearty or light and tasty. I have enjoyed them in frontier camps as well as in the most elegant metropolitan cafes. Universal though it may be, there is still one thing a pudding must avoid: it must not weep.

When serving, you may want to hold out a little portion for a late snack or tomorrow's light lunch. Keep this little nugget in the refrigerator and try it smothered with cold milk. You will find it tasty and filling.

∽ Chocolate Steam Pudding

Ingredients

3 tablespoons butter
⅔ cup sugar
1 egg, beaten
2¼ cups flour
4½ teaspoons baking powder

½ teaspoon salt
1 cup milk
2½ squares unsweetened
    chocolate

Directions (Serves 6)

Cream and blend together butter, sugar, and egg.
Sift together dry ingredients and mix into the above.
Add milk to mixture.
Melt chocolate and add to mixture. Turn into molds, filling no more
    than ½ full. Steam 2 hours and serve with sauce.

Sauce

Ingredients

¼ cup butter
1 cup powdered sugar
½ teaspoon vanilla

Pinch of salt
¼ cup whipping cream

Directions

Work butter until very soft.
Gradually add sugar to the butter.
Add vanilla and salt to mixture.
Whip cream and fold into the sauce.

∽ Suet Pudding

Mrs. Roy B. Morningstar, Bowling Green, Kentucky

Ingredients

½ teaspoon salt
1¾ cups flour
½ cup chopped suet
½ cup sorghum molasses

½ cup buttermilk
½ teaspoon soda
1 cup raisins

Directions (Serves 6 to 8)

Mix salt, flour, and suet together.
Mix molasses, milk, and soda. Add to this enough of the flour
    mixture to make a stiff batter (not dough).
Flour raisins lightly and add to the above mixture. Fill cans ½ full

and steam for 3 hours. (Use three 12 oz. baking powder cans or any similar containers.) If pressure cooker is used for steaming, go by chart for steaming puddings. Serve with Wine Sauce or Clear Brown Sugar Sauce and top with whipped cream. Note: Be sure to use suet that can be easily broken into pieces and is free from fine fibers; ask the butcher for kidney fat.

ᴄᴜ Steamed Blackberry Pudding

Ingredients

2 cups sifted flour	4 tablespoons butter
4 teaspoons baking powder	1 ¾ cups milk
1 teaspoon salt	1 cup blackberries

Directions (Serves 6 to 8)

Sift together dry ingredients into bowl.

Cut butter into flour mixture with pastry blender until coarse crumbs are formed.

Add milk to the above mixture and stir until blended.

Add berries to the above mixture and stir until mixed. Pour batter into greased mold and steam for about 1 ½ hours. Serve with cream or Brandy Sauce. (*See* Dessert Sauces section.)

ᴄᴜ Cranberry Steamed Pudding

Ingredients

1 cup boiling water	½ cup molasses
1 cup chopped cranberries	1 ½ cups sifted flour
2 tablespoons butter	1 teaspoon salt
1 egg, well beaten	1 teaspoon soda
½ cup sugar	

Directions (Serves 8)

Pour water over cranberries and butter.

Add sugar and molasses to beaten egg. Add above mixture and stir until well blended.

Sift together dry ingredients and stir into the above mixture. Pour into well-greased 1-quart mold. Steam for 2 hours. Serve with Foamy Sauce. (*See* Dessert Sauces section.)

～ *Steamed Vanilla Pudding*

Ingredients

1½ cups sifted flour
½ teaspoon salt
3 teaspoons baking powder
¼ cup butter

½ cup sugar
1 egg, well beaten
1 teaspoon vanilla
⅔ cup milk

Directions (Serves 6)

Sift together dry ingredients.

Cream butter and sugar together until light and fluffy. Add egg and beat well. Stir in vanilla.

Add dry ingredients alternately with the milk to the above mixture. Pour into greased and sugared 1-quart mold. Cover. Steam for 1½ hours. Serve with Fruit Sauce. (*See* Dessert Sauces section.)

～ *Raisin Pudding*

(Serves 6)

Use recipe for Steamed Vanilla Pudding, adding 1 cup raisins with the creamed mixture. Serve with Lemon Sauce.

～ *Plum Pudding*

Mrs. Charles Normand, Belton, Texas

Ingredients

½ lb. citron
¼ lb. candied lemon peel
¼ lb. candied orange peel
1 lb. raisins
1 lb. currants
1 lb. suet
¼ teaspoon cloves

⅓ teaspoon cinnamon
¼ teaspoon allspice
6 eggs, beaten
2 cups sugar
1 cup sherry wine
2 cups flour
2 teaspoons baking powder

Directions (Serves 8 to 10)

Chop fruit.

Put suet through food chopper. Mix with cloves, cinnamon, and allspice.

Mix sugar and eggs together and stir into above mixture.

Thicken the wine with flour and baking powder and pour over fruit mixture. Dip a cloth in hot water and line with flour. Pour the pudding into the cloth, and tie. Have the water boiling and keep it boiling for 6 hours. Keep the pudding covered with water during this process.

∾ English Plum Pudding

Anchorage-by-the-Sea, Mattapoisett, Massachusetts

Ingredients

1 cup flour
1 lb. seedless raisins
4 oz. candied citron, cut fine
4 oz. candied lemon peel, cut fine
4 oz. candied orange peel, cut fine
½ cup chopped almonds
½ lb. bread crumbs
½ cup sugar
1 teaspoon baking powder

1 teaspoon ground cinnamon
½ teaspoon ground allspice
½ teaspoon ground cloves
1 teaspoon salt
1 cup suet, chopped fine
3 eggs, beaten
1 cup molasses
1 cup pickled peach syrup or
　other fruit juice

Directions (Serves 10 to 12)

Sift flour over fruit and mix well. Set aside.

Mix almonds, bread crumbs, sugar, baking powder, cinnamon, allspice, cloves, and salt.

Work suet, evenly, into the above mixture.

Add remaining ingredients with the floured fruit to the above mixture. Pour mixture into buttered molds, filling ⅔ full. Cover; place in steamer of boiling water; steam slowly and steadily for 4 to 8 hours, according to the size of the molds. When ready to serve, reheat by steaming ½ hour or more. Serve with Hard Sauce or Wine Sauce.

∾ Chocolate Bread Pudding

Robert G. Brehmer Jr., Fond du Lac, Wisconsin

Ingredients

2 tablespoons butter
4 squares unsweetened chocolate
½ cup sugar
¼ teaspoon salt
4 egg yolks, beaten

½ cup milk
2 cups fresh bread crumbs
1 teaspoon vanilla
½ cup nut meats
4 egg whites, beaten

Directions (Serves 8)

Melt butter and chocolate in double boiler.

Add sugar and salt to the above.

Add yolks and milk to mixture and cook until slightly thickened.

Add bread crumbs, vanilla, and nut meats to the above and mix
thoroughly.

Fold egg whites into mixture. Turn into molds, filling about ½ full.
Steam for 25 minutes. Serve with Butter Sauce or whipped cream,
either hot or cold.

∾ *Raisin Puffs*

Ingredients

½ cup butter	2 teaspoons baking powder
1 cup sugar	1 cup milk
2 eggs, beaten	1 cup raisins, cut up
2 cups flour	

Directions (Serves 8 to 10)

Cream together butter and sugar.

Add eggs to above mixture.

Sift together dry ingredients and add to mixture, alternately with
milk.

Flour raisins and add to mixture. Steam in cups ¾ hour. Serve with
whipped cream.

∾ *Persimmon Pudding*

Mammoth Cave Hotel, Mammoth Cave, Kentucky

Ingredients

1 cup persimmon pulp	1 cup flour
1 tablespoon butter	1 teaspoon vanilla
1 cup sugar	1½ teaspoons baking powder
2 teaspoons soda	Pinch of salt
½ cup milk	

Directions (Serves 6 to 8)

Mix together all ingredients and turn into molds, filling ⅔ full.
Steam for 3 hours. Serve with sauce.

Sauce

Ingredients

2 egg yolks, beaten

1 cup sugar

½ cup sherry wine

½ pint whipping cream, whipped

Directions

Beat together yolks and sugar.

Add wine to eggs.

Add cream to mixture just before serving.

ᕦ *Pudding Saxon*

Ingredients

2 cups sugar

4 eggs, beaten

3 oz. citron peel, chopped

6 oz. raisins

1 pint milk

8 slices bread, diced

Rind of 1 orange, grated

3 oz. melted butter

Directions (Serves 8)

Mix all ingredients and blend. Pour into a greased mold and set in
hot water. Bake in 375° oven for 30 minutes. Serve hot. This is a
man's dessert.

ᕦ *Raisin Pudding*

Mrs. K's Toll House Tavern, Silver Spring, Maryland

Ingredients

1 cup sugar

1 cup flour

2 teaspoons baking powder

½ cup sweet milk

1 cup raisins

1⅓ cups brown sugar

2 cups hot water

1 tablespoon butter

Directions (Serves 6 to 8)

Mix first five ingredients together in order given and pour into
greased baking dish.

Dissolve brown sugar in hot water and add butter. Stir until melted.
Pour over above mixture and bake in 350° oven for 45 minutes.

∿ Queen of Pudding

Treadway Inn, Rochester, New York

Ingredients

2 slices bread
1 pint fresh milk
2 egg yolks, lightly beaten
Rind of ½ lemon, grated
1 tablespoon butter

½ cup powdered sugar, sifted
2 egg whites
4 tablespoons granulated sugar
2 tablespoons coconut
¼ teaspoon vanilla

Directions (Serves 6)

Cube the bread; heat milk to scalding point. Pour milk over bread cubes. Mash through strainer.

Add to the above mixture the egg yolks, lemon rind, butter, and powdered sugar. Place mixture in lightly greased baking pan and bake in 350° oven for 1 hour or until done.

Beat egg whites until fluffy. Add granulated sugar, gradually beating until stiff peaks are formed. Fold in coconut and vanilla. Spread evenly over pudding. Toast meringue under broiler or in hot oven and serve hot or cold.

∿ Chocolate "Brot"

Ingredients

3 squares unsweetened
   chocolate, melted
4 oz. almonds, chopped
6 egg whites

⅛ teaspoon salt
1 cup powdered sugar
1 teaspoon vanilla

Directions (Serves 6 to 8)

Combine chocolate and chopped almonds.

Beat egg whites and salt until stiff. Add sugar, 2 tablespoons at a time, and continue beating until blended. Add vanilla. Fold in chocolate-almond mixture. Pour into greased square pan and bake in slow oven at 300° for 45 to 50 minutes.

∿ Brown's Rice Pudding

Brown's Restaurant, Ft. Lauderdale, Florida

Ingredients

¼ cup raw rice
1 quart whole milk
¼ cup sugar
½ teaspoon vanilla

Pinch of salt
Pinch of cinnamon
½ cup raisins

Directions (Serves 4)

Wash rice thoroughly and place in earthenware casserole.
Add milk, sugar, vanilla, salt, and cinnamon.
Cook in 250° oven for 3½ hours, stirring frequently.
Then add ½ cup raisins, more if you like, and cook ½ hour longer.
Raisins will curdle milk if added before pudding is almost done.

∿ Baked Indian Pudding

The Toll House, Whitman, Massachusetts

Ingredients

3 cups milk
3 tablespoons Indian meal
⅓ cup molasses
½ cup sugar
1 egg, beaten

1 tablespoon butter
½ teaspoon ginger
½ teaspoon cinnamon
¼ teaspoon salt
1 cup milk

Directions (Serves 8)

Scald the milk.
Mix meal and molasses together; stir into hot milk and cook until it
thickens. Stir constantly to prevent scorching. Remove from fire.
Add sugar, egg, butter, ginger, cinnamon, and salt to mixture and mix
thoroughly. Pour into a buttered baking dish and put in 300° oven.
In ½ hour pour the milk over it and continue baking for 2 hours.

∾ Butterscotch Graham Cracker Pudding

Baron Steuben Hotel, Corning, New York

Ingredients

1 quart milk	2 eggs
3 tablespoons butter	½ teaspoon salt
¾ cup brown sugar	1 teaspoon vanilla extract
2 cups graham crackers, ground	¼ teaspoon nutmeg

Directions (Serves 6)

Scald milk in top of double boiler.

Melt butter; add ½ cup of sugar; stir and cook until brown. Add to scalded milk in top of double boiler and stir as it cooks.

Add graham crackers to above mixture.

Beat eggs and remainder of sugar together. Stir into the milk.

Add remaining ingredients to mixture. Pour into greased pan. Place pan in a water bath and bake at 350° for 75 minutes. Serve warm or cold with whipped cream, Hard Sauce, or Vanilla Sauce. (*See* Dessert Sauces section.)

∾ Grated Sweet Potato Pudding

Mayfair Hotel, Searcy, Arkansas

Ingredients

½ cup sugar	2 cups sweet milk
½ cup butter	1 teaspoon salt
½ cup chopped nuts	1 teaspoon nutmeg
3 eggs	1 teaspoon cinnamon
4 cups grated sweet potato (raw)	1 teaspoon cloves
1 cup corn syrup (light or dark)	

Directions (Serves 12)

Cream butter, sugar, and nuts.

Add eggs, one at a time, and beat well.

Add grated potato, syrup, milk, and spices and bake 2 hours in moderate oven in well-buttered iron skillet. When brown crust forms on top, stir down and let brown again. (If pudding gets to dry while baking, add another cup of milk, stir lightly, and let brown again.) Serve plain or with whipped cream, either hot or cold. This pudding makes a delicious cold weather dessert and handed down from the old days of Dutch oven baking.

◟ Riz à l'Impératrice

Grand Hotel Victoria-Jungfrau, Interlaken, Switzerland

Ingredients

⅓ cup citron, chopped
⅓ cup candied lemon peel,
  chopped
⅓ cup candied orange peel,
  chopped
3 oz. Kirschwasser
2 cups milk
1 tablespoon vanilla or one
  1-inch stick vanilla

½ cup water
½ cup sugar
¾ cup rice
2 tablespoons (2 envelopes)
  unflavored gelatin
½ cup cold water
1 pint heavy cream

Directions (Serves 10 to 12)

Combine fruits and marinate in Kirschwasser while making the
  pudding. Stir occasionally.

Add vanilla to milk and heat in top of double boiler.

Combine water and sugar in saucepan and let come to a boil. Wash
  and drain rice and drop into boiling syrup. Cook 5 minutes,
  stirring constantly. Drop the rice mixture by spoonfuls into above
  hot milk and let cook about 1 hour until almost all of the liquid is
  absorbed. Stir occasionally.

Soak gelatin in water about 5 minutes and add to above mixture; stir
  to dissolve. Let set until cool.

Whip cream until almost stiff and add to fruits and Kirschwasser.
  Add whipped cream and fruits to rice mixture and pack into a
  2-quart oiled mold. Let stand overnight or until well set. Unmold
  and serve with sauce.

Sauce

Ingredients

1 box frozen strawberries or
  raspberries

½ cup sugar

Directions

Combine ingredients in saucepan and simmer until well blended.
  Chill and serve over Riz à l'Impératrice.

◌◟ Old-Fashioned Indian Pudding

Ingredients

4 cups milk

5 tablespoons Indian meal

2 tablespoons butter

1 teaspoon salt

$1/2$ teaspoon ginger

$1/2$ teaspoon cinnamon

1 cup molasses

2 eggs, well beaten

1 cup sweet apples, sliced very
thin

1 cup cold milk

Directions (Serves 8)

Scald milk in double boiler.

Gradually add meal to the above and cook 15 minutes, stirring
constantly.

Add butter, salt, ginger, cinnamon, molasses, and eggs to the mixture.

Stir apples into mixture and turn into buttered baking dish.

Pour cold milk over all and bake in 325° oven for 1 hour. Serve with
vanilla ice cream.

Frozen Desserts

Believe it or not, ice cream has been known for centuries, but for many years it was served only to royalty.

There is some disagreement as to who discovered ice cream, but Emperor Nero is usually credited with being the first to serve this dish to his guests. As the story goes, his slaves ran down from the mountaintops carrying fresh snow, which was then flavored with juices and fruits by his kitchen staff.

Many years later, Marco Polo returned to Venice from Japan with a recipe for frozen milk ice. This was probably the first of our prepared frozen desserts. Eventually cream was substituted for the milk, and this was called "cream ice." This new dessert spread quickly through Europe, and the recipe was no longer the property of royalty alone. When Charles I of England heard about this dessert, which was so popular on the Continent, he immediately hired a French chef to make it for him. The popularity of ice cream grew steadily in England, and when the colonists came to America, they brought the recipe with them. Years later, when Dolly Madison served this dessert, she reversed the name on the White House menu, and we have the first recorded reference to ice cream.

In the United States we eat more ice cream than all the rest of the world combined. This is not surprising because we have a flavor for every taste. For example, in California it is possible to buy avocado ice cream; in the South, buttermilk ice cream; and in upstate New York, green corn ice cream. There is even a baked bean and ketchup ice cream! However, no matter how many different flavors we have available, the three most popular continue to be chocolate, vanilla, and strawberry.

Ice cream is not the only frozen dessert. This group can be classified into four definite types:

- Ice creams made of cream sweetened or flavored with or without a custard base or other thickening.
- Ices made of fruit juices sweetened and combined with water.
- Sherbets, which are a water ice to which milk, beaten egg whites, or gelatin have been added to change the flavor and texture.
- Mousses and parfaits, which are whipped cream desserts, frozen without stirring. A mousse may or may not have a foundation thickened with gelatin or another material. A parfait has a foundation of syrup cooked with beaten egg whites or yolks.

All these mixtures can be frozen by packing in a freezing unit of a refrigerator or, if available, a home freezer.

There are many party desserts made of an ice cream or sherbet base. They are simple and easy to make, but they add that extra gourmet's touch to your meals. Ice cream tarts, pies, and that very special treat, Baked Alaska, all are worthy additions to the frozen dessert section.

I am passing on to you many recipes for frozen desserts and suggest that you vary the old favorites with different fruits or sauces.

ᕼ How to Make Ice Cream in the Crank Freezer

1. Chill the freezer can and the mixture first.
2. Put the can in the freezer tub. Set dasher in place. Fill can with ice cream mixture ⅔ full to allow for expansion. Put on cover and adjust crank.
3. Pack freezer tub ⅓ full of crushed ice. Add remaining crushed ice alternately with layers of coarse rock salt until the tub is full. (Use 3 to 6 parts ice to 1 part salt, depending upon how fast you want the ice cream to freeze. More salt will bring quicker results, but the ice cream is not as smooth.)
4. Turn crank slowly at first. Then turn rapidly until the crank turns with difficulty.
5. Draw off water. Wipe off lid and remove it. Take out dasher; plug opening in lid; scrape dasher; and pack down ice cream.

ᕼ How to Make Ice Cream in Automatic Refrigerators

1. Use a thickening ingredient such as gelatin, eggs, flour, or corn-starch to get a smooth ice cream.
2. Set control at highest point. Pour mixture into freezing tray.
3. Beat or stir mixture several times while freezing to make a smooth creamy mixture.
4. Freeze until firm. Turn down control so it will not be too hard.

ᕼ Vanilla Ice Cream

Forestwood Lodge, Grantsburg, Wisconsin

Ingredients

3 pints cream
1 ¼ cups sugar
8 egg yolks

¼ teaspoon salt
1 teaspoon vanilla
⅛ teaspoon almond extract

Directions (Makes 3 quarts)

Scald cream in double boiler.

Add sugar to hot cream and stir to dissolve sugar.

Beat egg yolks until thick and creamy. Add sugar and cream mixture gradually, beating well to make custard.

Stir remaining ingredients into above. Let cool. Freeze, using 2 parts cracked ice to 1 part rock salt.

ᵔ French Vanilla Ice Cream

Ingredients

¾ cup sugar
1 tablespoon flour
⅛ teaspoon salt
2 cups milk

*6 egg yolks, slightly beaten
2 teaspoons vanilla
2 cups light cream

Directions (Makes 2 quarts)

Mix together sugar, flour, and salt. Then stir in milk. Cook over
boiling water, stirring constantly, until slightly thickened. Put on
cover and continue to cook 10 minutes longer.

Stir a little of the hot milk mixture into the eggs. Then add it to the
above mixture. Cook over hot water (about 5 minutes), stirring
constantly, or until mixture coats the spoon. Remove top section
of double boiler from hot water. Chill.

Add remaining ingredients to the chilled mixture. Freeze according
to directions given for ice cream in a crank freezer.

*For an ice cream that is less rich, use 2 whole eggs.

ᵔ Banana Ice Cream

Ingredients

2 cups mashed, ripe bananas
  (5 or 6 bananas)
1½ tablespoons lemon juice
½ cup sugar
½ teaspoon salt

2 eggs, well beaten
1 cup milk
2 teaspoons vanilla
2 cups whipping cream

Directions (Makes 2 quarts)

Mix together bananas, lemon juice, and sugar.
Add salt, eggs, milk, and vanilla to banana mixture.
Stir whipping cream into above mixture. Freeze in hand or electric
freezer until firm.

ᵔ Butter-Crunch Ice Cream

Use recipe for French Vanilla Ice Cream, adding ⅔ lb. finely crushed
butter-crunch just before serving.

ᨠ Graham Cracker Ice Cream

Ingredients

1 cup graham crackers, crushed
⅓ cup granulated sugar

1 pint coffee cream
1 teaspoon vanilla

Directions (Serves 6 to 8)

Combine graham crackers, sugar, and cream.
Add vanilla, pour into refrigerator tray, and freeze. Stir once in tray
during freezing; otherwise the crumbs are likely to come to the
top of the mixture.

ᨠ Chocolate Ice Cream

Ingredients

2 eggs, beaten
1 cup sugar
1 tablespoon flour
1 quart milk
3 squares unsweetened
chocolate, melted

1½ cups sugar
1 teaspoon vanilla
Pinch of salt
1 quart cream

Directions (Serves 20)

Cream together first three ingredients.
Scald milk and mix a little with the chocolate, making a smooth
paste. Add the balance of the milk, and pour over the egg mixture.
Cook in double boiler, stirring until a custard.
Add remaining sugar to custard and cool.
Add remaining ingredients to mixture. Put in freezer and freeze.

ᨠ Macaroon Ice Cream

Ingredients

24 stale macaroons
1 quart whipping cream
½ pint sherry wine

1 cup sugar
1 cup shredded almonds

Directions (Makes 3 pints)

Roll macaroons to a crumb.
Scald cream and whip.
Dissolve the sugar in wine. Combine the two liquids.
Add almonds to combined liquids. Fold in crumbs and put in freezer.
Freeze and pack for at least 4 hours.

∾ Coffee Ice Cream

Use recipe for French Vanilla Ice Cream. Add ⅓ cup ground coffee to 2 cups milk. Cook over medium heat until milk reaches the scalding point. Strain through a piece of fine cheesecloth and then proceed as directed for French Vanilla Ice Cream, using the coffee-milk mixture for the 2 cups of milk.

∾ Lemon Ice Cream

Ingredients

24 marshmallows
½ cup lemon juice
1 pint sweet milk
2 egg yolks

½ cup sugar
Grated rind of 2 lemons
1 pint whipping cream

Directions (Makes 2 quarts)

Put marshmallows in top of double boiler with lemon juice and let
  melt.
Scald milk.
Beat egg yolks until thick; add sugar gradually and beat until light
  colored. Gently pour in scalded milk and mix well. Add marshmallow mixture and lemon rind.
Mix well and let cool.
Whip cream and fold into lemon mixture. Pour into ice cream tray
  and freeze.

∾ Peppermint-Stick Ice Cream

Use recipe for French Vanilla Ice Cream. Omit sugar and vanilla;
when ready to freeze add 2 cups (½ pound) finely crushed
peppermint-stick candy.

∾ Persimmon Ice Cream

Ingredients

2 ripe Japanese persimmons,
  sieved
1 tablespoon sugar

¼ cup lemon juice
1 cup heavy cream, whipped

Directions (Serves 4)

Combine together persimmons, sugar, and lemon juice.

Fold whipped cream into the above mixture. Pour into refrigerator tray and freeze until firm.

∽ Pistachio Ice Cream

Use recipe for French Vanilla Ice Cream, reducing vanilla to 1½ teaspoons and adding ¾ teaspoon almond extract. Add 1 cup finely chopped blanched pistachio nuts and green coloring just before freezing.

∽ Raspberry Ice Cream

Use recipe for French Vanilla Ice Cream. Just before freezing, add 2 cups crushed raspberries, sweetened, with ½ cup sugar.

∽ Sherry Almond Ice Cream

Ingredients

1 envelope (1 tablespoon) unflavored gelatin	6 egg whites, beaten
¼ cup cold water	⅓ cup sherry
1 cup boiling water	½ teaspoon almond extract
1¼ cups sugar	1 cup almonds, chopped

Directions (Serves 8)

Soak gelatin in cold water for about 5 minutes.

Add boiling water and sugar to gelatin, and stir well until dissolved. Cool. When it begins to set, beat with an egg beater until frothy.

Fold egg whites into mixture.

Add sherry and almond extract to mixture.

Fill ring mold with alternate layers of mixture and nuts. Put in deep freeze and let set for 2 hours.

Sauce

Ingredients

6 egg yolks, beaten	½ teaspoon vanilla
1 pint milk	3 tablespoons sherry
¼ cup sugar	½ pint whipping cream, whipped
⅛ teaspoon salt	

Directions

Cook yolks and milk in double boiler until mixture coats a spoon.

Add sugar, salt, and vanilla to mixture and let cool.

Add sherry to cooled mixture.

Just before serving, fold whipped cream into mixture, and fill the
center of the mold.

ᕦ Lime Sherbet

Ingredients

1¼ teaspoons unflavored gelatin
¼ cup cold water
¾ cup water
⅔ cup sugar

½ cup lime juice
2 drops green coloring (about)
2 egg whites, stiffly beaten
Pinch of salt

Directions (Serves 4)

Soak gelatin in cold water about 5 minutes.

Combine sugar and water in saucepan and boil for 10 minutes.
Dissolve soaked gelatin in hot syrup. Cool.

Add juice and coloring to the above mixture.

Fold beaten egg whites and salt into the mixture. Pour into refrigerator tray and freeze until firm. Stir or beat once or twice to give
a smoother sherbet.

ᕦ Lemon Sherbet

Ingredients

2 teaspoons unflavored gelatin
¼ cup cold water
2¼ cups water
¾ cup sugar

1 teaspoon grated lemon rind
¾ cup lemon juice
2 egg whites, stiffly beaten
Pinch of salt

Directions (Serves 4 to 6)

Soak gelatin in ¼ cup cold water about 5 minutes.

Combine sugar and 2¼ cup water in saucepan and boil for 10 minutes. Dissolve soaked gelatin in hot syrup. Cool.

Add rind and juice to the above mixture.

Fold beaten egg whites and salt into the above mixture. Pour into
refrigerator tray and freeze until firm. Stir or beat once or twice to
give a smoother sherbet.

∿ Lemon Sherbet

Mrs. Ralph Prince, Gladewater, Texas

Ingredients

3 cups sugar
1 cup lemon juice
Grated rind of 4 lemons

2 quarts whole milk
¼ teaspoon salt

Directions (Makes about 3 quarts)

Combine sugar, lemon juice, and lemon rind, and let set 1 hour.
Combine milk and salt with the above mixture. Put in electric or
hand freezer and freeze. (Do not get upset if it appears to curdle;
it's all right.)

∿ Orange Sherbet

Ingredients

2 teaspoons unflavored gelatin
¼ cup cold water
1 cup water
⅔ cup sugar
1 teaspoon grated orange rind

1 teaspoon grated lemon rind
1½ cups orange juice
⅓ cup lemon juice
2 egg whites, stiffly beaten
Pinch of salt

Directions (Serves 4 to 6)

Soak gelatin in ¼ cup cold water about 5 minutes.
Combine 1 cup water and sugar in saucepan and boil for 10 minutes.
Dissolve soaked gelatin in hot syrup. Cool.
Add rinds and juices to the above mixture.
Fold beaten egg whites and salt into the above mixture. Pour into
refrigerator tray and freeze until firm. Stir or beat once or twice to
give a smoother sherbet.

➥ *À la mode your desserts: chocolate brownies, fruit tarts, Indian
pudding, dessert dumplings, hot gingerbread or chocolate cake, baked
fruit, hot doughnuts, pies, and warm fruit cake slices.*

~ "Five Threes" Sherbet

Mrs. E. E. Forbes, Greenville, North Carolina

Ingredients

3 cups sugar
3 cups water
3 lemons, juice
3 oranges, juice

3 bananas, mashed through a
   sieve
1 small can pineapple
½ pint cream (optional)

Directions (Makes 2 quarts)

Combine sugar and water, and boil about 2 minutes. Not until it
   strings, but just enough to dissolve sugar thoroughly.
Add remaining ingredients to syrup and freeze.

~ Three Fruit Ice

Mrs. Wallace J. Rigby, Larchmont, New York

Ingredients

2 cups sugar
3 cups water
3 bananas

1 cup lemon juice
1 cup orange juice

Directions (Makes 2 quarts)

Heat water and dissolve sugar in water. Let cool.
Slice bananas thin and make puree by passing through sieve. Add
   to above with juices. Freeze in refrigerator. If an old-fashioned
   freezer is used, then it is not necessary to puree the bananas, only
   to chop them fine.

~ Black Raspberry Ice

Virginia McDonald's Tea Room, Gallatin, Missouri

Ingredients

2 quarts black raspberries
5 cups sugar

3 cups hot water
Juice of 6 lemons

Directions (Makes about 2½ quarts)

Run raspberries through colander; then squeeze through coarsely
   woven cloth, extracting every possible bit of pulp but no seeds.
   Mix sugar and hot water; stir and bring to boil. Boil for 15 minutes.
   Combine lemon juice, raspberries, and syrup. Cool and freeze.

∽ Coffee Parfait

Ingredients

⅓ cup sugar   2 egg whites, stiffly beaten
½ cup strong coffee   1 pint whipping cream, whipped

Directions (Serves 6 to 8)

Combine sugar and coffee in saucepan. Cook over medium heat, stirring constantly, until sugar is dissolved. Then boil without stirring
until the syrup spins a thread (238° F.).

Gradually add the hot syrup, in a fine stream, to the beaten egg
whites, beating constantly until the mixture is cool. Chill.

Fold whipped cream into above mixture. Pour into individual molds
or freezing tray and freeze until firm.

∽ Maple Parfait

Ingredients

6 egg yolks, slightly beaten   Pinch of salt
¾ cup maple syrup   1 pint whipping cream, whipped

Directions (Makes 1 ½ quarts)

Combine first three ingredients in top of double boiler. Cook and stir
over boiling water until mixture is thick and coats a metal spoon.
Remove top section of double boiler from boiling water. Pour into
a bowl and beat with egg beater or wire whisk until it is cold.

Fold whipped cream into the above mixture. Pour into refrigerator
trays or mold and freeze until firm.

∽ Maple Walnut Parfait

Use recipe for Maple Parfait, folding in ½ cup finely chopped
walnuts with the whipped cream.

∽ *Apple Mousse*

The Derings, Green Lake, Wisconsin

Ingredients

1 cup thick, strained, sweetened applesauce
1 tablespoon lemon juice
1 cup whipping cream
½ cup sugar

Directions (Serves 4)

Combine the applesauce and the lemon juice. Whip the cream and add to it the sugar. Fold the two mixtures together and turn into freezing trays or a mold to freeze.

∽ *Gooseberry Mousse*

Ingredients

1 quart gooseberries
½ lb. sugar
½ pint water
1 tablespoon brandy
A little green coloring
1 pint whipping cream, whipped

Directions (Serves 6)

Combine gooseberries, sugar, and water, and cook slowly until tender enough to put through a sieve.
Add brandy and coloring. Let cool.
Fold whipped cream into mixture. Put in refrigerator trays and freeze. Any fresh fruit, minus the coloring, may also be used.

∽ *Raspberry Mousse*

Use recipe for Strawberry Mousse, substituting 1 pint fresh raspberries for the strawberries.

∽ *Strawberry Mousse*

Ingredients

1 pint strawberries, washed and stemmed
1 cup sugar
2 egg whites, stiffly beaten
1 pint whipping cream, whipped
Pinch of salt
1 tablespoon lemon juice (optional)

Directions (Serves 8)

Crush berries. Add sugar to berries and heat until sugar is dissolved. Chill.

Fold remaining ingredients into the above mixture. Pour into freezing tray and freeze.

➥ Parfait *comes from the French meaning "perfect." It is less cold and more creamy than ice cream.* Mousse *is French for foam.*

∾ Baked Alaska

Ingredients

3 egg whites
6 tablespoons sugar
Pound cake

1 pint very firm brick ice cream, any flavor

Directions (Serves 4)

Beat egg whites until foamy throughout. Add sugar, 2 tablespoons at a time, beating after each addition until blended. Continue beating until stiff peaks are formed.

Cut cake slices ½ inch thick. Place on board or baking sheet covered with heavy paper. Cut ice cream into 4 slices, slightly smaller than cake slices; place on cake. Spread with meringue, covering completely. Bake in hot oven at 450° for 5 minutes or until lightly browned. Serve at once.

∾ Butterscotch-Almond Ice Cream Cake

(Serves 4)

Line bottom of freezing tray with strips of pound cake. Spread with 1 pint softened coffee or vanilla ice cream. Pack ice cream down smoothly. Freeze. Serve slices with Butterscotch Sauce (*see* Dessert Sauces section) and toasted slivered almonds.

∾ Ice Cream Royale

Ingredients

1 pint chocolate ice cream
1 pint vanilla ice cream
1 pint strawberry ice cream

½ pint heavy cream, whipped
Walnuts, chopped

Directions (Serves 4)

Layer the ice cream in parfait glasses with the chocolate on the
   bottom, then vanilla and strawberry.
Top with whipped cream and chopped walnuts.

∾ Biscuit Tortoni

Ingredients

1 pint heavy cream, whipped
⅓ cup powdered sugar
1 teaspoon vanilla
3 tablespoons sherry wine

Pinch of salt
2 egg whites, stiffly beaten
1 cup macaroon crumbs

Directions (Serves 4 to 6)

Combine first five ingredients.
Fold beaten egg whites and macaroon crumbs into the above
   mixture. Pour into individual paper cups or freezing tray. Sprinkle
   with finely chopped, blanched toasted almonds, if desired. Freeze
   until firm.

∾ Ice Cream Pie

Ingredients

2 squares unsweetened chocolate
2 tablespoons butter
2 tablespoons hot milk

⅔ cup sifted confectioners' sugar
1½ cups coconut, toasted
1 quart vanilla ice cream

Directions (Serves 6)

Melt chocolate and butter over hot water, stirring until blended.
Combine milk and confectioners' sugar. Add to chocolate mixture,
   stirring well.

Add coconut to above mixture and mix well. Spread on bottom and sides of greased 9-inch pie pan. Chill until firm. Fill with ice cream just before serving. Serve with Chocolate Sauce, if desired. (*See* Dessert Sauces section.)

∾ *Marshmallow Ice Cream Pie*

Ingredients

1 egg white	2 cups coconut, finely cut
2 tablespoons sugar	1 ½ pints firm vanilla ice cream
1 tablespoon light corn syrup	1 cup crushed, sweetened
1 teaspoon vanilla	strawberries, drained

Directions (Serves 8)

Beat egg white until foamy throughout. Add sugar and beat until mixture will stand in soft peaks.

Add corn syrup and vanilla to the egg white mixture.

Fold cut coconut into the above mixture. Press firmly into the bottom and sides of a well-buttered 9-inch pie pan, using the back of a fork to press the mixture into the pie pan. Bake in moderate oven at 350° for 15 minutes or until lightly browned. Cool.

Spoon ice cream into cooled shell.

Spread crushed strawberries over ice cream. Reserve juice for meringue. Cover with marshmallow meringue. Seal the edges carefully. Bake in hot oven at 450° for 5 minutes or until golden brown. Chill at least 2 hours before serving.

Marshmallow Meringue

Ingredients

16 marshmallows	Pinch of salt
2 tablespoons strawberry juice	¼ cup sugar
2 egg whites	

Directions

Combine marshmallows and juice in top of double boiler. Cook over boiling water until marshmallows melt. Cool slightly.

Beat egg whites and salt until foamy throughout. Add sugar gradually, and continue beating until mixture will stand in stiff peaks. Carefully fold in marshmallow mixture.

～ Refrigerator-Tray Pie

Ingredients

1½ cups chocolate wafer crumbs   1½ pints vanilla or coffee ice
¼ cup butter   cream, softened
¼ cup sugar

Directions (Serves 6)

Cream butter and add crumbs and sugar. Blend together. Pack half
the crumb mixture into a refrigerator tray. Chill.

Spoon ice cream over crumb mixture and pack down well. Press
remaining crumbs on top of the ice cream. Spread with whipped
cream, if desired. Return to refrigerator to freeze.

～ Frozen Praline Pie

Anderson Hotel, Wabasha, Minnesota

Ingredients

4 egg whites   2 quarts vanilla ice cream
½ teaspoon cream of tartar   1 cup whole pecan halves
1 cup sugar   1 cup ground pecans

Directions

Beat egg whites until frothy and add cream of tartar. Beat whites stiff
and dry.

Add sugar slowly and beat until mixture is glossy. Line a 9-inch
springform pan with meringue. Bake in 300° oven for 50 to 60
minutes. Cool. While the meringue is baking, make the Butterscotch Sauce.

When the Butterscotch Sauce is done and cool, soften 1 quart ice
cream in mixer until sufficiently soft to spoon into meringue shell.

Pour over ice cream a thick layer of Butterscotch Sauce and cover
with pecan halves. Put in freezer and let get firm, about 1½ hours.
Soften the other quart of ice cream and put on top of frozen
filling. Top with Butterscotch Sauce, reserving some of the sauce
for serving with the wedges. Cover entirely with ground pecans.
Wrap tightly with aluminum foil and freeze. Unwrap and serve in
wedges with a spoonful of sauce on top.

Butterscotch Sauce

Ingredients

1¾ cups light corn syrup
2 cups sugar
1 cup butter

1 cup cream
1 teaspoon vanilla

Directions

Combine first three ingredients in a saucepan and cook until it
   reaches the soft-ball stage.
Add cream to the above and let cook until the candy thermometer
   says 218° F.
Add vanilla.

∿ Ice Cream Tarts

Fill baked tart shells with fresh, sliced, sweetened peaches or strawberries. Top with a scoop of vanilla ice cream. Serve with additional
fruit, if desired

∿ Chocolate Meringues

Fill cooled Meringue Shells (*see* Pie section) with scoops of chocolate
ice cream. Top with Chocolate Sauce. (*See* Dessert Sauces section.)

∿ Frozen Eggnog

Ingredients

5 egg yolks, beaten
1¾ cups sugar
¾ cup bourbon

Nutmeg to taste
5 egg whites, beaten
1 pint whipping cream, whipped

Directions (Makes 2 quarts)

Beat yolks and sugar together until light and creamy.
Add bourbon and nutmeg to mixture.
Fold beaten egg whites into mixture.
Add whipped cream to mixture. Put in freezer and freeze. Pack until
   ready to serve. This can also be made in refrigerator trays.

Strawberry Meringues

Fill cooled Meringue Shells (*see* Pie section) with scoops of vanilla ice cream. Top with crushed, sweetened strawberries.

Chocolate Charlotte

Ingredients

Ladyfingers, split
3 tablespoons sherry wine

1 pint chocolate ice cream,
    softened
Whipped cream

Directions (Serves 6)

Line bottom and sides of freezing tray with ladyfingers.
Sprinkle sherry wine over ladyfingers.
Spread ice cream over the ladyfingers. Freeze.
Just before serving, spread with whipped cream.

Cookies

COOKIES CAN BE DIVIDED into five general classes: dropped, spread, rolled, refrigerator, and pressed. Rolled, pressed, and refrigerator cookies are made with a stiffer dough than are the dropped and spread cookies. Dropped, rolled, refrigerator, and pressed cookies should be baked on a lightly greased baking sheet. This allows for even heat conduction and makes removal of the baked cookies easier. They should be baked on the top shelf of the oven to eliminate the chance of burning on the bottom. When the cookies are done, remove them immediately from the baking sheet, using a flat knife or spatula. Place the cookies on a wire rack to cool.

Spread cookies, on the other hand, are baked in a greased sheet pan. They are usually cooled in the pan before removing, as this prevents them from drying out. Store the cooled cookies immediately, with crisp and soft cookies stored separately in tightly covered boxes, cans, or jars. To keep soft cookies from drying out, add a piece of bread or a slice of apple.

Cookies may be decorated by sprinkling with chopped nuts, candied or dried fruit, coconut, colored candies, or grated chocolate before baking. Rolled cookies may be cut into unusual shapes with a cookie cutter, and especially at holiday time, attractive and appropriate designs can be prepared.

∾ Betty Cass's Brown Sugar Cookies

Mrs. R. T. Cooksey, Madison, Wisconsin

Ingredients

2 cups brown sugar
½ cup shortening
½ cup butter
2 eggs

2 cups flour
1 teaspoon baking powder
2 teaspoons vanilla
1 cup chopped pecans

Directions (Makes about 5½ dozen)

Mix ingredients in the order given and drop from a teaspoon onto a buttered baking sheet. Press a pecan half into each one. Bake in 350° oven for 15 minutes.

∾ Quick Brown Sugar Drop Cookies

Ingredients

1 lb. butter
2 cups brown sugar
2 egg yolks

3½ cups flour
2 teaspoons vanilla
1 cup chopped nuts

Directions (Makes about 7 dozen)

Mix all together, except nuts.

Drop mixture from the end of a teaspoon into the nuts. Then place on baking sheet and bake in 400° to 450° oven about 10 minutes, or until done.

∾ Soft Molasses Cookies

Ingredients

2 cups sifted flour
½ teaspoon salt
1 teaspoon soda
1 teaspoon ginger
1 teaspoon cinnamon

½ cup soft vegetable shortening
⅓ cup sugar
1 egg
½ cup molasses
¾ cup sour milk

Directions (Makes about 4 dozen)

Sift together first five ingredients. Set aside.

Combine shortening, sugar, egg, and molasses, and beat well.

Add flour mixture to the above, alternately with sour milk, mixing well after each addition. Drop from teaspoon onto lightly greased baking sheet. Bake in moderate oven at 375° for 8 to 10 minutes.

◡ French Cookies (Tulles)

Villa LaFayette, Mountain View, California

Ingredients

4 egg whites, beaten
1 cup sugar
1 teaspoon vanilla

1 cup almonds
¼ lb. butter, melted
1 cup flour

Directions (Makes 40)

Beat together egg whites, sugar, and vanilla.
Blanch and grind almonds fine. Add to the above.
Add butter to mixture.
Stir flour in slowly. Drop from a teaspoon onto a buttered pan. Bake in 350° oven for 15 minutes. Let cookies cool on rack before putting them away.

◡ Rocks

Ingredients

1 cup butter
1 cup granulated sugar
4 egg yolks
2¼ cups flour
1 teaspoon cinnamon
1 teaspoon cloves

1 cup black walnut meats
1½ cups raisins
1 teaspoon soda
1½ tablespoons boiling water
4 egg whites

Directions (Makes 4 dozen)

Cream butter and add sugar, beating until smooth.
Beat in the egg yolks.
Sift flour, cinnamon, and cloves together. Add walnuts and raisins to the flour.
Stir this mixture into the above, mixing well.
Dissolve soda in boiling water and add to batter.
Beat whites until stiff and fold into batter. Drop from teaspoon onto baking sheet and bake in 350° oven for 15 to 20 minutes or until done.

❧ Cherry Nut Cookies

Richards Treat Cafeteria, Minneapolis, Minnesota

Ingredients

1⅓ cups butter
2 cups brown sugar
4 cups flour
1 teaspoon soda
1 teaspoon salt

3 eggs
1⅓ cups nuts (peanuts or
  walnuts)
1⅓ cups candied cherries
1⅓ cups dates

Directions (Makes 60 cookies)

Cream together butter and sugar.

Sift flour, soda, and salt together and add a portion to the above.

Add the eggs to the creamed mixture and continue mixing. (If an electric mixer is used, the bowl and beater should be scraped down thoroughly.) Add nearly all the remaining flour.

Chop the nuts, cherries, and dates; dredge with the remaining flour, and add to the mixture. Drop cookies on a greased and floured sheet pan and bake about 15 minutes in 375° to 400° oven until brown. This dough can be kept in refrigerator and baked as needed.

❧ Cornucopias

Ingredients

1 egg
⅓ cup sugar

2 tablespoons water
½ cup sifted cake flour

Directions (Makes 1 dozen)

Beat egg slightly in small deep bowl. Add sugar and continue beating until very thick.

Add water gradually to the above mixture, beating constantly until very thick and light.

Add flour all at once, and fold in until just blended. Grease baking sheet and dust lightly with flour, tapping sheet to remove any excess flour. Drop dough from tablespoon onto sheet, spreading each cookie with a spoon into a very thin 5-inch circle. (Best to bake only 3 at a time so they may be rolled quickly when baked.) Bake in moderate oven at 350° for 10 minutes, or until golden brown. Immediately remove from baking sheet with a spatula and roll at once into a cone. (If necessary, place baking sheet over low heat or return to oven for a minute or two in order to remove cookies easily.) Set aside to cool. When cold, fill with Strawberry Whipped Cream, Cocoa Whipped Cream, or Lemon Whipped Cream. Serve at once.

∾ Salted Peanut Cookies
The Ruttger's Lodge, Deerwood, Minnesota

Ingredients

1 cup butter, melted
2 cups brown sugar
2 eggs
2 cups flour
1 teaspoon baking powder

1 teaspoon soda
1 teaspoon salt
2 cups oatmeal
1 cup cornflakes
1 cup whole salted peanuts

Directions (Makes about 5 dozen)

Blend together butter and sugar.

Beat eggs well and add to above.

Sift together flour, baking powder, soda, and salt, and add to mixture.

Stir remaining ingredients into mixture and drop from teaspoon onto a greased cookie sheet. Bake in 350° oven for 15 to 20 minutes.

∾ Chocolate Drop Cookies with Icing
Grace Peterson Adams, Chicago, Illinois

Ingredients

½ cup butter
1 cup brown sugar
1 egg, beaten
2 cups sifted flour
½ teaspoon salt
½ teaspoon soda

¾ cup milk
2 squares unsweetened chocolate, melted
½ cup nuts, chopped
1 teaspoon vanilla

Directions (Makes 36 cookies)

Cream together butter and sugar.

Add egg to the above.

Sift dry ingredients and alternately add to the mixture with the milk.

Blend together remaining ingredients and add to the mixture. Drop from teaspoon onto greased baking sheets and bake in 400° oven for 15 minutes.

Icing

Ingredients

2 tablespoons butter
2 squares unsweetened chocolate
4 tablespoons cream
2 cups powdered sugar
Pinch of salt
1 egg, beaten

Directions

Melt together chocolate and butter in double boiler.

Blend cream, powdered sugar, and salt, and add chocolate and butter mixture. Beat until smooth.

Fold beaten egg into mixture and spread on cookies.

> *When recipe calls for sour milk or cream, and you have none of your own, you may add 1 tablespoon vinegar or lemon juice to each cup of sweet milk, and sour your own.*

Lebkuchen

Ingredients

2½ cups sifted flour
½ teaspoon cinnamon
½ teaspoon cloves
¼ teaspoon soda
¼ teaspoon allspice
2 eggs
1 cup sugar
⅓ cup honey
¾ cup unblanched, slivered almonds
⅓ cup chopped candied orange peel
2 tablespoons chopped candied lemon peel

Directions (Makes about 3 dozen)

Sift together first five ingredients. Set aside.

Beat eggs and sugar together until light and fluffy.

Add honey and almonds to the above and mix well. Add dry ingredients and blend.

Add fruit to the batter and mix well. Chill. Roll ½-inch thick on lightly floured board. Cut with cookie cutter. Place on lightly greased baking sheet. Bake in moderate oven at 350° for about 20 minutes.

∿ Shortbread

Mrs. David Donald, Pittsfield, Massachusetts

Ingredients

1 lb. butter, soft, but not melted   1½ cups sugar
6 cups flour   1 egg

Directions (Makes about 4 dozen)

Cut butter into flour until like coarse sand, as for a pie crust.

Mix all ingredients together and roll or knead into larger cakes about
½-inch thick and cut with a cookie cutter. Prick each piece several
times with a fork. Place on baking sheet and bake in 300° oven for
20 to 30 minutes.

∿ Orange Cookies

Villa LaFayette, Mountain View, California

Ingredients

½ cup butter   ½ cup orange juice
1 cup sugar   3 cups flour
Rind of 1 orange, grated   4 teaspoons baking powder
1 egg, beaten

Directions

Mix all ingredients in the order given. More flour may be required.
Roll into a sheet; cut in rounds. Place on lightly greased baking
sheet. Dredge with sugar and bake in 350° oven for about 20 minutes, or until brown. This recipe makes soft cookies; if crisp ones
are desired, use ¼ cup of orange juice.

∿ Butter Cookies

Francis E. Fowler Jr., Los Angeles, California

Ingredients

1 lb. butter   6 cups flour
1 cup sugar   Pinch of salt

Directions (Makes about 5½ dozen)

Cream together butter and sugar.

Sift flour and salt and add to mixture. Roll out thin; cut. Place on
lightly greased baking sheet and bake in a 375° oven for 10 to 12
minutes.

∽ Sugar Cookies

Ingredients

2 cups sifted flour
2 teaspoons baking powder
½ teaspoon salt
½ cup soft butter

1 cup sugar
2 eggs
1 tablespoon milk
½ teaspoon vanilla

Directions (Makes about 3 dozen)

Sift together first three ingredients. Set aside.

Cream butter and sugar together until light and fluffy.

Add remaining ingredients to the above mixture and beat well. Chill several hours. Roll out thin on lightly floured board. Cut with cookie cutter. Place on lightly greased baking sheet. Bake in hot oven at 400° for 10 to 15 minutes.

∽ Filled Cookies

(Makes about 1 ½ dozen)

Prepare recipe for Sugar Cookies. Roll out the dough thin on a lightly floured board. Cut into rounds with cookie cutter. (The upper round may be cut with a doughnut cutter to permit the filling to show through.) Place jam or filling (for filling see below) between 2 rounds, or place the filling on half a round and fold over the other half. Seal the edges of the cookies with a floured fork. Bake as directed for Sugar Cookies.

Filling

Ingredients

1 cup chopped raisins, figs, or
    dates
⅓ cup sugar
⅓ cup boiling water

½ teaspoon grated lemon rind
1 tablespoon butter
Pinch of salt

Directions

Combine all ingredients in saucepan; cook and stir over medium heat until thick.

∾ Soft Ginger Cookies

Ingredients

½ cup sugar
½ cup butter
½ cup molasses
3 cups flour
2 teaspoons soda
1 teaspoon ginger

1 teaspoon cinnamon
¼ teaspoon cloves
Pinch of nutmeg
½ teaspoon salt
½ cup sour milk

Directions (Makes 2 to 3 dozen)

Cream sugar and butter. Stir in molasses.

Sift together flour, soda, spices, and salt. Add flour mixture, alternately with the sour milk, to the above mixture. Roll out on lightly floured board about ¼-inch thick. Cut. (Can be sprinkled with sugar.) Place on lightly greased baking sheet and bake at 400° for about 10 to 15 minutes or until lightly browned.

∾ Ginger Snaps

Ingredients

½ cup butter
1 cup sugar
½ cup lard
2 eggs, beaten
½ cup molasses

4½ cups flour
3 teaspoons ginger
1 teaspoon salt
1 teaspoon soda

Directions (Makes about 30)

Cream together butter, sugar, and lard.

Stir eggs into the above.

Add molasses to above and mix well.

Sift together remaining ingredients and stir into the above. Let stand in refrigerator overnight. Roll out thin on lightly floured board and cut with round cookie cutter. Bake in 400° oven for 15 to 20 minutes.

ᕀ Dream Cookies

Ingredients

1 cup butter	2 teaspoons vanilla
¾ cup sugar	40 blanched almond halves
2 cups sifted flour	(about)
1 teaspoon baking powder	

Directions (Makes about 40)

Melt and brown butter slightly in saucepan. Cool.

Add sugar to butter and beat until fluffy.

Sift together dry ingredients. Stir into above mixture. Add vanilla, and stir until blended and smooth.

Shape dough into balls about the size of a walnut. Place on lightly greased baking sheet. Press almond into each cookie. Bake in slow oven at 250° for 30 minutes or until golden brown.

ᕀ Swedish Oatmeal Cookies

Ingredients

3 cups finely ground quick-cooking oats	½ cup sugar
	1 teaspoon vanilla
¾ cup soft butter	36 pecan halves (about)

Directions (Makes about 3 dozen)

Mix together oats, butter, sugar, and vanilla thoroughly with hands. Shape into small balls and place on lightly greased baking sheet. Place a pecan half on top of each. Bake in a slow oven at 325° for 15 to 20 minutes or until lightly browned.

ᕀ Peanut Butter Cookies

Ingredients

1 cup butter	3 cups flour
1 cup granulated sugar	2 teaspoons soda
1 cup brown sugar	Pinch of salt
2 eggs	1 teaspoon vanilla
1 cup peanut butter	

Directions (Makes 3 dozen)

Cream butter; add both cups sugar gradually and beat until smooth.
Drop in eggs and beat until blended. Add peanut butter and stir until
well blended.

Sift flour; measure and sift again with soda and salt. Stir into above
mixture and stir until smooth. Add vanilla. Flatten small balls
between palms and crisscross with fork tines. Place on greased
cookie sheets and bake in 350° oven for 12 to 15 minutes or until
done.

◌ Pecan Puffs

Mrs. Louis M. Weathers, Elkton, Kentucky

Ingredients

½ cup butter
2 tablespoons sugar
1 teaspoon vanilla

1 cup pecans, put through a meat
  grinder
1 cup cake flour, sifted
Powdered sugar

Directions (Makes about 2 dozen)

Beat butter until soft.

Add sugar and vanilla and beat until creamy.

Mix pecans and cake flour together and stir into the butter mixture.
Roll into small balls and place on greased baking sheet. Bake in
300° oven for 45 minutes. While hot, roll in powdered sugar, and
when cooled, roll again in powdered sugar.

◌ Pecan Cookie Balls

Mrs. Alfred North, Philadelphia, Pennsylvania

Ingredients

1 cup shortening
1 teaspoon salt
2 teaspoons vanilla
½ cup confectioners' sugar

2 cups sifted flour
2 cups finely chopped pecans
Powdered sugar

Directions (Makes 10 to 12 dozen)

Blend shortening with salt and vanilla; add the sugar gradually.
Cream well.

Sift flour; add flour and chopped nuts to the above mixture. Beat
well. Shape the stiff dough into little balls, slightly larger than a

marble. Place on greased cookie sheet and bake about 15 minutes in moderate oven at 350°. Remove from pan and quickly, but carefully, roll the hot cookies in sifted powdered sugar. This forms a frosting-like coating over the cookies. Cool; then roll again in powdered sugar. Store in an airtight container.

-❧ *Recrisp "once crisp" cookies in a slow oven for about 5 minutes before serving them.*

❧ *Refrigerator Cookies*

Ingredients

4 cups sifted flour
1 teaspoon baking powder
¼ teaspoon soda
1 teaspoon salt
1⅓ cups soft butter

1 cup firmly packed brown sugar
⅔ cup sugar
2 eggs
1½ teaspoons vanilla

Directions (Makes about 6 dozen)

Sift together first four ingredients. Set aside.
Cream together butter, sugars, and eggs until light and fluffy.
Add vanilla with flour to the creamed mixture; blend thoroughly.
   Shape into rolls 3 inches in diameter. Wrap in waxed paper and chill thoroughly. Cut into thin slices with a sharp knife. Place on an ungreased baking sheet. Bake in hot oven at 400° for 5 to 8 minutes or until lightly browned.

❧ *Chocolate Refrigerator Cookies*

(Makes about 6 dozen)

Use recipe for Refrigerator Cookies, adding 4 squares unsweetened chocolate, melted and cooled, to the creamed mixture.

❧ *Coconut Refrigerator Cookies*

(Makes about 6 dozen)

Use recipe for Refrigerator Cookies, adding 1¾ cups finely cut coconut to the creamed mixture.

∾ Date-Nut Refrigerator Cookies

(Makes about 6 dozen)

Use recipe for Refrigerator Cookies, adding 1 cup finely chopped walnuts and 1 cup finely chopped, pitted dates to the creamed mixture.

∾ Nut Refrigerator Cookies

(Makes about 6 dozen)

Use recipe for Refrigerator Cookies, adding 1 cup finely chopped black walnuts or pecans to the creamed mixture.

∾ Refrigerator Nut Cookies

The Maine Maid, Jericho, Long Island, New York

Ingredients

2 cups brown sugar	3¾ cups all-purpose flour
1 cup butter	1 teaspoon salt
2 eggs	1 teaspoon vanilla
1 teaspoon soda	1 cup chopped nuts
1 teaspoon water	

Directions (Makes about 6 dozen)

Cream butter; add sugar and beat until creamy. Beat eggs and add.
Dissolve soda in water and add to sugar mixture.
Sift salt with flour twice and add to above mixture; mix well.
Add vanilla and nuts. Line loaf pan with waxed paper; pack in cookie mixture. Chill overnight in refrigerator. Next day slice thin. Place on lightly greased baking sheet and bake in 325° oven for 10 to 15 minutes. This will keep several days in the refrigerator.

∾ Pinwheel Refrigerator Cookies

(Makes about 6 dozen)

Prepare Refrigerator Cookies. Divide the dough into two parts. To one part add 2 squares unsweetened chocolate, melted and cooled. Leave the other part plain. Roll each part as thin as possible on a lightly floured board. Place one on top of the other and roll jelly-roll fashion. Chill; slice and bake as directed.

Ᏼ Ginger Crisps

Miss Katharine L. Little, Chicago, Illinois

Ingredients

1 cup shortening
1 cup granulated sugar
2 eggs, beaten
½ cup molasses

4½ cups flour
3 teaspoons ginger
1 teaspoon soda
1 teaspoon salt

Directions (Makes 36 cookies)

Cream shortening until soft and waxy.

Add sugar gradually to above and cream until fluffy.

Stir in eggs.

Add molasses and beat until well blended.

Sift together remaining ingredients and add to the mixture. Mold
into roll and place in refrigerator until thoroughly set. Slice as thin
as desired. Place on lightly greased baking sheet. Bake in 325° oven
until the cookies are brown.

Ᏼ Easy Mix Cookies

Duncan Hines Division, Nebraska Consolidated
Mills Company, Omaha, Nebraska

(Using White or Spice Cake Mix)

Ingredients

2 eggs
¼ teaspoon soda
¼ lb. soft or barely melted butter
or margarine

1 package (19 oz.) White or Spice
Cake Mix
¾ cup sifted all-purpose flour

Directions (Makes 2 to 3 dozen)

Beat eggs with soda.

Add shortening to above mixture and beat well.

Stir cake mix package contents into butter-egg mixture until all
moistened.

Add flour to the above and mix well. Drop by heaping teaspoonfuls,
2 inches apart, on ungreased cookie sheet. Bake at 350°, on rack
above center, 12 to 15 minutes. Remove from pan at once. Note:
For crisp cookies, use 1 egg and 2 tablespoons water instead of
2 eggs.

ᕁ Oatmeal Cookies

Use recipe for Easy Mix Cookies (using either White or Spice Cake Mix) and substitute ¼ cup flour and 1 cup rolled oats for the ¾ cup sifted flour. (Add fruit variations as desired.) Bake as directed for Easy Mix Cookies.

ᕁ Lemon Coconut Drops

Use recipe for Easy Mix Cookies (using either White or Spice Cake Mix) and add ⅔ cup cut coconut and ¼ teaspoon lemon extract. Stir these ingredients in with the flour. Bake as directed for Easy Mix Cookies.

ᕁ Fruit Cookies

Use recipe for Easy Mix Cookies (using either White or Spice Cake Mix) and add ⅔ cup finely cut raisins or dates and ½ teaspoon vanilla. Stir these ingredients in with the flour. Bake as directed for Easy Mix Cookies.

-➤ *Boiling water poured over seedless raisins makes them plump.*

ᕁ Refrigerator Cookies

Use recipe for Easy Mix Cookies (using either White or Spice Cake Mix) and increase flour to 1 cup. Use fruit variation desired. Shape in long rolls. Wrap in waxed paper. Store in refrigerator until used. Slice thin. Place on ungreased cookie sheet. Bake about 10 minutes at 350°.

✆ Easy Mix Cookies

Duncan Hines Division, Nebraska Consolidated
Mills Company, Omaha, Nebraska

(Using either Yellow or Devil's Food Cake Mix)

Ingredients

2 eggs	1 package (19 oz.) Yellow or
¼ teaspoon soda	Devil's Food Cake Mix
¼ lb. soft or barely melted butter or margarine	½ cup sifted all-purpose flour

Directions (Makes 2 to 3 dozen)

Beat eggs with soda.

Add shortening to above mixture and beat well.

Stir cake mix package contents into butter-egg mixture until all moistened.

Add flour to the above and mix well. Drop by heaping teaspoonfuls, 2 inches apart, on ungreased cookie sheet. Bake at 350°, on rack above center, 12 to 15 minutes. Remove from pan at once. Note: For crisp cookies, use 1 egg and 2 tablespoons water instead of 2 eggs.

✆ Fruit Cookies

Use recipe for Easy Mix Cookies (using either Yellow or Devil's Food Cake Mix), adding ⅔ cup finely cut raisins or dates and ½ teaspoon vanilla. Stir these ingredients in with the flour. Bake as directed for Easy Mix Cookies.

✆ Oatmeal Cookies

Use recipe for Easy Mix Cookies (using either Yellow or Devil's Food Cake Mix) and substitute 1 cup rolled oats for the ½ cup sifted flour. (Add fruit variations as desired.) Bake as directed for Easy Mix Cookies.

∾ Chocolate Chip Cookies

Use recipe for Easy Mix Cookies (using either Yellow or Devil's Food Cake Mix), adding ⅔ cup semisweet chocolate bits. Stir in with the flour. Bake as directed for Easy Mix Cookies.

∾ Refrigerator Cookies

Use recipe for Easy Mix Cookies (using either Yellow or Devil's Food Cake Mix), increasing flour to ¾ cup. Use fruit variation as desired. Shape in long rolls. Wrap in waxed paper. Store in refrigerator until used. Slice thin. Place on ungreased cookie sheet. Bake about 10 minutes at 350°.

∾ Brownies

Ingredients

2 squares unsweetened chocolate
½ cup butter
1 cup sugar
2 eggs
1 teaspoon vanilla

1 cup nuts, broken
¾ cup flour
½ teaspoon baking powder
½ teaspoon salt

Directions (Makes about 2½ dozen)

Melt together chocolate and butter over hot water.

Add sugar and eggs to above and beat thoroughly.

Add vanilla and nuts to mixture.

Sift together remaining ingredients and add to mixture. Stir in thoroughly. Pour into a greased and floured 12 × 12 × 2-inch baking pan and bake in 350° oven for 25 to 30 minutes. When cool, cut into squares. These may be iced before serving.

∾ Date Squares

Ingredients

1½ cups rolled oats
1½ cups flour
1 cup brown sugar
½ teaspoon soda

¾ cup shortening—half butter
    and half vegetable shortening
½ teaspoon salt

Directions (Makes 10 to 12)

Mix all ingredients together like pie crust. Divide and spread half
the mixture on the bottom of a greased 9 × 9 × 2-inch square pan,
patting down mixture with hands.

Filling

Ingredients

¾ pound dates, cut up   ½ cup water
½ cup sugar   Juice of ½ lemon

Directions

Cook all ingredients until transparent (about 5 minutes). Cool and
spread over first layer. Cover with remaining mixture. Bake 25
minutes in 350° oven. When cold, cut in squares and serve with
whipped cream as dessert. Or may be cut in smaller squares like
brownies and served with tea.

〰 *Fudge Squares*

Ingredients

½ cup butter   ⅛ teaspoon salt
2 squares unsweetened chocolate   3 eggs, beaten
    or ⅓ cup cocoa plus 1 table-   1 teaspoon vanilla
    spoon butter   ¾ cup chopped nuts (walnuts or
½ cup cake flour   pecans)
1¼ cups sugar

Directions (Makes about 16)

Melt butter and chocolate.
Sift dry ingredients twice and add to above.
Mix remaining ingredients into mixture. Pour into a greased
    9 × 9 × 2-inch square pan. Bake in 350° oven for 25 minutes.

➔ *You will not have burned cookies if you use a small timer clock or
the clock on the range.*

ᔆ Penuche Coconut Bars

Ingredients

½ cup soft butter
½ cup firmly packed brown sugar
1 cup sifted flour
½ teaspoon salt
1 tablespoon milk
2 eggs, well beaten

1 cup firmly packed brown sugar
1 teaspoon vanilla
2 tablespoons flour
½ teaspoon baking powder
¼ teaspoon salt
1½ cups coconut, finely cut
1 cup chopped pecans

Directions (Makes about 3 dozen)

Cream together butter and ½ cup brown sugar until light and fluffy.

Sift together 1 cup flour and ½ teaspoon salt, and add to sugar mixture. Blend well.

Stir milk into above mixture and mix well. Spread mixture in a lightly greased 9 × 9 × 2-inch pan and bake in slow oven at 325° for 20 minutes or until lightly browned.

Add 1 cup brown sugar and vanilla to beaten eggs and continue beating until thick and lemon colored.

Stir remaining ingredients into the above mixture and mix well. Spread over baked mixture and return to oven; bake 25 minutes longer or until golden brown. Cool and cut into small bars.

ᔆ Jackson Cookies

Mrs. Mathew Jackson, Chicago, Illinois

Ingredients

1 cup butter
1½ cups sugar
3 eggs, beaten
¼ cup milk
½ teaspoon soda
Pinch of salt

2 cups flour
1 teaspoon nutmeg
1 teaspoon cinnamon
1½ cups raisins
½ cup chopped pecans or walnuts

Directions (Makes 2 dozen)

Cream together butter and sugar.

Add eggs to above.

Stir milk, soda, and salt into mixture.

Sift together flour and spices and add to mixture.

Mix raisins and pecans well and stir into mixture. Spread on shallow well-greased pans and bake in 375° oven for 10 to 12 minutes. Remove from oven and cut into squares.

↶ Carmens

Ingredients

1 cup butter
2 cups brown sugar, sifted
4 egg yolks, beaten
2 egg whites, beaten
1 cup milk
1 teaspoon vinegar
1 teaspoon soda
2¼ cups pastry flour

1 teaspoon cinnamon
½ teaspoon cloves
1 teaspoon allspice
1 teaspoon vanilla
3 egg whites, beaten stiff
1 cup brown sugar
½ cup chopped nuts

Directions (Makes 1 cookie sheet)

Cream together butter and 2 cups sugar until light.

Add eggs to the above.

Mix milk and vinegar together.

Sift together dry ingredients. Alternately add a little of the milk mixture, then the flour mixture to the butter and eggs. Mix well.

Fold vanilla into the mixture and spread on cookie sheet about ⅜-inch thick.

Mix remaining 1 cup brown sugar with the nuts and sprinkle on top of the dough.

Make a meringue and spread over the nut-topped dough. Bake about 40 minutes in 350° oven. Cut in small pieces. These are very delicate and should be carefully handled.

↶ Berliner Krautzen

Mrs. Howard Gilbert, Sioux Falls, South Dakota

Ingredients

1 lb. butter
1 cup sugar
4 egg yolks, hard cooked and
  mashed

3 egg yolks, raw
3½ to 4 cups flour
1 egg white, slightly beaten
Loaf sugar, crushed

Directions (Makes about 5 dozen)

Cream butter and sugar together.

Add hard-cooked egg yolks and then add raw egg yolks, one at a time. Beat well.

Add enough flour to roll out the dough. Roll with palm of hand to the size of a pencil. Shape into a figure 8. (Cookie press may be used.)

Dip in egg white and then in sugar. Place on lightly greased baking sheet and bake in moderate oven at 350° about 10 minutes or until light brown.

∾ Spritz

Ingredients

1 cup soft butter
⅔ cup sugar
3 egg yolks

1 teaspoon vanilla
2½ cups sifted flour
Pinch of salt

Directions (Makes about 6 dozen)

Mix first four ingredients together thoroughly with hands.
Add flour and salt to the above mixture and work with hands until well mixed. Force the dough through a cookie press onto an ungreased baking sheet, using any desired design. Bake in moderate oven at 400° for 8 to 10 minutes. (Cookies do not brown on top.)

∾ Cocoa Kisses

Ingredients

1 cup sifted powdered sugar
2 egg whites
1 cup chopped walnuts
1 cup chopped dates

¼ cup sliced glaceéd cherries
1 large tablespoon cocoa
1 teaspoon vanilla
Pinch of salt

Directions (Makes about 2 dozen)

Beat egg whites stiff. Add sugar slowly. Stir in gently all other ingredients. Drop from a teaspoon onto a greased cookie sheet. Bake in 325° oven for 15 minutes, or until done, but not dry. These should be gummy when cool. Must be removed from tin quickly.

⁓ Nut Macaroons

McDonald Tea Room, Gallatin, Missouri

Ingredients

2 cups powdered sugar, sifted
½ cup flour, sifted
1 teaspoon baking powder

5 egg whites
1 lb. chopped nuts

Directions (Makes 6 or 7 dozen)

Blend first three ingredients.

Do not beat egg whites. Stir into the dry ingredients.

Add the nuts. Drop from a teaspoon onto a greased cookie sheet.
    Bake in 300° oven 15 minutes or until set. Do not bake too hard,
    or they won't be good.

Dessert Sauces

A SAUCE SHOULD ENHANCE a dessert by adding color, texture, flavor, and moistness. It should never mask the true flavor of the dessert. Too few people realize the importance of a sauce on the right dessert.

There are two kinds of dessert sauces, cooked and uncooked. Cooked sauces are usually thickened with whole eggs, egg yolks, flour, cornstarch, or tapioca. When you want a fruit sauce to have a bright clear color, thicken with cornstarch or tapioca. An appetizing color will greatly add to your sauce's eye appeal. Liquor, fruit juice (when used as a flavoring), and all other flavoring ingredients should be added only when the sauce is cool. If they are added when the sauce is still hot, then some of the flavor will evaporate.

Some desserts that are improved by the use of a sauce are: ice creams, sherbets, steamed puddings, simple puddings, dumplings, plum puddings and sponges, and angel food and pound cake squares.

Rum, sherry, brandy, and Madeira all add a good flavor and piquance to a dessert sauce. However, be sure to serve the right sauce with the right pudding, as not all flavors blend well together. There are a few simple rules that should be followed when choosing a sauce for your pudding. A sauce should complement the pudding. If a pudding is citrous, then serve a bland sauce with it; if the pudding is bland, then serve a rich sauce. If you have a rich dessert, then shun whipped cream and try a fruit sauce. The success of the pudding and the sauce will depend on your own discrimination.

A "hard sauce" with a butter foundation is a traditional supplement for many desserts that are served warm, such as baked and steamed puddings, dumplings, and some fruit pies. A chilled hard sauce served over such a dessert has a delicate flavor that mingles well with the hardier flavor of the pudding.

A sauce does not need to be complicated to be good. The most important point is to learn the correct combination of flavors. A simple sauce, such as a custard or lemon sauce, can be transformed into a sauce of fluffy consistency by adding beaten egg whites or whipped cream. An easy uncooked fruit sauce can be made from leftover fruit, fresh or stewed, with the flavor enhanced by the addition of a little wine or cordial.

Most cooked sauces require low heat or the use of a double boiler. In making a cooked sauce it is a good idea to use a saucepan large enough to allow for cooking without danger of overflowing, but not so large that the mixture forms only a thin layer at the bottom of the pan. Your sauce will have a better consistency if it is deep enough in the pan to enable easy stirring.

Most chefs classify a sauce as a "pick up," which is their term for a finishing touch that will add a dash of glamour and distinction to a dessert. Especially in ice cream, sauces are used to create color contrast. Popular crushed strawberries or raspberries over vanilla ice cream are good examples of this touch. This combination makes a good taste contrast too.

Any restaurant owner will tell you that one of the most popular desserts on the menu is ice cream served as a sundae. No matter how full you may be, there is always just a little room left for this dish with a special sauce. In this section I discuss several sauces that are well suited for ice cream desserts. I know you will enjoy the caramel fudge, butterscotch, pecan, and brandy sauces when you try them.

�❧ *Remember that every picture has a frame, and the frame for the dessert is the serving dish. Crystal, colorful china, or pottery should be carefully chosen, keeping in mind the enhancement of the dessert.*

Remember that the right sauce can greatly enhance the appeal of a steamed or baked pudding. An "everyday" sauce can be "dressed-up" for company dinner with a dash of brandy, rum, or nutmeg.

ᕦ Chocolate Sauce for Ice Cream

Ingredients

½ lb. marshmallows
2 squares unsweetened chocolate

2 squares sweet chocolate
½ cup cream

Directions (Makes about 1 ½ cups)

Cut marshmallows into small pieces.
Shave the chocolate. Place with marshmallows in a double boiler and
  let stand over boiling water until dissolved. Stir often. Serve on ice
  cream. Will keep well in covered jar in refrigerator.

ᕦ Regal Chocolate Sauce

Ingredients

½ cup light corn syrup
1 cup sugar
1 cup water
Pinch of salt

3 squares unsweetened chocolate
1 teaspoon vanilla
1 cup evaporated milk

Directions (Makes about 2 ½ cups)

Combine corn syrup, sugar, water, and salt in saucepan. Cook to the
  soft-ball stage or to a temperature of 236° F. Remove from heat.
Add chocolate to the above mixture and stir until chocolate melts.
  Add vanilla. Slowly add evaporated milk and mix thoroughly.
  Serve on ice cream.

➧ *Don't forget the whipped cream! Spoonfuls of whipped cream
around the edge of a pie will give it that professional touch, and
although it may add calories, it's worth it! A dab of whipped cream
also goes well on gelatin desserts, puddings, and baked desserts.*

ᕦ Chocolate Sherry Sauce

Old Southern Tea Room, Vicksburg, Mississippi

Ingredients

4 squares unsweetened chocolate
2 cups confectioners' sugar
¾ cup cream

1 tablespoon butter
¼ cup sherry

Directions (Makes about 3 cups)

Melt chocolate in top of double boiler. Add sugar, cream, and butter. Stir well and cook for 7 minutes. Let cool.

When sauce is cool, add sherry. Serve over vanilla ice cream in parfait glasses. Also may be served on a square of angel food cake with white icing on top, a scoop of vanilla ice cream, chocolate sauce, and then a red cherry. Dessert is called "Angel Food Sherry Delight."

⟶ *Caramel Sauce*

Ingredients

3 cups sugar	¼ teaspoon salt
2 cups hot water	1 teaspoon vanilla
2 tablespoons butter	

Directions (Makes 1½ cups)

Heat sugar in heavy skillet over low heat, stirring constantly until sugar has melted and changed to a golden brown syrup. Remove from heat and slowly stir in hot water. Return to heat and boil slowly until mixture thickens. Remove from heat.

Add remaining ingredients to above mixture.

⟶ *Caramel Fudge Sauce*

Ingredients

1½ cups sugar	1 tablespoon butter
1 cup boiling water	¾ teaspoon vanilla

Directions (Makes 1 cup)

Melt sugar in heavy frying pan over low heat, stirring constantly. When golden brown in color, remove from heat and stir in water. Add butter and return to heat. Boil until very soft-ball stage has been reached or to a temperature of 230° F.

Remove from heat and add vanilla. Stir. Serve hot or cold on ice cream.

➤ *Always remember that cold desserts should be served cold, and hot desserts should be served hot.*

ᕰ Butterscotch Sauce

Ingredients

¾ cup firmly packed brown
    sugar
1 cup light corn syrup

⅓ cup butter
1 cup light cream

Directions (Makes 3 cups)

Boil sugar, syrup, and butter for 5 minutes, stirring until the sugar is
    dissolved.

Add cream and bring to a boil. Serve hot or cold on ice cream.

ᕰ Foamy Sauce

Ingredients

½ cup butter
1 cup powdered sugar, sifted
1 egg yolk

1 teaspoon vanilla
1 egg white, stiffly beaten
Pinch of salt

Directions (Makes about 2 cups)

Cream butter until soft. Add sugar gradually and cream together
    until light and fluffy. Add egg yolk and vanilla and beat until
    blended. Place the sauce over hot water and beat and cook until
    slightly thickened. Remove from heat.

Fold egg white and salt into the above mixture. Serve hot or cold.

ᕰ Eggnog Sauce

Ingredients

2½ tablespoons sugar
1 tablespoon flour
Pinch of salt
1 egg yolk
1¼ cups milk

Pinch of nutmeg
1 tablespoon rum
1 egg white
1 tablespoon sugar

Directions (Makes about 2 cups)

Combine first three ingredients in top of double boiler. Add egg yolk
    and beat well. Gradually add milk, stirring constantly. Cook over
    rapidly boiling water 5 minutes, stirring occasionally. Remove
    from heat. Cool.

Add nutmeg and rum to the above.

Beat egg white until frothy. Add sugar gradually, beating until mixture will stand in soft peaks. Fold in cooled custard mixture.

∾ Fruit Sauce

Ingredients

1 cup unsweetened fruit juice
⅔ cup sugar
1 tablespoon cornstarch
2 teaspoons lemon juice

3 tablespoons butter
1 cup crushed fruit, fresh or stewed

Directions (Makes 1½ cups)

Combine first three ingredients in saucepan. Stir and cook until mixture comes to a boil. Remove from heat.

Add lemon juice and butter to the above mixture. Cool.

Add fruit to sauce mixture. Return to heat and cook and stir until thick. Serve over cake, pudding, or ice cream.

∾ Gold Sauce

Ingredients

4 egg yolks
¼ cup sugar

⅛ teaspoon salt
½ teaspoon vanilla

Directions (Makes about 2 cups)

Beat egg yolks in top of double boiler until very thick and lemon colored.

Beat sugar and salt into the above mixture. Beat until the sugar is dissolved. Place top section of double boiler over hot water. (Never let water boil.) Cook sauce, beating constantly for about 5 minutes or until mixture is the consistency of whipped cream. Remove from heat and add vanilla. Serve hot or cold over puddings and cakes.

∾ Brandy Gold Sauce

(Makes 2 cups)

Use recipe for Gold Sauce, adding 3 tablespoons of brandy just before removing sauce from heat. Beat into mixture thoroughly.

∾ Orange Gold Sauce

Purefoy Hotel, Talladega, Alabama

(Makes 2 cups)

Use recipe for Gold Sauce, adding ⅛ cup orange juice and 1½ teaspoons grated orange rind before cooking the sauce. Omit vanilla.

∾ Lemon Sauce

Ingredients

½ cup sugar	1 egg yolk, beaten
1 tablespoon cornstarch	3 tablespoons butter
⅛ teaspoon salt	2 tablespoons lemon juice
1 cup boiling water	

Directions (Makes about 1½ cups)

Mix sugar, cornstarch, and salt. Add boiling water slowly, stirring constantly. Boil for 5 minutes. Remove from fire.

Pour above mixture over beaten egg yolk, and add butter and lemon juice. This is good with pineapple or apricot upside down cake.

∾ Orange Sauce

Ingredients

1½ tablespoons cornstarch	1 cup orange juice
⅓ cup sugar	½ cup water
1½ tablespoons grated orange rind	1 tablespoon lemon juice

Directions (Makes about 1½ cups)

Combine cornstarch, sugar, and rind in saucepan. Stir in orange juice and water. Bring to a boil, stirring constantly. Boil until clear. Add lemon juice. Serve hot or cold on steamed puddings.

‿ *Pecan Sauce*

Ingredients

1 cup light brown sugar	1 cup cold water
Pinch of salt	3 tablespoons butter
2 tablespoons cornstarch	⅔ cup chopped pecans

Directions (Makes about 1 ½ cups)

Mix sugar, salt, and cornstarch in saucepan. Stir in cold water. Cook, stirring constantly, over low heat. Boil until clear. Remove from heat.

Add butter and pecans.

‿ *Pineapple Sauce*

Ingredients

1½ tablespoons cornstarch	¾ cup water
½ cup sugar	1 ½ tablespoons lemon juice
1 cup canned, crushed pineapple	

Directions (Makes about 1 ½ cups)

Combine cornstarch and sugar in saucepan. Stir in crushed pineapple and water. Bring to a boil, stirring constantly. Boil until clear. Chill.

Add lemon juice. Serve on puddings or ice cream.

‿ *Clear Sauce*

Ingredients

1 cup sugar	2 tablespoons butter
2 tablespoons cornstarch	½ teaspoon nutmeg
2 cups boiling water	¼ cup whiskey

Directions (Makes about 2 cups)

Mix sugar and cornstarch together in a saucepan.

Stir boiling water in gradually. Bring to a boil and boil for 1 minute or until clear, stirring constantly. Remove from heat.

Add remaining ingredients. Serve hot over Bread Pudding.

❧ Plain Custard Sauce

Ingredients

2 cups milk
2 eggs, slightly beaten
¼ cup sugar

⅛ teaspoon salt
1 teaspoon vanilla

Directions (Makes about 2 cups)

Scald milk in the top of a double boiler. Combine eggs, sugar, and salt
  in bowl.
Add scalded milk gradually to the egg mixture, stirring constantly.
  Return mixture to top of double boiler. Cook custard over hot
  water, stirring constantly until thickened and will coat a metal
  spoon without running off. (Takes 15 to 20 minutes.) Remove
  from heat and pour into a bowl or jar to cool. (Cover with waxed
  paper to prevent a scum from forming.)
Add vanilla when cool.

❧ Russian Sauce

Purefoy Hotel, Talladega, Alabama

Ingredients

4 egg yolks
1 cup sugar
1 tablespoon flour
Juice and pulp of 2 oranges

Grated rind of 1 orange
2 tablespoons coconut
½ pint whipped cream

Directions (Makes about 2½ cups)

Mix first five ingredients in double boiler and cook until mixture
  thickens.
Add coconut while still hot. Let cool and add whipped cream. Serve
  over slices of angel food cake.

❧ Brandy Sauce

Dolores Restaurant, Oklahoma City, Oklahoma

Ingredients

1 cup sugar
1 tablespoon cornstarch
¼ teaspoon salt

1 tablespoon butter
1 cup boiling water
¼ cup or more brandy

Directions (Serves 8)

Mix together dry ingredients. Add butter and boiling water. Mix well and cook 6 minutes or until clear.

Add brandy after you remove saucepan from the fire. Serve quite warm over any little plain cake or pudding.

ᕫ Hard Sauce (cooked)

Ingredients

1 lb. brown sugar
½ lb. butter
½ teaspoon nutmeg

2 egg yolks
½ cup whiskey

Directions (Serves 8 to 10)

Cook sugar, butter, and nutmeg together in double boiler until smooth, stirring constantly. Take from fire.

Beat egg yolks well and add to above.

Add whiskey to above. You may use more or less of the whiskey as you desire. This may be stored in a covered jar in the refrigerator and used as needed. Serve over plum pudding and gingerbread.

ᕫ Ethel's Famous Brandy Pudding Sauce

Water Gate Inn, Washington, D.C.

Ingredients

1 quart whipped cream
1½ tablespoons powdered sugar

3 egg yolks
Brandy or rum

Directions (Makes 1 quart)

Blend sugar with the whipped cream.

Beat egg yolks until frothy and combine with whipped cream. Add brandy or rum to taste.

ᕫ Fluffy Sauce

Ingredients

1 egg white, stiffly beaten
¾ cup powdered sugar
Pinch of salt

1 egg yolk
½ cup whipping cream, whipped
2 tablespoons brandy

Directions *(Makes about 1 ½ cups)*

Add sugar gradually to beaten egg white, beating until mixture
stands in peaks and holds its shape.

Beat salt and yolk into the above mixture.

Fold in whipped cream and brandy. Chill thoroughly.

∾ Sauce for Mince Pie

Boston Oyster House, Chicago, Illinois

Ingredients

3 tablespoons butter	2 oz. rum
2 teaspoons sugar	2 oz. brandy
1 tablespoon lemon juice	1 pinch nutmeg
¼ cup hot water	

Directions *(Serves 6)*

Melt together butter and sugar and mix well.

Add remaining ingredients to above and, when hot, pour over slices
of pie.

*-❧ Fresh and frozen fruits and berries add color and texture to the
plainest dessert. It is easy to decorate the serving dishes with clusters
of grapes or berries, fresh flowers, or leaves.*

∾ Hard Sauce (uncooked)

Ingredients

½ cup butter	1 ½ cups powdered sugar

Directions *(Serves 8 to 10)*

Cream butter and add sugar gradually, beating well. The longer
the beating, the creamier the sauce will be. Variations may be
made in this sauce by adding 2 tablespoons of brandy, Cointreau,
Grand Marnier, or any other flavoring desired. If vanilla is used,
then ½ teaspoon should be sufficient. Serve over plum puddings,
gingerbread, and the like.

Miscellaneous Desserts

(Fritters, Pancakes, Waffles, Cream Puffs, Doughnuts)

INCLUDED in this section are recipes that are sometimes over-looked as dessert possibilities. They are easy to serve and easy to eat.

Pancakes and waffles are a natural for informal entertaining. Modern electrical equipment for baking waffles and pancakes is streamlined-looking, and therefore the hostess need not hesitate to bring it into the living room where places can be filled and replenished readily. Living room service also lends an air of charm to your entertaining.

Waffles make an ideal dessert base for ice cream, crushed fruit, or whipped cream. The plain pancake can be "dressed up" by making thin pancakes, spreading them with jam or jelly, rolling up jelly-roll fashion, and sprinkling with confectioners' sugar. Pancakes can also be stacked in layers, spread with filling in between, and served with a sauce. For a change, the pancake or waffle batter can be enhanced by adding grated orange or lemon rind, blueberries, or chocolate chips. Cream puffs or éclairs may be filled with whipped cream, ice cream, or a custard filling, with its many possible variations. Even doughnuts can be decorated with tasty glazes, fruit sauces, or the versatile whipped cream. Fritter batter can be used for coating many fruits, such as pineapple, apple slices, apricots, bananas, strawberries, and many others.

As for the origin of the pancake, waffle, doughnut, and cream puff, again we must give credit to the Europeans. Pancakes, once called "hearth cakes," have been known since the days when man first mixed flour and water to make a batter. As the original name implies, they were baked over the hearth. The dessert pancake, however, went through many stages of development before it was perfected to the light delicate dish we now know. Crêpes Suzette, the most elegant of this family, was first created to be served with afternoon tea for Louis XV and his hunters. This glorified pancake was invented for the French knight by Princess (Suzette) de Carignan, who was in love with his royal highness.

The first waffle, as the story goes, came about accidentally in the thirteenth century. A Crusader, wearing his armor, absentmindedly sat on some freshly baked oat cakes, which his wife had placed on a bench to cool. The cakes were flattened, and deep imprints from the Crusader's steel links were made in them. Nevertheless, he spread butter on the oat cakes and ate them. His wife was delighted and fascinated with the way in which the butter stayed in the imprints made from the armor, and from then on, once a week, she had her husband put on his outfit and sit on her oat cakes.

The first doughnuts were nothing more than balls of yeast dough, and back in sixteenth-century England, they were called "imported doughty cakes." Doughnuts were brought to America by the English and Dutch settlers and were eventually perfected. However, the Indians have their own version of how doughnuts began. It seems that one day, back in the seventeenth century, an Indian, to display his skill with his bow, playfully shot an arrow through a fried cake a squaw was making. The squaw was startled, and she dropped the perforated cake into a kettle of boiling grease, which was on the fire; thus she created the first doughnut.

∾ French Pancakes or Crêpes Suzette with Southern Comfort Sauce

Mr. Francis E. Fowler Jr., Los Angeles, California

Ingredients

3 eggs, beaten
1 cup milk
⅓ cup water
1 cup flour
¼ teaspoon baking powder

½ teaspoon salt
3 tablespoons sugar
1 jigger Southern Comfort to a cake

Directions (Makes 5 to 6 cakes)

Mix together eggs, milk, and water.
Sift together dry ingredients and add to mixture. The batter should be very thin.
Take about ½ cup to a griddle. Bake on hot greased griddle. Turn carefully and brown the other side. When done, put on a dinner plate, sprinkle with powdered sugar and jelly, and roll up.
Pour Southern Comfort over pancake and light with a match.

∾ Polichinkas (Yugoslavian Crêpes Suzette)

Mrs. Frank Dieterich, Culver City, California

Ingredients

2 egg yolks
2 tablespoons sugar
Pinch of salt
1 cup sifted flour

¾ cup milk
2 egg whites
Apricot jam
Powdered sugar

Directions (Makes about 5)

Beat together egg yolks, sugar, and salt.
Add flour and milk and beat until smooth.
Beat egg whites stiff and fold in. Batter should be thin. Pour on hot greased griddle, tipping so that batter will spread over bottom. Brown one side, and turn and brown the other. When done, spread with a thick apricot jam or any other desired jam. Roll up and sprinkle roll with powdered sugar.

ᏉᎧ *Banana Suzettes*

Silver Grille, The Higbee Company, Cleveland, Ohio

Ingredients

2 bananas
2 egg whites
2 tablespoons flour

2 egg yolks, beaten
4 tablespoons cream

Directions (Makes 16)

Dice bananas in ¼-inch slices. Beat egg whites very stiff. Mix
remaining ingredients in order given. Fry golden brown in butter.
Suzettes should be size of silver dollar. Serve with New England
Sauce.

New England Sauce

Ingredients

1 cup sugar
1 tablespoon cornstarch
1 teaspoon vinegar

2 cups water
2 tablespoons butter

Directions (Makes 1 cup)

Mix all ingredients together in saucepan. Simmer over low heat for
about 50 minutes until transparent and the consistency of thin
custard.

ᏉᎧ *Swedish Pancakes*

Ingredients

1 ½ cups sifted flour
1 teaspoon salt
1 tablespoon sugar
3 eggs, well beaten

3 cups milk
3 tablespoons melted butter
Tart jelly

Directions (Serves 6 to 8)

Sift dry ingredients together into bowl.
Add milk and melted butter to beaten eggs. Pour into flour mixture
and stir until blended. Pour about ½ cup batter onto hot greased
griddle. Turn over when delicately brown and bake the other side.
Stack the baked pancakes in layers, spreading each layer with tart
jelly. Sprinkle top with confectioners' sugar.

❧ Apple Pancakes

Ingredients

1 cup sifted flour	4 eggs
¼ teaspoon salt	3 large tart apples, peeled and
2 teaspoons sugar	cored
1½ cup milk	½ cup lemon juice

Directions (Serves 4 to 6)

Sift together first three ingredients into a bowl.

Stir milk into the above mixture to make a smooth paste.

Add eggs to the above, one at a time, beating well after each addition.

Cut apples into thin strips and cover with lemon juice. Fold apple strips into the batter. Fry in butter in a small, hot frying pan until delicately brown; turn and brown the other side. Serve with sugar and cinnamon.

❧ Apple Fritters

Ox Yoke Inn, Amana, Iowa

Ingredients

1 cup bread flour	2 tablespoons melted butter
¼ teaspoon salt	3 tablespoons lemon juice
2 tablespoons sugar	6 large, ripe apples, peeled and
⅔ cup milk	cored
2 eggs, separated	

Directions (Serves 8)

Sift flour, salt, and sugar together into a bowl.

Add milk, egg yolks, and butter to the above mixture. Beat until smooth. Beat egg whites until stiff and fold into batter.

Cut apples into ½-inch slices. Pour lemon juice over them. Dip each slice in batter. Fry in deep hot fat at 356° F. until nicely browned. Drain; sprinkle with confectioners' sugar.

> ➥ *To glaze doughnuts, add ⅓ cup boiling water to 1 cup sifted confectioners' sugar. Beat until smooth and well blended. Dip the warm doughnuts into the warm glaze.*

ᕙ Apricot Fritters

Hotel Roanoke, Roanoke, Virginia

Ingredients

1 teaspoon sugar
1¼ cups flour
⅓ teaspoon baking powder
Pinch of salt

2 eggs
⅓ cup milk
½ tablespoon butter
Apricots

Directions (Serves 6)

Sift dry ingredients together.

Beat eggs well; add eggs, milk, and butter to the above mixture. Mix as a stiff batter.

Remove stones from apricots and cut fruit into quarters. Dust with flour and dip each apricot into batter. Drop into deep hot fat. Fry until brown. Serve with Rum Sauce.

Rum Sauce

Ingredients

1 cup mixed fruit juice
¾ cup granulated sugar

¼ teaspoon red coloring
¼ cup rum flavoring

Directions

Mix all ingredients and cook slowly for 1 hour. Stir occasionally.

ᕙ Banana Fritters

Ingredients

3 ripe bananas
½ cup cake flour
2 tablespoons sugar
2 teaspoons baking powder
⅛ teaspoon salt
2 eggs, beaten

¼ cup sweetened condensed milk
¾ teaspoon vanilla
¼ cup coarsely chopped, salted nuts
⅔ cup raisins

Directions (Makes about 3 dozen)

Mash bananas.

Sift together dry ingredients.

Combine eggs, milk, and vanilla, and add to flour mixture. Stir until just blended.

Fold nuts and raisins with the banana pulp into the above mixture. (The batter should be the consistency of drop cookies.) Drop fritters into deep hot fat at 365° F. and fry for 2 to 3 minutes or until golden brown.

ᕙ Maple Fritters

Ingredients

2 cups sifted flour
2 teaspoons baking powder
¼ teaspoon salt
1 cup milk

1 egg, well beaten
Confectioners' sugar
Hot maple syrup

Directions (Makes 16)

Sift together dry ingredients into a bowl.

Add milk to beaten egg and add to flour mixture. Stir until just blended. Drop from tablespoon into deep hot fat at 370° F. and fry for about 5 minutes, or until well puffed and golden brown. Drain on absorbent paper.

Sprinkle fritters with confectioners' sugar and serve with hot maple syrup.

ᕙ Pineapple Fritters

Ingredients

1 cup sifted flour
1 teaspoon baking powder
¼ teaspoon salt
2 tablespoons sugar

1 egg, slightly beaten
¾ cup milk
1 tablespoon butter, melted
1 large ripe pineapple

Directions (Serves 6)

Sift together dry ingredients.

Combine eggs, milk, and melted butter. Stir into dry ingredients.

Pare and core pineapple. Cut in ¾-inch slices and then cut in fourths. Dip in batter and fry in deep hot fat at 370° F. for 3 to 4 minutes or until golden brown. Drain. Sprinkle with confectioners' sugar.

> ᕙ *A heavy griddle is best for even browning of pancakes. Modern griddles require no greasing; however, to ensure success, make a salt bag by cutting a large piece of cheesecloth, doubling the cloth, and making a sack. Fill the bag with salt. This salt bag cleans the griddle as well as prevents sticking.*

⌒ Histulas (Little Fruit Doughnuts)

Anderson Hotel, Wabasha, Minnesota

Ingredients

½ cup sugar
2 egg yolks, beaten
½ cup sour milk
½ teaspoon soda
2 cups sifted flour
¼ teaspoon salt

½ cup pecans, finely chopped
¼ cup raisins, finely chopped
¼ cup dates, finely chopped
Grated rind of 1 orange
2 tablespoons orange juice

Directions (Makes 3 to 4 dozen)

Combine sugar and egg yolks.

Mix milk and soda and add to egg mixture.

Sift flour, measure, then sift with salt. Add to above.

Add pecans, raisins, and dates to above mixture.

Add the orange rind and juice. Drop from teaspoon into deep hot
fat at 325° and fry until light brown. Turn while cooking. Remove
from fat and drain on absorbent paper. Sprinkle with sugar.
(Histulas should be quite small, only slightly larger than the hole
in an ordinary doughnut. It helps to drop the amount spooned out
of the dough briefly into flour. Then each ball can be molded by
hand. The coating of flour keeps the grease from soaking in.)

⌒ Doughnuts

Helen Gougeon, *Weekend Magazine*, Montreal, Canada

Ingredients

½ lb. butter
¾ lb. white sugar
6 egg yolks
1 cup milk

6 cups flour
1 tablespoon baking powder
1 wine glass brandy
6 egg whites, stiffly beaten

Directions (Makes 6 dozen)

Cream butter and add sugar gradually.

Beat egg yolks, and add with milk to above mixture; beat well.

Sift flour and baking powder together. Add to the above, mixing well.

Add brandy and egg whites to above mixture. Pat out dough on
lightly floured board. Cut doughnuts and let stand from 5 to 15
minutes before frying. Fry in 370° F. fat until brown on one side;
turn and brown on the other side. Remove and drain on paper
towels. Frost with icing or sprinkle with fruit sugar.

~ Cake Doughnuts

Ingredients

1 ½ cups brown sugar
2 eggs
4 tablespoons melted butter
1 cup whole milk

4 cups sifted flour
4 teaspoons baking powder
½ teaspoon cinnamon
½ teaspoon salt

Directions (Makes 35 doughnuts)

Beat whole eggs until they are light and stir into sugar.

Stir butter and milk into above.

Add baking powder, cinnamon, and salt to flour and sift again. Add to above, stirring only enough to get ingredients thoroughly blended. Place in refrigerator to chill, at least 24 hours if possible. (This prevents the doughnuts from soaking up the fat when fried.) Roll out a little of the dough at a time on floured board; cut with doughnut cutter. Fry in deep hot fat about 365° until brown on one side. Turn over and brown on the other side. Drain and roll in powdered sugar. This dough may be kept at least a week in a covered dish in the refrigerator. Break off and cook only enough of the dough at a time to fill your requirements, as freshly cooked doughnuts are better than those left standing overnight.

~ Orange Doughnuts

Vera Kirkpatrick, San Mateo, California

Ingredients

2 eggs
½ cup sugar
¼ teaspoon salt
½ cup thick cream
2 ½ cups flour

2 teaspoons baking powder
6 tablespoons butter, melted
1 teaspoon nutmeg
½ cup orange juice
Grated rind of 1 orange

Directions (Makes 12 doughnuts)

Beat eggs until light. Add sugar, salt, and cream.

Sift flour, measure, and sift again with baking powder. Add to sugar and egg mixture.

Stir butter into above mixture.

Add nutmeg, orange juice, and rind, and stir until blended. Chill. Roll out and cut with doughnut cutter. Fry in deep hot fat at 350° F. When cold, dust with powdered sugar.

Waffle Brownies

Ingredients

1½ cups sifted flour
½ teaspoon salt
¾ cup shortening
⅔ cup sugar
2 egg yolks
¾ cup milk
2 squares unsweetened chocolate, melted
½ cup chopped nuts
2 egg whites, stiffly beaten

Directions (Makes 4 waffles)

Sift together flour and salt. Set aside.

Cream shortening and add sugar gradually. Beat until light and fluffy. Add egg yolks and mix well.

Add milk to the above mixture, alternately with flour.

Fold in remaining ingredients. Bake in moderately hot waffle iron about 5 minutes. Serve with a scoop of vanilla ice cream or whipped cream topped with chocolate sauce. (*See* Dessert Sauces section.)

Gingerbread Waffles

Ingredients

1½ cups sifted flour
1 teaspoon ginger
½ teaspoon salt
1 teaspoon soda
1 teaspoon baking powder
3 eggs
¼ cup sugar
½ cup molasses
1 cup sour milk
⅓ cup melted butter

Directions (Serves 6)

Sift dry ingredients together. Set aside.

Beat eggs until light and fluffy.

Add sugar to eggs and beat well. Combine the remaining ingredients and flour mixture. Bake waffles in waffle iron until golden brown. Serve with whipped cream, fruit, or ice cream.

Use a deep-fat-frying thermometer for frying doughnuts and fruit fritters.

ᶜᵔ Dessert Waffles

Ingredients

1 ½ cups butter
3 cups sifted cake flour
3 eggs

1 ¼ cups sugar
¼ teaspoon salt

Directions (Makes 6 to 8 waffles)

Cream butter and add flour. Beat well.

Beat eggs slightly. Add sugar and salt, and continue beating until light and fluffy. Add to above mixture and beat well. Bake in a moderately hot waffle iron about 3 to 4 minutes. Serve with crushed, sweetened strawberries, raspberries, or blueberries.

ᶜᵔ Cream Puffs

Ingredients

1 cup sifted flour
¼ teaspoon salt
½ cup butter

1 cup boiling water
4 eggs

Directions (Makes 1 dozen)

Sift together flour and salt. Set aside.

Combine butter and boiling water in saucepan. Cook and stir over low heat until butter melts. Add flour mixture, all at once, and stir vigorously over low heat until mixture forms a ball and leaves the sides of the pan. Remove from heat.

Add unbeaten eggs, one at a time, beating well after each addition. Continue beating until a thick dough is formed. Drop by table-spoonfuls onto an ungreased baking sheet, about 2 inches apart. Bake in hot oven at 425° about 30 minutes. When cool, cut a slit in the side of each and fill with Cream Filling. (*See* Frostings and Fillings section.) May be filled with sweetened whipped cream. Serve with Chocolate Sauce. (*See* Dessert Sauces section.)

-● *Most waffle irons require no greasing after first seasoning.*

⌒ Chocolate Cream Puffs

(Makes one dozen)

Use recipe for Cream Puffs, melting 1 square unsweetened chocolate with the butter and water mixture. Cool and fill with sweetened whipped cream and sprinkle with confectioners' sugar.

⌒ Éclairs

(Makes 1 ½ dozen)

Use recipe for Cream Puffs. Force mixture through a decorating tube onto baking sheet in strips about 1 inch wide and 4 inches long. Bake about 25 minutes. When cool, slit and fill as for Cream Puffs. Frost with Chocolate Confectioners' Frosting. (*See* Frostings and Fillings section.)

⌒ Fried Cream

Ingredients

3 egg yolks	2 cups warm cream
1 tablespoon Jamaica rum	¼ teaspoon cinnamon
⅛ teaspoon salt	¾ cup graham cracker crumbs
¼ cup sugar	(about)
3 tablespoons cornstarch	1 egg, beaten
3 tablespoons milk	¼ cup warm Jamaica rum

Directions (Serves 2 to 4)

Combine egg yolks, rum, salt, and sugar, and beat together until well blended.

Combine cornstarch and milk and mix to make a smooth paste. Stir into the above mixture.

Add cream, to which the cinnamon has been added, gradually to the egg yolk mixture. Cook mixture in double boiler over boiling water, stirring constantly, until thickened. Pour mixture into a lightly buttered pan to a depth of about ¾ inch. Cool and cut in squares.

Roll squares in cracker crumbs and dip in beaten egg. Fry squares in deep hot fat at 360° F. until lightly browned.

Place squares on serving dish and pour rum over. Ignite rum and bring to the table.

❧ Alsatian Pudding

Mrs. Bland Farnsworth, Bowling Green, Kentucky

Ingredients

½ lb. butter
2½ cups powdered sugar
8 egg yolks
½ cup strong cold coffee

1 dozen ladyfingers, split
Rum
Shredded, toasted almonds

Directions (Serves 8 to 10)

Cream together butter and sugar until very light and fluffy.

Add yolks to the above and beat well.

Add coffee very slowly to the above.

Line an oblong pan with waxed paper and place a layer of split lady-fingers on bottom and sprinkle with rum. Next a layer of creamed mixture. Another layer of ladyfingers and sprinkle with rum, and so on until mixture is used, ending with a layer of ladyfingers. Put into refrigerator overnight.

Just before time to serve, turn out of pan, slice, and sprinkle each slice with almonds.

❧ Date and Nut Confection

Gurney's Inn, Montauk, Long Island, New York

Ingredients

1 cup pitted dates, diced
½ cup black walnuts, broken
1 cup granulated sugar

1 teaspoon baking powder
Pinch of salt
4 egg whites, beaten

Directions (Serves 4)

Thoroughly mix together first five ingredients.

Fold egg whites into above mixture and bake in buttered tin in 300° oven for 20 minutes. When cool, serve with whipped cream.

➥ *Fill cream puffs with whipped cream into which has been folded sweetened strawberries, raspberries, or sliced peaches.*

ᑫ Ozark Bakeless Pudding

Hotel Taneycomo, Rockaway Beach, Missouri

Ingredients

½ cup butter
1 cup sugar
2 eggs, well beaten
1 cup chopped nuts

1 small can crushed pineapple,
  drained
½ lb. graham crackers

Directions (Serves 6)

Cream butter and sugar. Add well-beaten eggs, nuts, and pineapple.
  Crush the graham crackers, and in a dish place a thick layer of
  crackers, then the mixture, and top with remainder of crackers.
  Let set for 12 hours in refrigerator and serve with whipped cream.
  (Peaches may be substituted for the pineapple.)

ᑫ Peanut Brittle Delight

Hotel Roanoke, Roanoke, Virginia

Ingredients

2 cups peanut brittle
2 cups marshmallows
1 ½ cups whipping cream

½ teaspoon vanilla
½ cup sugar
1 cup peanuts

Directions (Serves 6 to 8)

Crush peanut brittle very fine. Quarter marshmallows. Whip cream;
  add sugar and vanilla. Fold peanut brittle and marshmallows into
  whipped cream. Let stand 2 hours before serving. Serve in sherbet
  glasses. Garnish with peanuts.

ᑫ Coffee Pudding Supreme

Rita Seech, Los Angeles, California

Ingredients

½ pint whipping cream
3 tablespoons confectioners'
  sugar

2 tablespoons instant coffee

Directions (Serves 4)

Whip cream until quite stiff. Stir all ingredients together and serve.

∽ Tapioca Cream Pudding

Grace E. Smith's Restaurant, Toledo, Ohio

Ingredients

½ cup pearl tapioca (scant)
½ cup water
1 quart sweet milk
½ cup granulated sugar

3 small egg yolks
1 ½ tablespoons sugar
¼ teaspoon vanilla
⅓ teaspoon salt

Directions (Serves 6 to 8)

Soak tapioca in water at least 12 hours.

Heat milk in double boiler and add soaked tapioca to hot milk. Cook 1 hour until tapioca is tender and clear. Stir occasionally.

Add ½ cup sugar to milk and tapioca and cook 1 hour.

Beat egg yolks and 1 ½ tablespoons sugar in mixer until light yellow and thick. Add a little of the hot mixture to the yolks. Turn off the fire. Stir yolks into milk and tapioca and mix well. Return to double boiler and cook until thickened, approximately 20 minutes.

Stir in vanilla and salt and let cool, stirring occasionally until lukewarm.

∽ Indian Tapioca Pudding

Ingredients

2 cups milk
2 tablespoons tapioca
2 tablespoons Indian meal
⅔ cup molasses
⅓ cup sugar
3 tablespoons butter

1 egg
1 teaspoon salt
1 teaspoon cinnamon
1 teaspoon ginger
2 cups cold milk
1 cup cold milk

Directions (Serves 8)

Scald milk.

Mix tapioca and Indian meal, and stir into the hot milk. Cook 20 minutes, stirring constantly until it thickens. Remove from fire.

Add molasses, sugar, butter, egg, salt, spices, and 2 cups cold milk to the above mixture; stir and pour into greased baking dish. Set dish in pan of hot water and bake 4 hours in 350° oven.

Add 1 cup cold milk about 1 hour before serving, but do not stir. Serve with whipped cream or Hard Sauce.

～ Apricot Cream Cheese Wafers

Ingredients

1 package (3 oz.) soft cream
cheese
½ cup soft butter
½ cup sugar
1 cup sifted flour

1 teaspoon grated lemon rind
Dried apricot strips
Milk
Sugar

Directions (Makes about 3 dozen)

Mix first five ingredients well. Shape dough in rolls 1 inch in diameter; wrap in waxed paper. Chill and slice thin.

On one slice place a thin strip of apricot and cover with another slice. Press edges together. Brush top of cookies with milk; sprinkle with sugar. Place on lightly greased baking sheet and bake in moderate oven at 350° for 5 to 8 minutes or until done.

～ Pecan Drop Cakes

Mrs. George P. Meier, Indianapolis, Indiana

Ingredients

1 egg white, beaten
1 cup brown sugar

1 cup pecans (whole or broken)

Directions (Makes about 30)

Beat sugar into egg whites.

Add nuts and drop from a spoon onto a buttered cookie sheet. Bake in 300° oven for 40 minutes. Should be a light brown when done.

> ⬥ When guests are invited to my home for seven o'clock dinner, we begin the meal promptly at seven-thirty, whether all have arrived or not. There is no reasonable excuse for thoughtless guests to spoil a good dinner for those who arrived at the appointed hour.
>
> I believe there isn't any profession that requires more artistry, talent, and experience than the careful preparation and cooking of good food.

᠊᠊ *Oat Cakes*

Mrs. David Donald, Pittsfield, Massachusetts

Ingredients

3 cups quick-cooking oats
½ cup cornmeal
½ cup butter or shortening
1 cup flour
3 teaspoons sugar

1 teaspoon salt
½ teaspoon soda
1 teaspoon baking powder
⅔ cup hot water

Directions (Makes 2 dozen)

Put oats through a meat chopper.

Add cornmeal, butter, flour, sugar, salt, soda, and baking powder to the above and mix thoroughly.

Add water to mixture. Roll thin; cut and place on lightly greased baking sheet. Bake in 350° oven for 30 to 40 minutes.

Coffee

❦

COFFEE, America's favorite beverage, can be the crowning glory of a meal. But if you serve poor coffee, then you can spoil the enjoyment of the best food.

Americans drink more than 100 billion cups of coffee each year, and consumption is still increasing steadily. In the United States we have many different methods of preparing coffee, and some people have developed special techniques of their own to produce coffee unlike anything else wrung from a coffee bean. Someone once said that coffee is handled by experts up until the crucial moment of brewing, and then an amateur takes over. Nevertheless, we do a pretty good job of coffee making. Otherwise, it would never have become the popular drink that it has since its introduction in the coffeehouses and cafes of Europe more than three hundred years ago.

The essentials to producing a good cup of coffee are few, but the results are well worth any effort. Buy a good brand of coffee and the right grind for whatever brewing method you wish to use. Fresh coffee makes the best coffee, so do not store your supply too long. Your coffeemaker should be clean and shiny. Soap has a tendency to cling to your coffeemaker and will spoil the flavor, so be sure your utensil or appliance is well rinsed. Use cold water and never, never start with hot or tepid water if you want the best flavor from your coffee. For medium coffee, use 1½ to 2 tablespoons of coffee per cup, and vary it either way for stronger or weaker coffee. Serve your coffee as soon as possible. Cooled coffee often loses its flavor if reheated. If your coffee must stand, then be sure it is not in contact with the grounds.

A good idea for your leftover coffee in the summertime is to pour it into an ice cube tray and freeze it. Then you will have coffee cubes for your spiced iced coffee.

The New Automatic Coffee Makers

I have found some of the new automatics to be very good. The higher cost of these units over the conventional-type pots is often offset by the pleasure you get from a better cup of coffee and from actually being able to brew a good drink with less coffee.

I especially like a coffeemaker that brews out all the goodness without boiling. This is important because boiling releases the acrid oils that make coffee bitter.

Percolator Coffee

(Automatic and Nonautomatic Coffeemakers) In the percolator coffeemakers, the water is measured into the percolator, and then the steam and basket, holding the desired amount of coffee, are inserted. When using the automatic percolator, follow the manufacturer's directions, as different makes of electric percolators have different automatic features. If the percolator is nonelectric, place over medium heat; lower the flame when the water begins to spurt; count percolating time from the first spurt. Percolating for 5 to 10 minutes makes coffee of medium strength when 4 to 6 cups are being made.

The principle involved in the percolator coffeemaker is that when the water is sufficiently heated it is forced up through the narrow stem and sprays over the coffee in the basket, which is held over the water. The spurts of water extract color and flavor from the coffee, and then return to the bottom of the coffeemaker.

Vacuum-Type Coffee

The vacuum-type coffeemaker consists of two separate containers. Measure the water into the lower bowl, using either cold or freshly boiled water, unless the manufacturer's directions specify just cold water. The coffee is placed in the upper bowl. Heat forces the water to rise through a tube into the upper section, where it mixes with the coffee. Steam pressure keeps the water there long enough to extract the desired flavor and color from the coffee. When all the water has risen to the top, the nonelectric coffeemaker is removed from the heat. This causes the lower section to cool off, and the pressure is reduced; the finished coffee then filters back into the lower section.

Since vacuum-type coffeemakers vary with the brand, the manufacturer's directions should be followed carefully. General directions do not apply in all cases.

Drip Coffee

Measure the coffee into the basket or middle section, which may either fit over the bottom section of the drip coffeemaker or may be attached to the top section. Fit the parts together, and pour freshly boiled water into the top section. The water drips down through the coffee and into the bottom section. Remove the section holding the grounds when all the water has dripped through to the bottom. Let the coffee stand 5 to 8 minutes before serving. (This "ripens" the coffee.) To keep the coffee hot, heat the bottom section, provided that the coffeemaker is not made of pottery or glass that cannot be placed over direct heat. With pottery or glass coffeemakers, scald the pot with hot water before using and then keep in a warm place.

Boiled Coffee

To make boiled or steeped coffee, select a rather coarsely ground coffee. Mix the ground coffee with a slightly beaten egg white and cold water just to moisten the coffee grounds. This helps to clarify the finished coffee. (Use about 1 teaspoon of egg white per cup of coffee.)

To make boiled coffee, pour fresh cold water over the coffee mixture. Place over a low flame and bring to a boil, stirring occasionally. Remove from heat at once.

To make steeped coffee, pour boiling water over the coffee mixture and place over low heat for about 10 minutes. Do not let the water simmer. Several tablespoons of cold water will help settle the grounds.

Cafe au Lait

Prepare double-strength coffee. Heat some milk to the scalding point. Then pour the coffee and milk at the same time into the coffee cups, usually adding equal amounts of each. More or less coffee may be added depending upon individual preferences. Top with unsweetened whipped cream, if desired.

ᐓ Spiced Iced Coffee

Ingredients

15 whole cloves
1 stick (5-inch) cinnamon
½ cup ground coffee
7 cups water, boiling or cold

1 cup powdered sugar
1 cup whipping cream
2 tablespoons sugar

Directions (Serves 6)

Add cloves, cinnamon, and coffee to water and brew as usual. Strain and add powdered sugar.
Pour into tall glasses half-filled with crushed ice.
Whip cream with sugar. Put a scoop of whipped cream in each glass.

ᐓ Cafe Brûlot

Ingredients

Peel of 1 orange, cut thin
4 sticks cinnamon
10 whole cloves

6 lumps sugar
½ cup brandy
4 cups prepared hot coffee

Directions (Serves 6 to 8)

Place the first four ingredients in a silver brûlot bowl or chafing dish.
Pour brandy over the above mixture. Ignite brandy and keep ladling brandy over ingredients in bowl until sugar is dissolved.
Gradually add coffee, and ladle mixture until the flame dies. Serve immediately.

ᐓ Cafe Diablo

Cameo Restaurant, Chicago, Illinois

Ingredients

6 demitasses of coffee
6 whole cloves
½ stick cinnamon
2 bay leaves
1 lemon peel
1 orange peel

¼ cup whole roasted coffee
  beans
6 lumps sugar
2 oz. Jamaica rum
4 oz. brandy

Directions (Serves 6)

Use your own favorite method to brew coffee.

Mix remaining ingredients in a deep chafing dish and set liquor
afire. Keep stirring the mixture with a ladle and very slowly add
the coffee, stirring all the time to keep the flame burning. Serve in
demitasse cups, using ladle and a spoon to remove coffee beans.

ᨓ Coffee for a Crowd

Ingredients

1 lb. ground coffee   2 to 2½ gallons water

Directions (Serves 40 to 50)

Place the coffee in one or more cheesecloth bags; never fill a bag more
than ½ full. Measure the water into a large coffeepot or kettle. Let
the water come to a boil. Drop the bag, containing the coffee, into
the boiling water and lower the flame. Heat without boiling for 10
to 15 minutes, moving the bag through the water several times.
Remove the bag; serve coffee immediately or keep hot. Another
method, using the same ingredients, is as follows: Immerse the
coffee bag in cold water. Bring the water to a boil. Remove from
heat immediately and keep the bag in the water for 3 to 5 minutes.
Remove the bag and serve coffee, or keep hot.

ᨓ Demitasse or After-Dinner Coffee

Prepare coffee, using double the amount of coffee usually used, and
figuring on two demitasse servings per measuring cup of water. The
coffee is served in small demitasse cups with demitasse spoons on
the saucers. It is not necessary to pass cream and sugar as it is usually
taken black. The hostess usually serves after-dinner coffee in the
living room.

Index